T0285217

The Parenthood Dilemma

The Parenthood Dilemma

PROCREATION IN THE AGE OF UNCERTAINTY

Gina Rushton

ASTRA HOUSE ʌ NEW YORK

Originally published in Australia in 2022 by Pan Macmillan Australia as *The Most
Important Job in the World*.

For information about permission to reproduce selections from this book, please contact
permissions@astrahouse.com

Astra House
A Division of Astra Publishing House
astrahouse.com
Printed in the United States of America

Library of Congress Cataloging-in-Publication Data

Names: Rushton, Gina, 1992– author.
Title: The parenthood dilemma : procreation in the age of uncertainty /
   Gina Rushton.
Description: First edition. | New York : Astra House, [2023] | Includes
   bibliographical references. | Summary: "THE PARENTHOOD DILEMMA
   is a bold, feminist investigation into the decision whether or not to become
   a parent"—Provided by publisher.
Identifiers: LCCN 2023009149 (print) | LCCN 2023009150 (ebook) |
   ISBN 9781662602382 (hardcover) | ISBN 9781662602375 (ebook)
Subjects: LCSH: Parenthood. | Childlessness. | Reproductive rights.
Classification: LCC HQ755.8 .R868 2023 (print) | LCC HQ755.8 (ebook) |
   DDC 306.874—dc23/eng/20230327
LC record available at https://lccn.loc.gov/2023009149
LC ebook record available at https://lccn.loc.gov/2023009150

First edition
10 9 8 7 6 5 4 3 2 1

Design by Richard Oriolo
The text is set in Minion Pro.
The titles are set in Bulmer MT Display.

For my mum, Cathy.

CONTENTS

AUTHOR'S NOTE

The people in this book were either self-selecting or approached as experts. Some of their names have been changed for privacy reasons.

Not all people with uteruses are mothers and not all mothers have uteruses. The words *woman* and *mother* are used throughout this book, particularly where people identified as such, alongside more inclusive terms like *parent* or *pregnant person*.

Introduction

THE QUESTION ARRIVED AS A sudden and unbearable cramp.

In January 2019, I found myself curled up in my boyfriend's bathroom, clawing at the tiles. I wanted to take a taxi to the hospital, but the heavy pain in my abdomen had fastened me to the floor, so he called an ambulance. An internal ultrasound revealed I was bleeding out of my uterus and into my pelvic cavity. I needed emergency surgery. I was handed a piece of paper to sign, giving the surgeon permission to remove an ovary and to show I was aware they could puncture other organs on the way in. The doctor told me my left ovary was "dead" after twisting and cutting off its own blood supply. I would go into surgery immediately because if the dead tissue was left inside of me it could cause blood poisoning. This operation would affect my fertility, but we could discuss that once it was out.

You don't have to write about reproductive health for a living to know that halving the number of sites where an egg is produced might impact your ability to conceive. The doctor left, drawing the curtain behind her. I turned away from my boyfriend, wanting to privately assess the feeling rising inside of me. I was humiliated by the tears spilling onto my white hospital gown, betraying a secret vacillation, a pathetic flinching in the face of an operation that shouldn't faze a woman who had decided a decade earlier that she didn't want to be a mother.

"I don't want kids, you know I don't want kids," I told him.

I didn't know why I was so upset, I explained. "It is probably just the morphine," I offered. I called my mum just before the operation and repeated, "I don't want kids, you know I don't want kids."

"I know," she said. There was an unfamiliar softness in her voice that I thought about afterward.

In my mission to reject the most rudimentary of patriarchal mythology—that if you have the physical potential for motherhood, it should be your "single destiny and justification in life"—I had internalized an unfortunate tendency of the kind of feminism I was raised on. I became a woman with a preference, in this case not to be a parent, which was meant to be purely and unequivocally empowering simply because it was mine. In fact, I felt small and disoriented.

In the end, a surgeon found that a large cyst had burst, but that the ovary itself was alive. They did however find endometriosis, a condition in which tissue that normally lines the uterus grows beyond it. It can, and probably will, impact my fertility. Just as I thought I might need longer to choose, I am accepting I might have even less time than the average thirty-year-old woman. I am reckoning with the cost of ambivalence, the calculus involved when your wish for something, anything—a life centered on work, the possibility of a family, an abstract sense of community—comes only in flashes and there is no hunger that lasts long enough to try satiating it.

I don't have loud enough answers for the questions I have barely whispered. My long-standing internal retort has been dismissive, uncoupled from any strong desire and defensively vague. Even if I was made of mother material, I would not volunteer for a position so chronically devalued. Moreover, the planet is dying of heatstroke. This sweeping verdict that the world is no place for another child and that I am not supposed to be a parent at least needs an appendix if it is to be my final adjudication. The diagnosis has turned a sand timer inside of me. I am at the page to decide whether I want to have children. I am here to investigate and interview. I am here to read, to reflect, and to write. My life is divided by deadlines, but only my body knows the true date of this one, so I want to make my decision before it arrives.

The question of who owns a body and who can intervene in its fate has consumed most of my working life so far. Every day for several years I worked as a journalist reporting on reproductive choice, which is to say I documented power and control. I wrote extensively about each push to decriminalize abortion and each corresponding reprisal. I now know the expertise I acquired was not in the legal, medical, or political technicalities—variations can be found the world over—but a deeper understanding of how the decision to have or not have a child is often at the whim of other people if you have a uterus. It is compromised. It is politicized. It is not the choice we believe it is.

This was a topic that only fleetingly captured the attention of other outlets, most often when the political debate had turned most inflammatory. I was determined to cover it so comprehensively that readers were taken outside of the halls of Parliament where men were talking about their bodies and examination rooms, emergency departments, homes, and relationships where patients were treated as mothers in waiting. I interviewed woman after woman about the ways social stigma, inequality, the law, and the state had each obstructed their access to contraception and abortion. Few people have been so professionally occupied with the risks of coercing people into parenthood. Even fewer have written hundreds of news articles about how compromised and conditional bodily autonomy can be. I know it has left me carrying an unreasonable need to prove to myself that this is a decision I am making without intervention. That this is my body, that this is my choice. I might come to the page with a singular paranoia, but I am also just another person, unsure of herself and her future, trying to make a decision.

Nothing so quickly confirms what you fear most about the world and yourself as the question of whether or not you want children. The graphs showing emissions and inequities, lines inching toward the top right corner of each square. The sense that everyone is hardening, digging their heels into dogmatism. The struggle to think of a single friend in a relationship with a man where there is a fair division of any kind of labor. The 200-and-something weeks of exposure to readers who believe women are overreacting, women are asking for it, women are incubators. Tracing the identities of one of my trolls and discovering he was a boy, not yet a man. The days where I hear a whisper in the wind: I'm broken and can't be repaired. Fires blazing along the Arctic Circle. Loving someone who is in addiction for a long time and learning how neither love nor time always heals. Every parliamentary debate I've reported on in which physical sovereignty was discussed by men who fetishized motherhood, the most important job in the world, while supporting policies that made life harder for mothers.

Nothing so quickly confirms what you love most about the world and yourself as the question of whether or not you want children. My friendships with women who are perpetually loving, blossoming, failing, forgiving, growing, reaching toward a better world with a grace that should never have been demanded of them. The kids, marching with their signs. The fathers in my life softening, the mothers taking space. My partner, gently challenging expectations of what a relationship with a man could be. My elderly neighbor leaving a single homegrown tomato on my doorstep in the middle of a pandemic. My unstoppable niece, half-naked, zooming on her scooter down a hill through a public park, refusing to heed or wear a shirt, speeding with the confidence and fearlessness of a middle-aged man, somehow yet to realize girls are expected to be obliging, sweet, and modest. My hubristic belief in my own ability to take good care of others. The bluebells I sold to my mother's friend as bulbs when I was a child still blooming each September two decades later. Other people's homes, stable in the way mine wasn't.

There are no deciding factors, only feelings.

At night I can hear the freight trains hiss and clatter past, 20 meters from my bedroom. My great-great-grandmother and namesake would have heard the trains scrape along the same line from her shack next to the tracks two stops east. She had ten children, eight of whom survived. For long stretches of time, she was alone with them while her husband was away moving livestock from place to place in the country. To survive, she worked as a wet nurse, breastfeeding richer women's children.

"How did she feed her own children then?" I ask my mother.

"She just had to hope there was enough milk left."

From all accounts, Letitia loved motherhood as she did her children, but her options were not as mine are now. The control she had over the number of kids she was having, and the frequency with which she was having them, was almost non-existent. It barely mattered how little time, how little support, how little money, how little milk she had for another human ten times over. A century later, I don't have to choose motherhood at all.

One more stop east on the train line is the house my mother lived in. She was married with three children by the age of twenty-three, and four by age thirty-four, when I was born. My parents were growing a family at a time when houses in our city cost around six times the average full-time income, not more than fifteen as they do now. Back then, there wasn't a widespread fear about how the climate crisis would impact the next generation, when fertility was rarely assisted and when gender roles were, if not set in stone, then a rigid default. My mother's decision to swap studying psychology and journalism for teaching, a more family-friendly profession, while my father pursued law, would be a different, longer conversation for me and my part-ner almost five decades later. I have choices my great-great-grandmother never did and more time than my mother had to make her own. This is not to patronize the women whose blood runs through mine but to acknowledge that while my body, my hopes, and my desires are still valued less than those of men, I have more agency than they would have had in years past. I have options, even if I'm learning they have an expiry date.

I am a member of a generation that often feels impotent in the face of endless uncertainty. The question of children thrusts us into a time beyond now, demanding we come up with more than whatever gets us through the present while the only assurance we've had about what lies ahead is that it will be worse.

I began seriously considering this question in a global pandemic, unfold-ing alongside a climate crisis. It feels especially foolish to want something specific from the coming years. How do we let ourselves imagine any future without being overpowered by despair or manipulated by hope? I am trying not to self-soothe in the ways millennials know best. I am trying not to reflex-ively temper my faith in the future with irony and fatalism. I am trying not to whip myself into a delusional frenzy so my despondency can't be heard over the hum of a mantra: If I work hard enough, grow enough, control my surroundings enough, believe enough, march enough, consume ethically enough, read enough, I will cool the planet and subdue behemoth institutions or insidious cultural forces that are completely beyond one person's control. Recycling and sharing memes in the group chat about global collapse won't sustain me into my thirties, with or without children. I want to map the differences between giving up and, as authors Pablo Servigne and Raphaël Stevens write in *How Everything Can Collapse: A Manual for Our Times*, accepting "the death of a future that was dear to us, a future that was reassuring, however irrational it might have been." At a time when the planet is warming and people are wondering how many, if any, children they should be having or adopting, I want to understand how much power and responsibility individuals have when it comes to family planning. I begin just as eight teenagers, supported by an eighty-six-year-old Catholic nun, take on the Australian federal government in court to stop the extension of a coal mine in my state. They invoke the environment minister's duty of care to protect young people against climate change. The children will eventually lose and the mine will extract 168 million tons of coal over the next few decades. What do we owe to our children who will fall heir to a planet different from the one we grew up in? What do we owe to the planet when it comes to adding another human to it? What do we owe to our own hopes and dreams when governments are allowing businesses to emit carbon with impunity?

I want to know how people parent without living in permanent denial or perpetual dread. I will find people who are watching species die, authoring papers on rising sea levels, studying renewable energy, and protecting their children's lungs from bushfire smoke to ask them where they put their hope and fear.

In Sophie Mackintosh's dystopian novel *Blue Ticket,* on the day of your first period you enter a lottery and you're handed either a white ticket, designating you as a person who will have to bear children, or a blue ticket, the coveted option, which grants you a compulsory contraceptive insertion and a childless future. Inevitably, some blue ticketholders wrench the devices from their uteruses and conceive and some white ticketholders try to abort their forced pregnancies. "Having a child is both the most rational and irrational decision possible, in this world," says Marisol, a blue ticketholder who is on the run from the authoritarian regime under which her pregnancy isn't allowed. "This fucking awful, beautiful world, which I can't stop loving, though I have considered it, I have evaluated and counted the ways."

To have a child feels like a leap of faith in myself as I am and this awful, beautiful world as it will be, or an act of faith in our ability as parents and children to survive transience. I find in myself and in others a fear about what children will inherit, not just in the earth where we plant them in but in their roots; a contemporary consciousness of how harm moves through generations. My mother had a single ultrasound across four pregnancies. It feels as though we now scan ourselves for complications before we even know if we want to be parents. When I was a child, to be inconspicuous was a virtue and it seemed parents were also less inspected. But now even hypothetical children feel visible to us and we feel visible to them in a way that feels new with all our flaws.

The question of whether or not to have children forces us to think deeply about our own impermanence while reminding us that we might be here just long enough to pass along what we love and fear. In my quest for answers to my own dilemma, I have sought out people who are scared about what their legacy might be when it comes to their genetics, their cultural mores, their trauma and their tendencies, and thinkers who could help me answer how much agency we have over this. Is an awareness of how you were raised and how you want to raise your children enough? How much are we trying to prevent harm and how much are we trying to control outcomes? What if all our kids actually absorbed was the millennial hyper-cognizance of consequences and we raise a generation of risk-averse neurotics?

For women in relationships with men, the question of motherhood intensifies many of the lessons we are unlearning about our place in our own partnerships. In considering whether to make an irreversible decision to have a child, we are often considering an investment in the longevity of dynamics we have spent years questioning. We still hear echoes of the messages we were told as children about how boys and girls should or should never express our needs and what we are allowed to ask of each other. The childfree women I know have already tasted motherhood. We have given unconditional love, care, domestic and emotional work to those around us, including partners, for our entire adult lives.

I am not the first dutiful daughter to resist the specter of maternal responsibility. The year I was born, *Men Are from Mars, Women Are from Venus* was published. The self-help bestseller answered the frustrations of heterosexual relationships, where gender was seen as the inherent cause of friction. In this book, the highest ranked work of nonfiction in the 1990s, women were encouraged to straddle a planetary divide by cajoling men into doing stuff they apparently weren't biologically wired for, like willingly contributing emotionally and domestically to a home and relationship. In its gender essentialism, the book assured readers that the origin of their relationship problems was inevitable and in doing so, "renormalized hetero-sexual misery for a new generation," as feminist author Jane Ward writes.

I want jokes in which women are mothers to childish men to be incom-prehensibly boring to my niece and nephew by the time they are in romantic relationships. At a time when heterosexuality has become the easiest conven-tion to satirize, how do we take relationships with men seriously? I don't want to start a family drenched in this pessimism, or worse, breathless with gratitude that my partner does as much as me. How do we test assumptions and expectations around love and labor, regardless of our gender and sexuality? How do we find symmetry in care and in communication that feels sustainable enough to hold a third human? How do we do so without expending more of the work we are weary from? At a time when we are often asking one person to give us, as Esther Perel says, "what an entire village used to provide," I want to name what we should expect from our partners and what we have failed to build in our other relationships, including in the one we have with ourselves.

I began writing this book at a time when we needed to social distance and sanitize. Each day we are reminded of our connectedness, our ability to keep each other safe, and how we have always breathed in the strangers we ignored. People were leaving toilet paper, cans of lentils, and loaves of bread for each other at the end of my street. I was surprised, then sad that I was surprised. I want to understand why I can't imagine building a community strong enough to support me into my old age without family. What does kin mean to someone born just before a divorce in a family that fractured in every direction? I want to understand why I imagine modern motherhood as inherently isolating, detached from community, when I was frequently minded by neighbors and friends of my mother and she would mind their children too. I want to find my way back to a proximity with other humans beyond the nuclear family, with or without my own children.

Revisiting my decision to reject motherhood forces me to reconsider what the word means. Why would anyone become a mother? Not a woman with a child but a mother. As I was first led to believe she should be—infinitely nourishing, serene, sweet, soft, without anger, without needs, without self and later, as she was revised, with a meaningful career. Author Deborah Levy writes in *Things I Don't Want to Know* that mother is the woman the whole world has "imagined to death" and still here I am, needing to revive and reimagine her again until the last unsavory archetypes I am holding on to crumble in my hands. I need to know precisely what I am saying "no" to. I need to acknowledge how witnessing my mother cook, clean, and care for four children who had different needs for their security and sanity has defined the word for me.

I need to examine everything I have learned about how rewarding a career is and how thankless parenthood would be. I am wary of romanticizing the unpaid work of motherhood. I have watched too many politicians prove that you can idealize something without valuing it. I have liveblogged their comments in parliamentary debates; I have fact-checked their claims. You can dehumanize someone by putting them on a pedestal because saints don't have needs. They don't need paid parental leave; they don't need affordable childcare or housing; they don't need freedom from punitive welfare programs; and they definitely don't need safe, affordable, and legal access to choose whether they continue a pregnancy. I don't want to be thanked once a year in May because I am need-less. I don't want to enter into something laden with guilt and judgment.

The sentimentalizing of motherhood as the God-given purpose of all women with uteruses lingers even though our parents' generation began to resist parenthood as the default. People my age are still pushing against this while simultaneously questioning what came in its wake: the ascendance of paid work as the primary place of self-fulfillment.

Revisiting my decision to reject motherhood will mean reconsidering whether a career is what I want to prioritize instead. The feminism I grew up with was anti-maternal or at least calling for women to become "more" than "just" mothers. Meaning-making happened outside the home. In parenthood we are expected to accept that laboring for love requires no compensation; in the modern workplace we are expected to accept that any love we have for our labor is worth so much it can even supplement cash in a paycheck. If the expectation now is to love what you do in parenthood and find a career that allows you to do what you love, I want to understand the fine print.

Revisiting my decision to reject motherhood will mean reconsidering what lives I might live if I move beyond defining myself through any form of labor. I want to fantasize about the space between the myths of woman as womb and woman as worker to consider a life in which my purpose is tied to neither. I want to consider a life in which my identity is not contingent on the labor my body produces in reproduction or production. A libido for other kinds of creation.

A friend who was nearing thirty called to talk about a change she could feel inside herself. It was not whatever smug biological clock-watchers think happens when you reach this age. It was something else. She doesn't want children. She liked her job, but had realized it would never be everything to her. She wanted to travel but couldn't because of the pandemic. The mess of her early twenties was over. The parade of men we knew never deserved her, they nonetheless taught her more about herself, the stress of study, the years of late nights partying then the years of late nights working, the traveling, the learning and unlearning, the knowledge of who she might be and what she might want. "I've done the work, I feel ready for something," she said. She was describing a richness within herself, an absence of toxicity, a readiness, an ability to sustain growth; a fertility. She was wondering where to plant her roots. She was ready to unfurl.

Many of the issues shaping individuals' decision process are universal. Some are not. I am a journalist in my thirties writing and speaking in English. This search to find an answer was first published in my home country, Australia, but you are reading something I had the chance to expand and refine. I am one woman, a lucky one, with a big set of liberties and a smaller set of burdens influencing my decision. I have had the immeasurable free-dom of time to consider this question in the abstract, which is not afforded to many people considering how and with whom to build a family, biologically or otherwise. I want to look beyond the doubts I have about myself and my own place in the workplace, in a relationship with a man, in a body that might be infertile, in a dynasty of dysfunction, in a country where color is draining from the coral and smoke will more frequently fill the sky. I don't want to draw myself into my own windowless hesitation, where I can't see storms nor appreciate how sheltered I am from them.

What are the stakes for a middle-class white woman considering middle-class white motherhood? I have spent years immersed in various battles for reproductive rights that have been organized around women like me—those who want to prevent pregnancy. I am learning. I am expanding my concept of reproductive oppression to include everyone with a uterus who is obstructed not only from preventing or ending pregnancy but from continuing them safely, free from violence and discrimination. How have my safe interactions with medical and legal institutions limited my understanding of how other women, especially women of color, experience them? Not one of the challenges posed by potential parenthood are borne evenly by everyone and they are rarely heaviest for white, cis-gendered, able-bodied women who are in relationships with men. I am hoping that the experiences of others will speak where I cannot and should not.

No one can now consider having children without confronting the unavoidable cost of raising them. Inflation is soaring and most people on Earth are enduring a cost of living crisis in which the price of everyday essentials like groceries, fuel, and rent, let alone house prices, have risen far quicker than wages or social support payments. For two-income families who aren't lucky enough to live in Japan, Scandinavia, or Germany—where stillbirth rates are in decline—most households are spending between 10 percent and 25 percent of their average earnings on childcare. The raw economics of parenthood will be for many people the deciding factor of whether they have kids and, if so, how many. While I am here to explore many of the cultural and structural barriers that stop us from socializing the cost of reproduction, I know for most people the financial question will be a personal one. The drastic difference between no child, one child, or multiple children is now economically undeniable.

"Whether I want kids is a secret I keep from myself—it is the greatest secret I keep from myself," Sheila Heti writes in *Motherhood*, a novel in which the protagonist tries to answer the same question I am. I start my own process feeling disconnected from myself and what I want from the rest of my life, unpracticed at accessing my own wanting without self-censoring. My friends and I, all millennials, bought Heti's book a few years ago believing we would finish it knowing one way or the other if we were going to be parents. I suspect some of my friends wanted a book that would reassure them that to have a child wasn't to fail at feminism, ruin a career, forfeit creative fulfillment, risk a relationship, or refuse action on climate change. I was foolishly hoping it would convince me of the opposite—I wanted an object that I could press into the hands of my loved ones to explain my decision not to have kids. Instead, we were left with more questions.

Inspired by the ancient Chinese divination text *I Ching*, Heti's main character creates her own kind of clairvoyance, posing yes–no questions while tossing three coins which give her answers. When I was a child, I was desperate to believe in God like my mother did. I wanted to bypass goodness, accountability, community, and anything else that might remediate the things that kept me up at night. I wanted a set of commands I could claim as morals. Now that I know how arbitrary and harmful these rules can be, now that I know you can't manufacture faith, now that I'm older, I just want a conviction that feels enduring enough to confront fear as I feel it. Unlike Heti's character, I am not just aiming to answer yes or no; I am also trying to legitimize the questions we are striving to answer and identify those that have been thrust upon us and from which we could liberate ourselves. I'm here to find priorities I can live with, love even, in the time it takes to grow a baby.

In a letter to his brothers in 1817, poet John Keats used the term *negative capability* to describe "being in uncertainties, mysteries, doubts, without any irritable reaching after fact and reason." I am trying to get more comfortable with the questions, curious not craving ones, calm about what I don't know. I want to get better at living in the in-between despite knowing I might have limited time to ask whether I should have children before I can ask whether I even can. Endometrial cells could continue to grow beyond my uterus regardless of what I choose. It's possible to feel indignant about the speed at which we need to consider these questions if we are to leave enough time for kids, should we want them, but I can't help but feel blessed by the urgency.

How lucky we are, as women with uteruses, to be conscripted by our own fertility into asking these huge philosophical questions in our adulthood and fighting for what we want from our future. It need not be an unresolvable burden but an opportunity to ask not just what we want from our own lives, but what kind of world we want to move toward whether we parent or not.

Gestation is depicted as a peaceful process but in fact it is biological paradox, a bloody war mediated by the placenta that protects the embryo from being immunologically attacked like any other foreign matter would. In pregnancy, you don't just grow a fetus but a whole new guardian organ that gathers food and defends your baby from the body's own desires and defenses. At first, the placenta distracts the body from this piece of nonself and then fights the uterus for blood to nourish the growing embryo. The parent within the parent before there is a child. I have never allowed space to grow the idea of myself as a mother and now, on the page, I will find the parent within so I can see the person I am renouncing. I make space for hypotheticals, I make space for honesty. I make time to call mothers, fathers, people who do not want children, experts, and friends. I make time to weave something through which I can filter hope and fear, mine and the fear I find in each conversation.

I always believed the answer would come before the question, as we're led to believe it does. The desire for children would just appear, unbidden and then unwavering.

I never heard that "yes" and so I assumed it was a "no." Instead, the question came first and fast, uncomfortable, and unanswered. I can't build a life around a preference; I need to make a choice.

———
1.
———

Reproductive Rights

AT FIRST, ROSITA HAD DISMISSED the notion, expressed by her daughter, that all our rights as women are provisional.

"How right she was," the crestfallen seventy-four-year-old concedes.

I am speaking to Rosita, a founding member of the Irish Women's Liberation Movement, in the wake of a leaked US Supreme Court decision that will overturn the country's constitutional right to abortion.

"The leading cause of death for a child in America now is from a gunshot and yet they're saying no to abortions," she says, shaking her head, days after nineteen children were shot dead at a Texas elementary school in Uvalde.

As someone who has felt the scalding heat of misogynistic reprisal, Rosita's optimism about the rights of women was hard-won.

In the early 1970s, she marched peacefully alongside mothers with babies and toddlers in baby carriages toward the Irish parliament, petitioning for the legalization of contraception. At the time, advertising or selling contraceptives was punishable with penal servitude in Ireland. A red-faced man emerged from the senate chamber toward the peaceful congregation, shouting, "Ye should all be fucked on your hands and knees like animals because that's all ye are."

"I remember being really shocked as it was the first time I came up against the viciousness of the patriarchal pushback," Rosita says. "I thought 'wow, this is really strong and really toxic.'"

She grew up in a country where there was no sex education, contraception, or protections against marital rape and where unmarried pregnant women were sent to mother and baby homes. At these "charnel houses," as Rosita calls them, babies died, others were adopted out or trafficked. She witnessed the end of the "marriage bar" where single women had to resign from their jobs upon marriage and married women could not apply for vacancies; she saw justice for widows, deserted wives, and unmarried mothers, and she saw the sale of contraception allowed.

One of nine children, Rosita has watched the disintegration of policies that, in practice, legislated forced birth. Now, as a grandmother, she watches her daughter and her friends find motherhood with a sense of agency.

"The babies are so loved, you've never seen anything like it because every single one of them has been chosen and they are absolutely adored," she says, smiling.

She fought for this expansion of choice, liberty, and autonomy—and won—but Rosita knows now it can be one step forward and one step back. In 1983, "the unborn" was given the same legal right to life as "the mother" in the Eighth Amendment of the Constitution. This was not repealed until 2018 via a referendum.

"Ireland is so small and the church is just this monster spider still sitting on top of women," she says.

We are speaking in 2022, shortly after the Irish parliament has approved plans for the National Maternity Hospital to move to a site owned by the Catholic Church, raising concerns that tubal ligations, contraception, and terminations might be compromised. Rosita tells me that "Nine of the big hospitals are still refusing to carry out abortions. Anyone who says they have conscientious objection can refuse to be involved." Even though abortion was decriminalized in Northern Ireland in 2019, 161 women traveled to England or Wales for an abortion in 2021. Around 40 percent of women of reproductive age live in places where abortion access is a crime or restricted—the grounds for abortion were all but abolished in Poland in

2021 and women are prosecuted for stillbirth and miscarriage in parts of Central America.

As *New Yorker* staff writer Jia Tolentino wrote, in the wake of the decision to overturn *Roe v. Wade* we have entered an era not only of unsafe abortion but of the criminalization of pregnant women and "anyone who comes into meaningful contact with a pregnancy that does not end in a healthy birth." That is how thirty-one-year-old dentist Savita Halappanavar was left to die of sepsis in Ireland after her request for an abortion was denied on legal grounds. The fight for fetal personhood will continue to trump the fight for bodily autonomy of pregnant people in many places for decades to come. "No other such obligation exists anywhere in our society, which grants cops the freedom to stand by as children are murdered behind an unlocked door," Tolentino writes.

These rights are provisional. Daughters will keep learning this even if their mothers didn't have to.

The right to use your body to bear children. The right not to. The right to make informed decisions about this, free from judgment, coercion, or deception. The people I interviewed while reporting on reproductive rights were often incredulous that these rights were compromised or on the precipice of revocation. "I had no idea it was still a crime. I had no idea I would have to borrow money. I had no idea a doctor could refuse to help me. I had no idea a doctor would lie to me. I had no idea I could be harassed outside a clinic. I had no idea I would have to travel across states. I had no idea I couldn't get it in the public system. I had no idea a hospital could turn me away if there was a complication. I had no idea I'd have to go into an induced labor on a maternity ward while hearing other babies crying and knowing I would not leave with ours." Their agency was more conditional than they knew. Journalists are just vessels through which stories travel, but we fool ourselves into thinking they don't change us in transit. Sometimes I think these interviews have left me shadowboxing, convinced I will not have the final say over how I use my body.

"There are a thousand different reasons why people go down that path and it is nobody's business why," Annie told me. Not long before I went into the hospital, I had interviewed Annie, a mother of two who had become pregnant as the result of a rape. She was at eight weeks' gestation, early enough for a medical abortion, but she booked a surgical termination because she did not want to cramp and expel the evidence of her trauma. Even if she had resources to raise a third child, she "didn't want to explain to this kid where they came from."

I had already reported on the clinic Annie attended because footage had been taken of protesters trying to hand a plastic fetal doll to another patient. "This is a little 12-week-old baby," a woman in the video says, following the patient toward the door. "That little one that you have has a heartbeat, ten fingers, ten toes and God hates the hands that shed his blood." The patient can be heard begging them to leave her alone.

When Annie and her father approached the same clinic, one picketer blocked her path and another touched her arm. "I just kept my eyes on the door or on the floor," she told me. "I felt embarrassed. I felt ashamed. People were grabbing me." I didn't include the last bit of our interview in the story, but it followed me into the emergency ward.

Annie told me that since her abortion, she'd had several miscarriages, all for planned pregnancies. She admitted sheepishly that she felt like this was "karma" even though she felt certain that her abortion had been the right decision. I told her it wasn't the first nor would it be the last time a woman I interviewed would explain to me this tension between a decision they felt was hard but right. We talked about how stigma can live on inside someone. I thought about the hate mail of my impending stories and saw them manifest before the message arrived on my screen. The words did not disappear even after I emptied the trash folder.

Access to abortion was not something I gave any thought to before 2016. I could only name a few women I knew who had undergone what I assumed was a seldom chosen but attainable procedure. It wasn't until learning that abortion was in fact incredibly common, but rarely accessible, that my editor and I found ourselves confronting a situation so undocumented that it would generate stories for the next four years. By 2020, I had probably spoken to more people in Australia about their abortions than anyone else in the country, apart from medical professionals or counselors. The patchwork of legality, the fragile network of doctors who had to become advocates, the travel, the prohibitive cost, mirrored the situation in many countries. Unfolding across the hundreds of articles I wrote were different versions of the same truth—reproductive choice expands and contracts according to the resources you have, the means to afford travel, accommodation, privacy, lost days of income, childcare, and the procedure. Unlike other common medical procedures, there is no widespread public access to abortion and people often need to find money at short notice to go to a private clinic.

When I began reporting on the issue, a woman in one state down in Australia's south could access a surgical termination at no cost at a public hospital while those in another state up north were paying private clinics AUD$800 for two pills that were supposed to cost AUD$38. Notorious "conscientious objectors," sometimes the only doctor for kilometers, judged and obstructed with impunity. Cash-strapped women's organizations fundraised on Facebook to cover the cost of abortion for people without housing or those experiencing violence. Abortion was decriminalized in four jurisdictions in as many years, but in failing to make healthcare affordable or available, governments forced patients to rely on good luck or goodwill to access the procedure.

Women, with or without uteruses, already know their bodies can be treated as public property. Week by week, I learned how many people can and will intervene in the choices women make about our own bodies and our own futures. Once you understand the body as public property, you begin to see how the state can also degrade what it owns through neglect.

After a couple of articles, a handful of people I knew messaged to tell me about their abortions. Within months, it was dozens. I found girls I had gone to high school with, journalists in other states, mothers and grandmothers who had had backyard abortions, all wanting to tell someone, often for the first time. Halfway through dinner, a friend took a sip of wine, closed her eyes and, keeping them shut, said, "I know you won't judge me." I moved the food out of the way, held her hand and waited. She turned her head to the right, looking past me, the tears on her left cheek catching the light, and only met my eye when she had finished her story. Over the next four years, people would tell me again and again that no matter what, whether the law, their doctors, or their families helped or hindered them, they would have ended their pregnancy somehow, safely or unsafely. A woman approached me at a bookshop and told me about her great-grandmother, who had many children and found herself pregnant for the last time. She tried to end the pregnancy herself out of desperation and when it went wrong, was too scared to get help as abortion was a crime. This woman said her own grandmother watched the white bed sheets turn red as her mother slowly died. "They kept changing the linen again and again. But it just kept getting soaked with blood. It was all they could do. *Change the linen, change the linen, change the linen.*"

In 2018, an Australian politician introduced a motion calling on the government to fund counseling for women who wanted to have abortions; this would inform them about the "development of the unborn baby," alternatives such as adoption, and the risks of abortion. "We have seen outrage over the destruction of kangaroos, yet where is the same compassion when it comes to an unborn human?" the senator—who later that year invoked a Nazi euphemism for genocide while arguing against Muslim migration— asked the chamber. The motion was redundant; anyone accessing abortion services publicly or privately is offered counseling and informed of any risks—but anti-abortion politicians around the world do this frequently. They pass meaningless motions or suggest unnecessary amendments to proposed legislation—a gestational limit that is already regulated by clinical guidelines, a caveat forbidding sex-selective abortions that would only work if doctors were mind readers, an amendment creating a separate criminal offense for anyone who pressures someone into having an abortion as if intimidation isn't already a crime. Their claims so rarely matched the lived experiences of each person I interviewed, and the grandstanding was never about practicality—for that you'd need truth—but the message it sent. Behind the propositions I fact-checked remained a suspicion of women and their capacity to make choices of any virtue for themselves.

I have interviewed women who could not fund the cost of a termination let alone the cost of raising a child. One of the first stories I published was about research that showed women in Australia were delaying paying bills and forgoing food and groceries to cover the cost of getting an abortion. There was the woman who said she paid for some of her abortion with 20-cent pieces from her friends' tip jars. The woman who told me she had lived on packet noodles for weeks afterwards. The woman who borrowed half and cashed in all of her accrued annual leave to cover the rest. All the pregnant people who relied on women's organizations to fundraise for them via Facebook statuses—a fourteen-year-old without accommodation who could not access her local Catholic public hospital, a young homeless woman who was pregnant after being sexually assaulted while staying in a squat and had tried to induce a miscarriage with over-the-counter medications, a mother of three whose ex-partner had been jailed for the physical and sexual violence he had perpetrated against her.

Jamie had been hospitalized for severe postpartum depression seven months after the birth of her son and started a relationship with her abuser a few months later. "I was in a women's-only mental health housing and a vulnerable person with a young child," she told me. Jamie's partner, who was eventually charged and jailed for assaulting her, refused to wear protection as it "didn't feel as good." "He knew I would take risks if he didn't want to use protection because in this abusive dynamic, I would have done anything to make him happy," she said. They had decided to terminate the pregnancy, but she wanted a few days to accept and process the decision. "He responded violently, assaulted me, stomped on my stomach, and grabbed me by the throat." Jamie said access to affordable abortion saved her life. "I could never condemn myself, my son, or that child to being tied to an abusive man for eighteen years, giving him that hold on me, giving him any right to contact me ever again," she said. "I had to make that sacrifice to sever that tie."

Laura had been a victim of domestic abuse after she fell pregnant and wanted an abortion. "I was coerced into keeping the baby due to my partner's emotional abuse, controlling and harassing tactics, which later escalated into physical abuse," she told me. "The entire nine months, I was trapped in his control, reliant on him, and subjected to emotional turmoil." The violence does not stop with the pregnancy; in fact, pregnancy can be a risk factor for violence. Australia's personal safety survey found that more than half (54 percent) of women living with abusive partners experienced violence during pregnancy, while a 2021 analysis of America's homicide data found pregnancy significantly increases a woman's risk of being killed by her partner.

"I think domestic violence is about control and [during pregnancy] she is starting to focus on this new life, her body is changing, she is developing that natural maternal care for the baby," Hannah Dahlen, a professor of midwifery, told me. "Men are starting to see their possession slip from their grip." It can also tighten their grip. I sat waiting with Isabelle in a small room next to the courtroom where her ex-partner was about to be sentenced for her rape. Her leg shook nervously as she read over her victim impact statement, preparing herself. She had a congenital heart condition, which meant she could not use the contraceptive pill when they were together and her pregnancies were high-risk. She had three children because her partner had refused to wear protection and she did not feel like she had any control over when they had sex. "It felt like an obligation and another chore, and I just gave it to him so he'd shut up, because I didn't want the fighting," she told me. She also had multiple abortions throughout their relationship, against his wishes. "He wanted me to have babies because that meant staying home another five years." Isabelle lost an enormous amount of blood in her final pregnancy because she also had placenta previa, a condition where the placenta lies low and may cover the cervix, blocking the baby's exit during birth. She nearly died. She looked at her partner after the birth and thought, "How dare you? And all because you wanted sex." A jury found him guilty of one count and not guilty of another count of rape. He was sentenced to four years' imprisonment with a non-parole period of two years and nine months.

"For me, the termination was an act of love for my other children and a reaffirmation of my love for my relationship," Kate whispered over the phone, so as not to wake her sleeping baby. She had had a medical abortion on the eve of Mother's Day a few years earlier. "If I hadn't had an abortion my life would be over. I know I would have taken my own life and left many children without a mum." Other women did not think they could survive going off their psychiatric medication for the duration of a pregnancy.

The majority of abortions happen in the first nine weeks of gestation. It was, for most people I spoke to, an instant decision to end a pregnancy even if doing so was complex or confronting. Liz, a Christian, was told at eleven weeks that her fetus had abnormalities. Her father told her if the Lord wanted her to keep the pregnancy, he would make that clear. She knew she wanted to terminate. "Abortion is portrayed in Christianity as being this cold and callous money-making business, and that if you have an abortion you'll never really get rid of the guilt because you'll suffer for the rest of your life," she said. "I felt really peaceful about it."

There were women who felt unadulterated relief about their decision and others who did not regret their abortions, yet they had a real sense of grief about them. Sadness, even regret, is not a medical condition, but I have repeatedly debunked a widely discredited phenomenon, coined "post-abortion syndrome" by American anti-abortion campaigner Vincent Rue in the 1980s, that suggests women who have terminated a pregnancy allegedly develop a condition in which they are more prone to suicidal ideation, alcohol, and drug abuse among other things. The tragic consequence of this misinformation is the women I interviewed who were sad about their abortions felt there was no space in the pro-choice movement to acknowledge their feelings without giving power to religious charlatans.

"It has taken me a long time to let myself feel sad because I am so pro-choice—I felt like that meant you're not allowed to be ashamed and you're not allowed to be sad," one woman told me. She was a lesbian who had gotten pregnant from one-night stand with a man on a cruise ship; she was grieving her partner of ten years, who had recently died. Another woman who had an abortion as a teenager said, "Any sign of weakness is co-opted by a narrative that I don't want to contribute to because I'm not grieving for the child I could have had. . . . Reducing it to a decision that you have to be 100 percent comfortable with really erases the experience of people who— for whatever reason—need to terminate a pregnancy but who would, in other circumstances, have kept it. It doesn't leave room for people who have conflicted emotions about it."

Just as I stopped writing about reproductive rights full-time, a landmark ten-year study was published that confirmed what I had always believed: not only that my interviewees' choices were painfully considered, as I could hear in their voices and through their tears, but that their self-knowledge could in fact be prescient. It wasn't an aimless prediction, a foolish clairvoyance, but an awareness of their own material conditions. Diana Greene Foster and her team of psychologists, epidemiologists, physicians, demographers, economists, and public health researchers conducted and analyzed almost eight thousand interviews of women who were either allowed or denied the abortion they wanted in the United States for *The Turnaway Study*. Some gave birth after they were denied an abortion because they had been just over a clinic's gestational limit and the rest were just under that limit and received an abortion. "When asked why they want to end a pregnancy, women give specific and personal reasons," Greene writes. "And their fears are borne out in the experiences of women who carry unwanted pregnancies to term." The data should not matter—agency should not only be afforded the prophetic—but it does matter because for decades women have been told they are making rushed, uninformed, selfish choices to end their pregnancies.

The *Turnaway Study* found women who were denied their abortions were more likely to live in poverty. It found that women who were unable to terminate their pregnancies were more likely to stay in contact with their violent partner. It found the children of women who had to carry an unwanted pregnancy to term scored worse on several measures of health and development than those whose mother was able to access the abortion she wanted. There were no differences in the women just over or just under the gestational limits when it came to baseline mental health, history of trauma, or drug and alcohol use—they were similar to national estimates. Those who had been denied an abortion had slightly worse mental health in the short-term but within a year the two groups found themselves back at similar levels. These women proved resilient to the experience of giving birth following an unwanted pregnancy. Greene found no evidence that abortion hurt women and found that women who had terminated their pregnancy were more frequently better off—physically, financially, professionally—than those who were denied one. Two women who were denied their abortions died of childbirth related causes.

The data does not say having a child makes your life worse. It says that when women want to end a pregnancy, there are real repercussions if they are denied that choice. It says that women know themselves and their families and use that knowledge to make choices. Women who were given their abortion were more likely to intentionally become pregnant in the next five years than women who were not.

In the United States, the legality of abortion now varies dramatically depending on where you live, with some states banning terminations altogether unless it is to prevent the death of the pregnant person or where the pregnancy is the result of rape or incest and other states only allowing abortions up to unworkable gestational limits like six weeks before most people know they are pregnant. Abortion still sits in criminal law in the UK, apart from in Northern Ireland, but people still access abortion every day. The Abortion Act, passed in 1967, allows abortion in England, Scotland, and Wales without prosecution of the patient or doctor if certain rules are followed. This includes two doctors agreeing that continuing the pregnancy would pose a greater risk to a woman's mental or physical health or to that of her existing children than having an abortion, that the abortion is necessary to save the woman's life or prevent grave permanent injury, or for fetal anomaly. The abortion may only be performed by a doctor and the places where an abortion can be performed are also defined in law.

"On paper the law looks cumbersome, but for most women it's a very straightforward process because continuing a pregnancy is statistically always riskier than not taking a pregnancy to term, and because health is interpreted in light of the World Health Organization definition, which is not just the absence of disease but the presence of wellbeing," Patricia Lohr, medical director of the British Pregnancy Advisory Service, tells me. "The law also allows for clinical discretion and, over the years, broad interpretation has meant that for most the law meets their need for an abortion whatever the reason. But the fact that abortion remains in criminal legislation, rather than being regulated in health legislation, still undermines the autonomy of women seeking an abortion, especially those in complex circumstances," Patricia says. A gestational limit that is codified by law can be "absolutely devastating" for the people who need a termination after that gestation. "Abortion for mental or physical health is only allowed to twenty-three weeks and six days of pregnancy. One day's difference and suddenly you can't get an abortion," she says.

What does it mean for doctors when a procedure lives in a gray concession of criminal law rather than regulated by health legislation? "It keeps us from providing evidence-based medical care," Patricia says, adding that it also ensures the procedure remains marginalized and stigmatized, disincentivizing medical professionals from training in abortion care. "Even though we know [abortion drugs] can be used safely at home beyond nine weeks and six days, that is the law in England and Wales and if you come in at ten weeks and zero days I cannot give those medicines to use at home even if studies show it is safe and effective. In addition, we have to tell women 'if you intentionally use these medications and you know you're over that gestation, it is illegal.'"

Even in a country like England with far more reproductive freedoms than others, these rights remain provisional. Patricia thinks an interplay between religious ideology, a belief that the rights of an embryo or fetus are paramount to a woman's, and a lack of trust in women as decision-makers has created a culture where it makes sense for these personal health decisions to be subjected to legal oversight. "At some point in pregnancy, the needs and rights of the woman who is pregnant don't exist anymore. This is a result of a patriarchal society where women are subordinate: They don't matter and the potential for life takes priority over them."

If you have the capacity for pregnancy, you can be simultaneously scrutinized and abandoned by a health system when abortion remains a crime, no matter how many loopholes there are. Sophie, a woman in an Australian country town, spoke to me when she was about to leave work and drive six hours to stay overnight at a hospital because every hospital near her house had refused to accept her as a patient. She had taken RU486 (mifepristone) but the second pill, which expels the pregnancy, had not worked. She could not believe that she was going to have to take sick leave and book a hotel to complete a procedure thousands of women do every week. She needed a D&C (dilation and curettage), an operation that every obstetric and gynecological ward around the world performs every day, whether for a spontaneous or induced miscarriage. "Whose values and morals does this woman have to abide by?" her doctor, who had been trying to get her into hospitals locally, asked me, his voice breaking over the phone.

I did not publish an article about it but around that time, the doctor called me again while he was in the midst of dealing with another woman who'd had a failed medical abortion in a regional area and needed a D&C. She was waiting anxiously in the emergency department of her large local hospital. They would not admit her as a patient. I am still not sure if it was obstruction by a staff member or an unwillingness to be involved in the aftermath of an abortion while the procedure remained in the state's criminal code. Her doctor was increasingly anxious that they would only see her once she was at great medical risk. It was not until I had called repeatedly and sent media requests to the head of the ward, asking for their policies on who was eligible to be admitted for a D&C, that she was quietly admitted. A situation so tenuous that the threat of bad publicity could change it.

Olivia, a single mother in another Australian country town, had an intrauterine device (IUD) inserted at her local hospital and then found out she had been pregnant when they gave it to her. The hospital refused to deal with the situation by terminating the pregnancy or removing the IUD and sent her away with painkillers, despite warning her that there was a high risk the device would perforate her uterus because she was pregnant. She told me that every doctor and nurse she dealt with was panicked, but they said it wasn't enough of an emergency to operate until something more drastic happened. Her mother took a day of carer's leave and drove her to a private clinic cross state. She paid the money she had saved for her son's first vacation to cover the abortion and IUD removal.

To write about abortion is to hear constantly from people who know what is going on and to hear nothing from people who can change it. It is hearing versions of the same truths from patients, gynecologists, obstetricians, counselors, surgeons, frontline domestic violence workers, volunteers, and lawyers who repeatedly offer you their expertise and to hear meaningless jargon from government departments. When the status quo denies people the choice to end a pregnancy, those who maintain it are complicit.

The most successful narrative the anti-abortion lobby has authored, is to frame the decision to terminate a pregnancy as a decision to reject motherhood. A desperate teenager or a selfish hussy might terminate a pregnancy, but a mother, she who has known what it is to give and sustain life, surely could not. This myth has proved powerful, affirming that women who have abortions are occupied with themselves only. They are not nurturing, they are not gentle, they are not maternal. In fact, it is estimated that more than half of women in Australia who have abortions are mothers. In the United States, around 60 percent of patients who have abortions are already mothers and half of them have two or more children. Figures in the United Kingdom from 2021 show the proportion of people who have terminations who were already mothers jumped from 51 percent to 57 percent in the preceding decade. The women in my stories were making decisions as mothers, even for the few who weren't already or would never become mothers. The idea that women do not have adequate information, intelligence, or intuition to make decisions for themselves but somehow have the innate ability to care for a child often dovetails neatly with the idea that abortion is to reject motherhood, either through selfishness, incomprehension that life is growing inside of them—here is an ultrasound—or ignorance about how easy and fulfilling parenting can be.

Nowhere was this myth more ruthlessly mongered than in the debate about abortions after the first or second trimester. Each push to decriminalize abortion has been met with an aggressive misinformation campaign about what anti-abortion campaigners termed "partial-birth abortions" or "abortion up to birth." Examining these claims in parliamentary and public debate took up too much of my reporting. One Australian Senator, Cary Bernardi, claimed later term abortions were when "you've known you're pregnant for thirty-four or thirty-five weeks and you decide you're going to have a termination. How can anyone justify the killing of a baby at that point?" he asked the chamber. "It is murder of an unborn baby that could exist outside of the womb, and it shouldn't be done on what I would say is the simple demand, or the selfish demand, of an individual involved." Of course, women can't just decide to have an abortion at thirty-four or thirty-five weeks.

As many doctors did, obstetrician and maternal-fetal medicine specialist Dr. Carol Portmann explained that if anyone wanted a termination at thirty weeks "they would just have to go on to have the baby." Terminations beyond the utmost gestational limit—twenty-two or twenty-four weeks in most areas—can't be done on a patient's whim, they are only permitted after strenuous medical consultation, often with an ethics board.

Patients are often denied abortions past a certain gestation point, but those who are granted them are in devastating situations. "It is mostly brain problems which weren't visible earlier on, and parents know their child will survive for a period of time with no quality of life, whether that is a matter of days or up to a year, and pass away. And parents feel they simply can't watch their child in suffering," she said. "These are conditions which are ultimately always lethal." Portmann told me in her more than two decades of clinical experience she had never been asked to perform a termination after twenty-eight weeks for psychosocial reasons. "It is always because a baby has [been] found to have such a severe heart or brain injury, or where the mother's life is at risk."

Emily, a mother who terminated a wanted pregnancy at nineteen weeks, told me about Maya. "She was really sick and it was unlikely that she would survive to term, but if she did she may have been born dead, died in the process or lived a short and painful life for a few days where she wouldn't see life outside the hospital. . . . It would have been cruel to force her to live through that pain." Emily described the agony of the process in which her labor was induced, and the unforgettable thud of her dead fetus hitting the bedpan. "Post-birth you have bleeding, which was almost reassuring that I had this connection to her," she said. "It almost made something that was very surreal seem quite real because while it was a day, it was not just a day you get over: You're forever changed by it."

Another male senator moved a motion to condemn abortion decriminalization saying, "I can hardly hold the thought: a baby who is seconds off being named, or even pre-named in many cases—certainly, in my family line and in most of the families I'm involved with—will be euthanized." Melanie McKenzie, who runs a not-for-profit organization to support women and their families who have received a poor or fatal diagnosis during pregnancy, testified in support of decriminalizing abortion: "These parents face perhaps the hardest decision of all when told of a fatal diagnosis of their unborn baby: whether or not to have a late termination," she said. "This is never a decision taken lightly or without much medical testing, diagnosis, and medical advice." In 2010, McKenzie's fourth son, Harrison, lived for just twenty-eight hours due to an incurable condition, a diaphragmatic hernia, diagnosed at twenty weeks' gestation. "We chose to continue with our pregnancy," she said. "I watched my son, who was in obvious pain, having to have invasive medical procedures."

Abby, a mother who terminated a pregnancy at twenty-four weeks, told me she waited for four days in hospital in unbearable limbo while her case underwent a legal review. She was told by doctors she needed to terminate as soon as possible as her fetus' heart was barely beating. "I was terrified of having a dead body inside of me," she told me. "I was in labor for five hours and scared the entire time because, on top of the immense pain, I knew I was going to give birth to a dead baby." The family had a private burial at a cemetery and they visit every day to lay fresh flowers at Harrison's grave.

The month after the male Australian senator spoke against abortion decriminalization, his colleague stood up, tears in her eyes, and said to her fellow senators in the chamber, "Most . . . late-term abortions are because there are issues with the development of the fetus, and that was certainly the case for mine, and yet [other senators] are willing to stand here in this place and call me a murderer. Anybody who wants to look at the facts about late-term abortions will see that a woman having a late-term abortion has gone through a huge thought process, discussion, and consideration of whether it's the right thing to do." Later, she told me privately, "I know how much impact those words have, and my emotion showed in the Senate."

I am no longer surprised about what people will blame on abortion. One politician said his region's diminishing share of tax profits was due to slow population growth because of abortion. The budget might be repaired if the government "promoted" women continuing unwanted pregnancies.

During the devastating 2020 Black Summer bushfires in Australia, my local anti-abortion organization told its members that the deadly blazes were ordered by God for our own good and would continue until we rejected moral degeneracy. Your body is shrinking tax revenue; your body is kindling. In my inbox, in the submissions to legislation, in their speeches to parliament, on their posters, on their billboards, people referred to abortion as "infanticide." These entities repeatedly and earnestly said that there was no difference between most abortions, which take place before nine weeks without surgery, and the murder of a child. I always found it jarring that these people, who described embryos and teenagers as children, refused to interrogate why having a child might be untenable for someone. If they believed this was murder, would they not be concerned that this woman with a killer's instinct, forced through legislation or neglect to carry the pregnancy to term, would then be responsible for a child?

Writer Jacqueline Rose argues motherhood should be "the central means through which a historical moment reckons with itself" and that mothers can contribute to our understanding of public and political space by dint of being mothers. Actual infanticide has always been instructive—the higher rates in poverty-stricken regions tell us where parents don't feel they have food for another mouth while the clusters of female infanticide show us where women are devalued so much that girls are unwanted. In Toni Morrison's novel *Beloved*, her protagonist Sethe, a runaway slave, slashes her infant daughter's throat as their capture is imminent. "It ain't my job to know what's worse," Sethe says of the choice between slavery and death. "It's my job to know what is and to keep [my children] away from what I know is terrible. I did that."

Sethe was based on the story of Margaret Garner who in 1856 said before her child was taken and made a slave, she would kill them, which she did. Her mother-in-law said that before Margaret cut her three-year-old daughter's throat with a butcher knife, she cried, "Mother, I will kill my children before they shall be taken back, every one of them." Morrison said in 1987 that her character Sethe did "absolutely the right thing" but that "she had no right to do it." "I think if I had seen what she had seen, and knew what was in store, and I felt that there was an afterlife—or even if I felt that there wasn't—I think I would have done the same thing," Morrison added. "But it's also the thing you have no right to do." Not all choices made by mothers are acts of maternal love or logic, that blanketing permissiveness most often sought by and granted to white, well-to-do mothers, but even choices that might seem unthinkable to an outsider are made by a human being who knows the truth of her own life so far.

The politicians and organizations who claim abortion is infanticide, who are hell-bent on intervening in a pregnancy to the point of birth or shortly after, have never been at the forefront of reforming the structures that make motherhood impossible for many women. Many anti-abortion politicians have blocked social security payment reform and gendered violence prevention funding while supporting policies that make life less safe and more precarious for marginalized mothers and their children. They are not campaigning to improve parental leave or wages or make childcare more affordable, and they refuse to support greater access to abortion at the earliest gestation and rather endorse detaining a toddler in an offshore prison. The lack of interest in the welfare of a child beyond the womb is instantaneous.

I read through hundreds of submissions to inquiries to decriminalize abortion in various states. There were many people arguing for abortion to remain a crime—one person asked lawmakers to imagine if Beethoven's mother had had an abortion, another said women were having abortions because they would rather pay for cable TV than diapers, and many compared safe and legal abortion to the Holocaust or to slavery. "Choosing to be sexually active and risk becoming pregnant these women already exercised 'control over their own bodies,'" one submission read. "Now indeed they do have a duty to exercise the control of their own bodies by giving birth." Another said a woman's body was property and abortion was most akin to breaking a lease: "The room/womb is let and a soul's agreement has been struck between landlady and tenant/un-born."

The message was always clear: The maternal archetype for those opposing abortion was a selfless virgin and now thousands of wayward women had gone and brought sex and self-interest into it. However, this hypothetical hypersexualized, or if they were feeling generous, sexually victimized, modern woman had a shot at redemption in motherhood. Every religious lobbyist I met made it clear that something like forgiveness awaited those who continued the pregnancy. If you don't take absolution, well, you've chosen damnation.

Dr. Alexandra Doig, an anti-abortion general practitioner, once gave me a list of alternatives to abortion. Her hypothetical scenarios were not ones I had encountered—a woman who had an abortion because she did not want morning sickness, another who had been unfaithful to her husband, and a pregnant child who had been sexually abused. She gave adoption as an option for most of them and in the case of an unviable pregnancy, she said the woman should be induced, the fetus born prematurely and palliated. Doig believed the priority for the pro-life movement was "protecting life at its earliest stage" but for pro-choice activists it was "sex without consequences." She said domestic violence was a "flow-on effect," a consequence of sexual liberty and that decades after the introduction of contraception, "we now have to teach all children how to identify a pedophile on the street or in their own homes."

I appreciated that she had said the quiet bit loud, that sex outside of procreation was not okay. In the hours of political debates I had sat through on abortion, some into the early hours of the next day, no one mentioned sex. It was always hovering above the conversation—sex before or outside marriage, sex with strangers and, importantly, sex for pleasure, not procreation. I have written stories about women whose partners sexually assaulted them and refused to use contraception, flushed their pills down the toilet, one smashing a hormonal implant in her arm, another ripping out her IUD. I spoke to doctors about what they offer women whose partners would turn violent if they knew they were using contraceptives—hormone progesterone discreetly injected, a hormonal IUD with the strings cut short or a copper IUD if he wants proof of menstruation. The ways in which pregnant women are coerced into keeping pregnancies they want to discontinue goes beyond the physical obstruction outside clinics. Reproductive coercion can include contraceptive sabotage, pressuring another person into falling pregnant, continuing a pregnancy, or ending a pregnancy, or forcing a person into sterilization. It can be so subtle sometimes you wouldn't know how to spot it.

I spent the day at a crisis pregnancy center, linked to vocal anti-abortion politicians and religious lobbyists and marketed as a "place to pause" before making a decision about an unplanned pregnancy. Behind the Tiffany-blue café serving tea and pastries there were two ultrasound machines used by a volunteer nurse who told me, "My standpoint is that life begins at conception." Unlike at all-options services, these ultrasound scans are not diagnostic but a tool to help achieve one outcome. This place did not help people navigate the often complicated path to an abortion or fund terminations for those without means. They existed to support parents in keeping their pregnancies by providing "pre-decision counseling" and "congrats starter packs" as well as baby carriage and car seat fitting and "mummy must-haves" hospital kits.

"I have never met a woman who hasn't regretted her abortion, whereas I've never met a woman who has regretted having a child," the organization's chief executive told me. "Women have fears of the material requirements that a baby might bring into their scenario, so usually it is not pregnancy that is the problem but other stuff around it." She showed me a storage room packed with donated cribs and strollers. If you wanted to continue your pregnancy and had no money, this place would be helpful. If you were trying to access an abortion and thought you had found support, this place would be hell.

I have seen how reproductive health needs are prioritized according to fertility, a quality that declines with age. This is not unique to older women—trans men and pre-menopausal infertile women have their own unique struggles—but in my work I have most closely observed the neglect of cis women past their reproductive prime.

I reported on the legal fight between Johnson & Johnson and women who had been implanted with transvaginal mesh for prolapse or incontinence. The court, as did a Senate inquiry into the devices from all brands, heard from women, mostly in their fifties and sixties, who were experiencing chronic pain, inability to exercise, sit, or sleep normally. They were unable to have pain-free vaginal sex due to adverse impacts from the mesh including, in many instances, the polypropylene device eroding through tissue and into other organs. At that point, I had interviewed a woman who was suicidal living with complications from mesh, a woman whose husband was stabbed by the device after it pierced through her vaginal wall, and a woman who spent tens of thousands of dollars putting her daughter who has special needs into care while she used all of her annual leave to fly to the United States to have the mesh removed after four corrective surgeries in Australia had failed. A video of a mesh insertion was tendered as evidence and played on multiple screens. We watched a series of metal tools plunging into sensitive pieces of tissue, knowing that for some women this piece of plastic would ruin their lives. The judge, a woman, remained stone-faced. The complainants in the courtroom moved uncomfortably in their seats as another incision was made, a knife into an apricot.

In the Australian Senate inquiry into multiple mesh products, women testified that they were repeatedly ignored by their doctors, who appeared uninterested in helping women who were too old to have sex for procreation, have it for pleasure. The women were in some cases told to "just have anal" sex. Half of the women who experienced adverse physical and psychological side effects after receiving a vaginal mesh implant also suffered a relationship breakdown after the procedure. I wondered whether their pain would have been taken more seriously if menopause did not exist.

I interviewed a twenty-two-year-old woman who had two children and was pregnant with her third. She had been on an implant and then the mini pill and condoms the entire time, but her contraception had failed her thrice. She had gestational diabetes with each pregnancy and was determined not to have a fourth child. She had been referred for a consultation to have tubal ligation but no doctor would consider sterilizing her because of her age. "I was reduced to tears by a medical professional who has no compassion what-soever," she said. She told me a specialist asked her, "What happens in ten years if one of your children passes away?" The woman told the doctor she did not need the option to "replace" her children, she needed to ensure she did not have a fourth. A doctor from the hospital agreed to give me a comment for my story and suggested the woman try a different contraceptive or that her husband get a vasectomy. I thought of each decision this mother had made every day to keep her children fed, clothed, and alive without interven-tion. And yet this final decision, to risk having another child, was not considered hers to make.

I began to understand how patients could be reduced to something not quite sentient, a set of organs to be fiercely preserved while they could repro-duce and ignored once they couldn't.

"I've never had an abortion," I correct a friend. They'd assumed I had because, they said, I had barely reported on anything else for years. The implication buried in the assumption made by others, was personal attachment. An obsession with your subject matter is what makes a good beat reporter, but none of the men I knew who had distinct reporting rounds would have their dedication mistaken as such—the court reporter must have been a victim or perpetrator of a crime, the business journalist must have a giant stock portfolio, the industrial relations reporter must have once been unfairly dismissed. I felt embarrassed. Did they think this is a sad kind of solipsism? Had I not turned down every opportunity to give my personal opinion on abortion until I had finished reporting on it full-time? Had I not repeatedly interviewed people on all sides of the debate? Had I not presented the facts as clearly as possible? Was the expertise of the doctors I interviewed also compromised? I thought of Caroline de Costa, the first woman to become a professor of obstetrics and gynecology in Australia. The first autopsy she attended as a student in Ireland was a twenty-three-year-old unmarried woman who had died as the result of a backyard abortion. Her uterus was so butchered it fell apart in the pathologist's hands. Does bearing witness to this compromise her forty years of clinical experience?

I realized this obsession with your specialty was only personal, even pathological, if you were a woman writing about issues that predominantly affected women. What does personal detachment and objectivity look like when you are a woman reporting on the pain of other women? I have always found opinion columns parading as journalism dishonest, but if you have made a genuine and good faith attempt to cover the complexity of an issue so fraught, what is the value in denying your interviewees' pain? What is the value of denying your own in reaction to it? Many of my interviewees cried. What is the purpose of pretending I didn't also cry sometimes once I'd hung up the phone? Does our humanity, do our bodies, make us worse journalists? I think the vitriol I received would have stung in a specific way if I had terminated a pregnancy, but I don't believe an abortion would have made me worse at my job.

I once worked on an investigation with another journalist who had survived a rape as, statistically speaking, many journalists would have. She taught me to offer victims and survivors as much agency as is possible in how their story was told. Choice had been taken from them, don't make them feel like everything was once again out of their control. I asked if they would like to know which quotes would be used, the probable headline, and the framing of the article. I told them what time the article was likely to be published and sent the link. I asked what pseudonym they might like. This journalist's life experience made her, and in turn me, better not worse at the job.

A well-meaning man with decades more experience than me encouraged me to change my focus to something "harder-hitting" before I was pigeon-holed as a journalist who only wrote about "women's stuff." I did not know how to say there might not be anything more political than the regulation of a body by the state without appearing too attached to my work. There was so much I could have said about how hard it should have hit him, how hard it had hit me. I understood he thought I had written myself into a corner not through professional dedication but gendered obsession. Eventually, I agreed that I had in some way boxed myself in and cut myself off. I had sacrificed something I didn't know how to name. I didn't have the words yet to say I believed it was motherhood.

When I first began writing about abortion, most places didn't have safe access zones protecting patients from picketers outside clinics. Many patients I spoke to had been harassed on their way in. A single mother, experiencing violence and undergoing radiotherapy in her uterus, who couldn't afford to travel to another state and found herself encircled by the religious picketers outside one town's only abortion clinic. These picketers carried rosary beads and signs emblazoned with dead fetuses. She told them about her medical situation and they told her the pregnancy was God's will. A Chinese-Australian woman secretly recorded a "sidewalk counselor" offering to help her with her immigration, legal, and visa status if she did not enter the clinic. A woman splashed with fake blood, those handed plastic fetal dolls, a sexual assault survivor photographed by picketers when she got back into her car, a nurse who had to comfort a patient when a protester told her four-year-old son that mummy was about to kill her sibling.

Kathy Clubb became the face of a renewed fight between religious groups and lawmakers and health professionals over safe-access zones. Clubb was the first person charged, convicted, and fined for breaching the zones around clinics in Melbourne, Victoria, when she handed a patient and her partner a pamphlet. The mother of thirteen would later appeal her case all the way to the highest court in the country, arguing that the zones themselves were unconstitutional as they impinged on her freedom of political communication. This one woman, and another picketer, were both threatening the legality of the zones in all states, and they had the financial backing of the Australian Christian Lobby, who had identified the cases as "strategic." Attorney generals across the country intervened, making submissions to the court against Clubb and arguing that trying to deter a person from making a personal and private medical choice was not political communication just because abortion had become politicized. She lost, but before she did, Clubb wrote a lengthy blog post about me, which she also posted on her Instagram. It was titled "Dear Gina, You're Helping Women Kill Their Babies." The stock image was of a distraught woman sitting in a car, her hands covering her face. Presumably I'd helped this woman to murder her child.

Clubb and I had corresponded for a few stories and our interactions had always been polite. It was a shock to realize she thought of me at all. Her diatribe focused on a story I had written about what was inside the bags anti-abortion picketers were handing patients entering an abortion clinic which were full of misinformed pamphlets. "Now I don't blame you for promulgating these falsehoods," Clubb wrote to me in her article. "You also haven't seen the glazed-over look of the women who come outside after their abortion." This was true, I did not regularly station myself outside clinics like she did. However, I had spoken to at least as many women about their abortions as religious picketers like her had. An interviewee who had read the blog post told me, "Of course women looked glazed-over. I had just been sedated and someone is coming at me with a pamphlet full of prayers."

As the only reporter writing about abortion regularly in Australia and with an international, mostly American, readership, I found myself a target for people like Clubb. By then I had been sent prayers, bible verses, and a rape threat, but something about her article, the boldness of the accusation in its title, derailed me. I felt sad and exhausted and completely isolated. Everyone I told dismissed her as an outlier, a voice from the fringes, a stranger. I didn't know a single person who would understand how I felt. I wanted to write about anything but reproductive rights.

Clubb has the same first name as my mother. My mother, who attended "pro-life" rallies at university. My mother, who believes life begins at conception. My mother, with whom I fell into an uncomfortable silence over my job. It was easier not to talk about it. The first time I mentioned my reporting, she defended protesters, explaining they were only trying to help and they should have the right to do so. She saw the eventual successful enactment of safe-access zones in our state as Clubb did, as a loss for freedom of speech. It felt as though it did not matter how many women told their stories, they would always be murderers and I would always be aiding and abetting them, complicit in something burning with shame, smoking with sin.

I was raised a Catholic but casually so. I went to church at Christmas and Easter, attended scripture classes and had a fleeting devout phase around the age of ten, when I began the sacraments of initiation. I would kneel before a shrine of Mother Mary I had resting in the unused fireplace in my room and thank Jesus for my good health before bargaining with him to reunite my parents, help my brothers, and make sure my sister passed her law exams. In my First Reconciliation, in which you have to go to confession for the first time, I confessed to the priest that my bedroom was messy. He gave me ten Hail Marys. I wore a white dress and patent leather shoes for my First Eucharist, in which you are given the body of Christ and his blood, a sip of red wine, for the first time. Then, finally, I had my Confirmation, in which you are given the gift of the Holy Spirit and the name of a saint. I chose Frances. I stopped believing soon after that.

More than a decade later, I arrived at one of Sydney's older courthouses to begin covering a murder trial for a newspaper. There was the same solemn hush of church, the same deference to a man in robes. It was a high-profile case, in which two men were accusing each other of pulling the trigger, and I had arrived slightly late. The wooden benches were long and shiny like pews and as I moved toward the row allocated for journalists, without thinking, I genuflected. I locked eyes with the judge as my knee kissed the carpet, my face warming. I shot upright and shuffled into my seat. He smirked, a TV reporter stopped chewing her gum, bewildered, and a juror looked at me sympathetically. Until I was about to go into emergency surgery to remove the "dead" ovary, this was the only indication that something of Catholicism had left its mark on me, a tattoo I found as permanent as I am.

As I sat on the edge of the hospital bed and signed the papers to have my ovary cut out, I felt scared but unsurprised. I couldn't express, even to myself, how inevitable it felt that my reproductive system would fail me. I observed the strict binary of what a mother could and could not be, unchallenged, even by my own reporting. This was the bolt of lightning I had been waiting for. It struck me for living in sin, for wanting a career, for not marrying, for using contraception, for writing about contraception, for writing so much about abortion, for being unsure about motherhood. If there was a God, would He not punish me for fact checking His disciples in multiple parliaments? For framing motherhood as anything other than destiny? For my ambivalence? For my criticism? My body was kindling. Two hundred milliliters of blood spilled into my pelvic cavity, clouding the ultrasound. I knew it was an unhinged, potentially morphine-induced thought but motherhood felt like a mirage, unreachable to a woman like me even if I should want it. *Where is your bodily autonomy now?*

Maybe religion has branded even non-believers, or maybe the stories we tell ourselves about women and the choices they make have less to do with theology and more to do with power. It took me a long time to realize that not every person opposed to abortion was holding rosaries. Most of them were just clutching pearls. Religion explained the hallucination of retribution, but not the inadequacy I felt. How fast I found myself capable of reproducing lies about my capacity to reproduce. In my mind I became the infertile woman as she has been historically—an object of suspicion, self-interested, uncaring, cold, unfeminine, scheming, more inclined to practice witchcraft.

Hippocrates thought women fell ill because their uterus was moving around the body, searching for moisture. This "wandering womb" stalked like an animal wanting to be inseminated, Terri Kapsalis writes, adding that if it went towards the throat, the woman would lose her voice, choke or cough, and if it got stuck in the ribcage, she might have difficulty breathing. In Ancient Greece, magicians prescribed hysterical women amulets to heal their wandering wombs, but as Kapsalis notes, the mischievous uterus was thought to relax into its proper place in pregnancy. "The triad of marriage, intercourse, and pregnancy was the ultimate treatment for the semen-hungry womb," she writes. "The uterus was a troublemaker and was best sated when pregnant."

By the nineteenth century hysteria, derived from the Greek *hystera*, meaning womb, was thought to be a psychological rather than purely physical disease. In 1873, a Harvard professor wrote that women should not pursue higher education because they might become "irritable and infertile" if blood traveled to their brains instead of nourishing their uteruses. The idea persists: if the womb isn't being used for its God-given purpose, it wreaks havoc. People told me that becoming pregnant would ease the symptoms of endometriosis. *Only for nine months*, I thought.

I want to feel in communion with other fleshy beings, united by the vulnerability and brevity of our shared existence on this Earth, impelled to face every existential threat as one. But in many places, we are still women before we are human. I am scared of the ways motherhood might enforce and cement my gender. This is what happens when you nail an identity to the womb—arms are just tubes ending in ovaries, legs descending straight down like a cervix, hopes and dreams expanding only as the uterus does. She nurtures, she supports the growth of others. *Woman as womb* makes fertility synonymous with functioning, makes procreation purpose. *Woman as womb* sidelines all the women without wombs—transgender women, cis women with Mayer-Rokitansky-Küster-Hauser syndrome or those who have had hysterectomies. *Woman as womb* insists family must be made there, as though people don't foster, don't adopt, don't make room at a table for a stranger who becomes a relative.

I have spent so much of my life feeling indignant about being, as poet Denise Riley says, "positioned antagonistically as a woman-thing." That gendered self-consciousness has, Riley writes, "mercifully, a flickering nature." I am reminded in flashes, usually by other people, of myself as a woman-thing. Rarely is it enjoyable—a burst of glowing solidarity with other woman-things, an unexpected flash of gratitude for being socialized to express my feelings. More often it is a feeling that your body is illuminated by an inextinguishable and volatile flame—a bolt of fear as a man yells at you out of his car window, a fiery flush when a boyfriend's mother asks if you feel maternal, the searing grief of reading about another murder at the hands of someone she trusted. The stinging reminder that your body isn't quite yours.

2.

Reproductive Justice

I AM SUSPICIOUS OF MOTHERHOOD for what I have been taught to believe it is—the ultimate expression of womanhood. When your gender is the primary, or the only, weight under which you have felt oppressed, there is fear of solidifying it. Why would you further associate yourself with what is deemed less valuable? I can feel my own reluctance, and that of women like me—white, university-educated, nondisabled, middle-class—to have a child if parenthood might mean relinquishing the political, sexual, and social power that has allowed us into places and conversations historically reserved for white men with money.

Who is encouraged to be a mother? Who is trusted as a mother? Who is protected as a mother? When suffragists first conceptualized "voluntary motherhood," decades before marital rape was a crime, they were doing so to liberate a type of woman whose right to be a mother is rarely challenged. Their experiences were never universal, and yet refusing motherhood remains a paramount right that mainstream feminism strives to protect above other social and reproductive liberties.

What does it really mean to fear motherhood as a white middle-class woman? To wonder if I will become invisible before I imagine myself surveilled. To resent the domestic realm when I am not strictly designated to stay there. To picture my eros fading while other bodies are mythologized as hypersexual. To know I am more likely to be depoliticized than criminalized as a mother. I knew the questions I would ask on the page were not borne proportionately by all women, but I wanted to understand why I felt pregnancy and parenthood would interfere with the place my body occupies in the world. If I'm going to sulk about a loss of power, of control, of agency, I need to explain how I have them in the first place. If I'm going to talk about reproductive health, I need to speak of violence as well as care.

Tinu's experience of the British maternity care system was defined by neglect from her first pregnancy to her third, when she was hospitalized weeks after her pleas for help were dismissed. After requesting a birth plan for her first pregnancy, finally, well into her third trimester, Tinu was asked by a new doctor whether she was going to have a vaginal birth or cesarean. She was clear she wanted a vaginal birth. No doctor had indicated there was any reason for her to have a C-section. But this doctor told her, without any medical explanation, that if she didn't have a scheduled cesarean, she would end up having an emergency one. This would be rushed and risky, the doctor explained, as they would frantically *"cut, cut, cut"*—Tinu replicates the slashing motion with her hands—exposing her and the baby to harm. "What kind of doctor uses that kind of emotive language to basically bully you into making a decision about your body and your baby? I felt like I had no rights in my body," she said.

Disappointed, Tinu and her husband, reluctantly accepted their scheduled C-section date. They turned up for the operation and the doctor on the ward that day was confused to hear this hadn't been the couple's first preference. He explained, "No, you don't have to do anything you don't want to do" and she was sent home without her baby. "It was so emotionally turbulent," she remembered. When Tinu returned for the vaginal birth she had requested, no one explained to her that there was a cut off point for different types of pain relief, and she was left to endure the final stages of labor with 'gas and air,' confused as to why she wasn't able to access better pain relief.

A 2016 report from the United States found half of the white medical students sampled endorsed false biological beliefs about pain perception in Black and white physiology. "I have quite a high pain threshold but childbirth is childbirth," Tinu said to me. A 2020 Turning the Tide report captured racism and stereotyping in National Health Service maternity care, revealing staff had acted on the falsehood that Black women had a higher pain threshold. Workers testified that "ethnicity" was given as a reason for induction and told not to challenge it, one claiming they were told that Black women didn't bruise and another explaining that all the training textbooks were based on the anatomy of white men. Lawyers quoted in the report described the dismissive and harsh nature of correspondence from midwives, obtained under court order, and clients who thought they were going to die.

"I remember feeling so invisible and not listened to," Tinu says. "I'm obviously an expert of my own body, but I don't know myself in pregnancy and it is a new situation. And so you end up surrendering a lot of decision-making to these professionals because you think they know best . . . their knowledge and your knowledge of your body should go hand in hand."

Tinu began to worry when she bled during her third pregnancy at about twenty-six weeks' gestation during COVID-19 lockdowns. She had previously experienced two miscarriages. Tinu booked an over-the-phone appointment with a doctor who told her she had a urinary tract infection then put her on antibiotics. The bleeding became heavier. When Tinu sought medical advice again, asking to be examined, she was told she just needed to give the antibiotics a chance to work. "I need someone to actually see me and examine me," Tinu implored. That night the blood got so heavy—"it was horrifying"—that she drove an hour down the highway to the hospital after having been dismissed again over the phone. Once again, Tinu was told she hadn't given the antibiotics a chance to work and told to go home. She cried and pleaded with staff, explaining that she was bleeding profusely and that she was scared. "I obviously thought I was losing my baby," she said. "I just needed someone to examine me." Eventually, she was told she could sit in emergency and wait, which she did until 1 a.m. Her urine sample was unable to be tested because it was so polluted with blood. She begged the available doctor to examine her and he refused, repeatedly. She begged the doctor to explain where the blood was coming from. She begged for another doctor to examine her. "Right now I'm carrying a child and all I can see is blood and this is not okay," she said.

"The amount of time that guy took to convince me I didn't need to be examined, he could have just examined me."

The next doctor also refused to examine her and she was sent home. When the sun came up she called an emergency maternity line. The "flabbergasted" midwife who answered instructed Tinu to go back to the hospital and that they were expecting her. "She said 'please, please go back there now,'" Tinu said. "So I'm pregnant, tired, emotional and thinking I'm losing my baby driving up and down this motorway wondering if I'm going to face another doctor like that." Finally, after requesting countless times, Tinu was examined by another doctor. She was hospitalized for two weeks, requiring two blood transfusions. They are still unsure about what caused the blood loss, but it was not a UTI. "Thankfully, as you can see, the baby is here, thank god, but so many women don't make it," she said, gesturing to the toddler perched on her hip. "This whole racial discrimination and dismissiveness and lack of autonomy . . . it is almost like a movie."

When Tinu told her GP that she didn't want to go back to the same hospital to have her baby, her doctor read through the hospital notes. The doctor looked up at Tinu and said "So you said you asked to be examined?" and Tinu responded "I *begged* him. I *begged and begged and begged*." Her doctor looked confused: "But right here it says 'you declined, that you refused examination.'" Tinu read the notes in disbelief. "What kind of a doctor writes the opposite to what actually happened and if he thought that his decision to not examine me was medically correct then why did he lie in the notes? What if I had died and they would read my notes and say 'well, we tried to help her and she declined.' It was like a horror show to be in a hospital, a place where it was supposed to be a place of safety and healing and to be turned away at my most vulnerable. It's unforgivable. What do doctors go into the medical profession for if it's not to help people? Is it only to help people who look like them? Am I different? Do I deserve less? Do I not bleed? I *was* bleeding. Do I not deserve the same respect, the same dignity?"

In mid-2022, British charity Birthrights released the findings of a year-long inquiry into systematic racial injustice in maternity care and collected testimony from pregnant and birthing people, healthcare professionals, and lawyers in the United Kingdom. The report was titled "Systematic Racism,

Not Broken Bodies," summarizing the thread throughout the horrific testimony, that it was a racist system not "defective" bodies that was impacting maternity outcomes and experiences. Patients felt unsafe, ignored, disbelieved, and dehumanized. They felt like their consent was disregarded. Asian women described being referred to as "princesses" or "precious" and Black women as "aggressive" or "angry." "The white staff did not recognize jaundice in a Black baby," the report quotes a woman whose baby was hospitalized for several weeks after staff had told her nothing was wrong with him. "There was one point in my labor right near the end where I remember looking at (my partner) and saying, 'I'm going to be a Black statistic,'" another woman said. One Black midwife said the idea that Black bodies are somehow faulty and "flawed" was "really embedded in the system" and that women of color were made to feel as though they should be grateful for any care they received.

In the US, Native American, Alaska Native, and Black women are two to three times as likely to die from a pregnancy-related cause than white women. Black women are four times more likely than white women to die in pregnancy or childbirth in the United Kingdom. "The statistics relating to women that have died are not even all the women who were near misses like me," Tinu says. "The stats are worse than what they appear to be because they don't encompass all the maltreatment that women of color have had to endure. I know one woman who said she's so traumatized after her birth she's not going to have any more kids. She said to me, 'What if I die?'" Tinu wrote a long letter during her hospital stay and was met with coldness and dismissiveness by the hospital bureaucracy. She doesn't feel like voicing her concerns made any difference. She was told she should have escalated her worries and insisted and complained. The irony of this was not lost on Tinu, who was painfully aware of the line she walked between asserting her right to be examined and given medical care and avoiding appearing combative. "The microaggressions are really hard to navigate when you're in a vulnerable position," she explained. "You want to be heard, you don't want to be misunderstood. You don't want to be perceived as being aggressive because as Black women we sometimes feel we are perceived as angry Black women, so that then fuels a kind of silence. We don't want to speak up, even if it is completely valid, the way you say it is often misinterpreted."

Leicester community sexual and reproductive health doctor Annabel Sowemimo has argued practitioners need to recognize the lasting legacy of racist and unethical foundations of obstetrics and gynecology. "Colonial history has taught us, and subsequently generations of clinical professionals, that Black women are not soft or gentle—the idea of where the angry Black woman comes from—and therefore we're often not seen as vulnerable," Sowemimo told *Glamour* magazine. "It's why pain is often underplayed by those treating them or why we're often disbelieved about the reality and severity of our symptoms. Should you choose to stick your head above the parapet and advocate for yourself, you're shutdown and told that it's not that serious or you're being aggressive or angry." When Tinu was hospitalized for the blood infusions, one of the doctors told her: "You're actually such a nice lady. You're so pleasant." "What happens when I'm not nice? What if I'm just having a bad day? I'm allowed to have bad days too and I still deserve good medical healthcare. Is it not a human right? Am I not human?" Tinu asked me now. "I was born here and it scares me to think about my children. I've got two daughters and what is going to happen to them?" In the United States, a 2019 study found Black, Latinx, and Native American healthcare workers were severely underrepresented. Research has also shown a clear underrepresentation of people of Black, Brown, and Mixed ethnicity in leadership and governance roles in the NHS. "You can't be like 'we love the NHS yay,'" Tinu said, clapping her hands as people did to cheer on healthcare workers during the pandemic. "But they just can just kill a few of us and it's okay? No. We appreciate the NHS for all the amazing things it does and the people it continues to help, but the systemic racism that is breeding beneath cannot be ignored."

"Hiii Auntie Gigi." My niece's head floats into frame as we video call the morning of her first day of school. She shows me the red ribbons in her hair, her new school shoes adorned with love hearts and rainbows, and her checkered school dress, so cartoonishly oversized my stomach cramps from what I can only attribute to cuteness. "I might not make any friends," she says quietly, a statement I know is a question. I reassure her, desperately wishing I could instantly catapult across state to do so in person. Sometimes I wonder how my sister can function alongside this immobilizing love. This feeling, this raw protectiveness and glistening delight, this soreness and sweetness I feel watching my niece grow and interact with the world. This pure and private feeling is stolen from families in Australia every day.

Naomi Williams should have been taking her son to his first day of school the same week my niece began kindergarten. "At the end of the day, she should still be here and her little boy should be starting school," her mother Sharon told me. In the early hours of New Year's Day in 2016, Naomi, an award-winning disability worker and Wiradjuri woman, died. She suffered a cardiac arrest caused by an overwhelming sepsis infection while en route back to the emergency department that had sent her home the previous day with two paracetamol, thirty-four minutes after she got there. She was twenty-two weeks pregnant.

In 2018, I reported on part of the coronial inquest into Naomi's death. We listened to evidence that Naomi had been to Tumut Health Service, a hospital in her area, eighteen times in the eight months leading up to her death, repeatedly complaining of symptoms including vomiting, nausea, and abdominal pain. In most cases, she was given anti-nausea medication and fluids, offered drug and alcohol and mental health counseling, and sent away. The inquest heard that in June 2015 Naomi had tested positive for *Helicobacter pylori*, a stomach bacteria that can cause pain and nausea, and in September that year was diagnosed with excessive morning sickness. The inquest heard that Naomi had used cannabis to alleviate her symptoms, but the drug and alcohol reviews had found she was not dependent on it or any other substances. "They had already made their mind up [that Naomi was a drug user]," Sharon said. Two months before her daughter's death, Sharon wrote to the head of nursing staff at Tumut Health Service explaining that her daughter needed a specialist referral for her ongoing symptoms of vomiting, nausea, and pain, and that the repeated referrals to drug and alcohol counseling were adding to her daughter's distress. "They have tried to apologize to me, but I will never forgive them," Sharon said. "They just dismissed Naomi like she was a nobody. It was absolutely disgusting. The amount of times she presented to the hospital and doctor would have to be a red flag for anybody."

The inquest heard Naomi's partner Michael explain that the day she died was not the first time she went to Tumut Health Service "begging for help." "During the time she was pregnant, she went there again and again for her nausea," he said. "She would come home and tell me how tired she was of just being ignored—just being turned away. She felt like nobody was there listening to her." Michael said the pain would never leave him, that he was barely holding things together since Naomi died in front of him and his twelve-year-old daughter. He said life was "almost perfect" three years earlier when he was waiting for the birth of their son and they were talking about getting married. "That dream was shattered in an instant on New Year's Day when I watched the love of my life and my baby boy die in front of my eyes," he said to a silent courtroom. "I just wanted to take a moment, so the court and all the lawyers and hospital staff here understand what that feels like, when the light in your life has suddenly been taken away and all that's left is empty darkness."

Sharon said she tried to focus on the good parts of her life and writes things down when it all became too much. "I've still got stuff here of hers that I have to unpack and I struggle with letting go a bit," she said. "We're getting there slowly and teaching the boys to be strong and proud, to speak out when something isn't right. They know and I know her story will flow through them." Sharon sent me photos of the healing garden she built as a tribute to Naomi.

The state's deputy coroner told the courtroom she herself, as a middle-class white woman, would not have been treated as Naomi had. "Naomi Williams went to a doctor many, many times and never got a specialist referral," she said. "If I look at it from my own experience as a middle-class woman in the eastern suburbs of Sydney, my perception is I would have got a referral and that is my strong perception. I would not have gone in eighteen times and not gotten a referral."

I remember frantically transcribing this as she voiced what I had been thinking all week. I was the same age as Naomi had been and I knew this never would have happened to me. The court heard that Naomi had already decided she would have her baby in another state, where she could access a local Aboriginal Medical Service because, as her mother relayed, they would better "hear what she was saying." I could not imagine my medical history, my pain, my mother's email having been ignored.

The coroner ruled that while the nurse and midwife on duty could not have known Naomi's symptoms were a sign of a life-threatening bacterial infection, her care at Tumut Health Service was inadequate and Naomi had "reduced expectations of care" in the hours before her death. "I am satisfied that had there been more curiosity and inquiry involved by those caring for Naomi at the time of her presentation, a fuller picture of her condition may have emerged," the coroner said. Naomi should have had an assessment of her pain and medical history and "at the very least" a doctor should have been called on for further medical advice.

During Naomi's inquest, Yin Paradies, a professor of race relations, was cross-examined about the implicit racial bias in hospitals, which meant Indigenous patients received worse levels of care. They had 30 percent fewer procedures than non-Indigenous patients even accounting for location, socioeconomics, gender, and age. He explained Indigenous patients were discharged from hospital, against doctors' advice, at a rate five times higher than non-Indigenous patients. This was due to six reasons: "racism, lack of cultural safety, issues of miscommunication, issues of mistrust, family and social obligations, loneliness and isolation." Outside the court, he spoke to another journalist and myself and elaborated: "Historically, we had the stolen generations . . . in hospitals, there has been a history of forced sterilization and babies being taken and so on."

As with so many deaths of women of color, no one was criminally charged, no one was fined, no one was personally held responsible for Naomi's death. While an inquest found systematic failures, recommendations were only to the specific local health district, namely to make sure an Aboriginal liaison health worker could be available twenty-four hours a day and to improve the employment of Indigenous people as health workers to reduce danger in an unsafe system for Aboriginal patients. The recommendations do little to address the racism from which Sharon could not protect her daughter. Sharon believes if Naomi hadn't been racially profiled, she would have been listened to. "She would have been taken more seriously and I think they would have checked her medical background, seen her history, and sent her straight to a specialist," she said to me. "She lay down and cried, she was anxious. They didn't act on it or treat her with respect. She was put in the corner, put on a drip and left. She was treated like a second-class citizen." Sharon listed what she wants to change in hospitals after her daughter's death. The demands were painfully modest—for all patients to be listened to, for all patients to be treated with respect, for all patients to know that if they have presented multiple times, they will be attended to. "We are the experts in our own bodies and we know when there is something not right." The infection that killed Naomi was treatable with antibiotics.

Author Layla F. Saad writes in *Me and White Supremacy* that white supremacy is "an ideology, a paradigm, an institutional system, and a worldview" white people are born into. "Whether or not you have known it, [white supremacy] is a system that has granted you unearned privileges, protection, and power," Saad writes. "It is also a system that has been designed to keep you asleep and unaware of what having that privilege, protection, and power has meant for people who do not look like you." It is white privilege to be able to ignore the role of race in my reproductive choices and in motherhood. I have spent too much time worrying how my experience of pregnancy or motherhood would entrench my own oppression and not urgently considering how they would solidify my presence in places where other women are mistreated.

Now that I am wondering how I would plan a family, I see how narrow my definition of family planning has been. There is reproductive health—on which I have reported, fact-checked, and myth busted. There are reproductive rights—on which I have documented the legal restrictions and legislative changes around abortion and contraception. I have not spent much time on reproductive justice, which values not just the right to not have a child but the right to have a child and to parent that child in a safe and healthy environment. It goes far beyond pro-choice feminism and was created by activist women of color to capture, as academic Loretta J. Ross described in *Radical Reproductive Justice* how gender, race, class, ability, nationality, and sexuality all intersect to produce a reproductive politics that goes far beyond ending or preventing a pregnancy. "In addition to supporting the pro-choice movement's goals of protecting abortion rights and securing safe and effective contraceptives, as people of color subjected to continuous population control strategies, we must fight equally as hard for the right to have children and to parent the children we have," she writes.

There are so many groups of women who seek reproductive justice within violent systems—pregnant asylum seekers detained in offshore prisons, parents denied affordable fertility treatments, mothers trying to access social support—but the lasting legacy of who is encouraged to procreate and protected to safely do so in Australia began with colonization. Similarly, colonizers from the United States and Canada allowed eugenics-based sterilization—by 1953 nearly one-fifth of Puerto Rican women, many of whom didn't know the procedure was irreversible, had received sterilization. As gender studies professor at the University of Redlands Jennifer Nelson writes in *Women of Color and the Reproductive Rights Movement*, Black Nationalist groups—including the Nation of Islam and the Black Panther Party—brought sterilization abuse to the public's attention in the 1960s and 1970s, pointing out that poor women of color in America were often sterilized without their knowledge. "Indeed, physicians in many states used eugenic sterilization laws, passed in the first two decades of the twentieth century, to justify the sterilization of poor and often very young women of color," she writes.

Waanyi writer Alexis Wright says that "since time immemorial" her ancestors managed to survive in fragile environments. "In the Aboriginal world, we know the apocalyptic realities of two-and-a-half centuries of continual invasion, an invasion informed by the Enlightenment project of colonization, which has been driving the major environment disasters of the Anthropocene and the harmful realities of globalization." Fears about pregnancy and motherhood need to be tethered to reality, to a context beyond yourself. The structures inside which I find liberty and safety can be places of violence for other women. The assumption that a woman can, should, and will reproduce, though restrictive, is not universal.

White people have always been encouraged to reproduce themselves in the colonies. As legal academic Larissa Behrendt has written, ever since British invasion there has been "a call for the right type of woman to reproduce the nation." In 1904, a Royal Commission into the declining birth-rate in New

South Wales delivered its report condemning white women for having fewer children and putting their own comfort ahead of reproducing. This selfishness had struck "at the welfare of the white race in Australia" and would generate "a weaker race of Australians," claimed a *Sydney Morning Herald* article published following the commission's report. The commission had been called in response to the huge decline in the Australian birth-rate during the 1890s, but it was more an "ideological exercise" than a "rational inquiry," as historian Neville Hicks observed. The deliberate limitation of fertility increasingly practiced by women in Australia was of concern to everyone from doctors to politicians to clergymen, who feared the social and moral implications.

It was clear, in the opinion pieces and letters to newspapers at the time, that population growth through immigration or by increasing the rate of the whole population was not the proposed solution. "They feared for the future of the Anglo-Saxon race in Australia," Hicks writes. This report came during a decade when Aboriginal parents didn't even have legal guardianship over their children in most jurisdictions—their kids were legal wards of the state and so could be torn from families and relocated. It is estimated that up to a third of all Aboriginal and Torres Strait Islander children were forcibly separated from their families between 1910 and 1970 alone. Despite the abolition of many of the initial policies, including that of assimilation, which took children from their parents and placed them in often abusive institutions and taught them to reject their Indigenous heritage, this state-sanctioned removal has not stopped. As Anishinaabe journalist Tanya Talaga writes in her book *All Our Relations*, "even in a country like Canada," generations of Indigenous children have grown up in communities without access to the basic determinants of health: "income and social status, access to clean water and air, safe houses and communities, supportive families and a connection to their traditions, and access to a basic education and health care services."

It would make me happy as a feminist to write about reproductive rights as a united and equal march toward bodily freedom but, as author and scholar Sara Ahmed says, if talking about racism within feminism gets in the way of feminist happiness, then we need to get in the way of feminist happiness. You can't talk about modern family planning organizations and movements without tracing their undeniably racist roots. "Failing to recognize how white supremacist ideology affects pro-choice organizations and jeopardizes our collective ability to defeat our mutual opponents and weakens the entire movement," Ross writes. You can pick almost any family planning organization older than a few decades to understand eugenic influence on the birth control movement.

Planned Parenthood in the United States was founded by a eugenicist nurse Margaret Sanger who spoke to the women's auxiliary of the Ku Klux Klan in the 1920s and endorsed forcible sterilization of "unfit" people. Two letters—the MS, standing for Marie Stopes, in MSI Reproductive Choices—tell a long story about a major global abortion provider. Marie Stopes was a white founding mother of the reproductive rights movement who has been lauded for defying the Catholic Church and opening Britain's first clinic offering birth control advice to married women. She was a classist, racist, disablist homophobe whose proposed eugenics program has been described as "slightly to the right" of that enacted by Adolf Hitler, to whom she sent a book of poetry in the 1930s. She wanted the "hopelessly rotten and racially diseased" to be sterilized. The biggest publicly funded contraception and sexual health service in my state, Family Planning NSW, was founded as the Race Improvement Society and then the Racial Hygiene Association of New South Wales. The third object of its first constitution was to improve the race on eugenic principles. The association said in 1932 it "openly advocates sterilization of the unfit" and that a "good or bad human race does not just happen—it is bred the same as sheep etc. can be bred."

The Race Improvement Society was concerned with preventing venereal diseases and, as historian Sylvia Bannah wrote in her PhD thesis on the history of family planning in Australia, the "promotion of racial fitness through premarital health checks." At the time, family planning organizations received backlash because of contraception rather than their blatant eugenics—population control was accepted in Australia long before birth control was. As historian Diana Wyndham suggests, the eugenics movement was only less active and organized in Australia than it was in other countries because these principles were already enshrined into our legislation and founding ethos.

Terra nullius, land belonging to no one, was the concept used by the British government to justify the colonization of Australia, and the brutal policies that followed were informed by the idea that colonizers were there to "smooth the dying pillow" for a "dwindling race"—the oldest living culture on Earth, spanning back more than sixty thousand years.

The White Australia Policy to restrict non-British migration to Australia was not completely eliminated until the 1970s. As "custodians of the white race," many feminists supported the White Australia Policy and wanted to preserve white racial purity because whiteness had become the uniting feature of Australian nationalism, writes author and Indigenous activist Aileen Moreton-Robinson. "The new enfranchisement for white women tied them to increasing the white population. Unlike white women, Indigenous women were not encouraged to produce offspring," she wrote.

Just as abortion rights activists in the United States failed to fight against the epidemic of sterilization abuse of disabled, Puerto Rican, Black, Chicanx, and Native American women, those in Australia failed to acknowledge these abuses against Indigenous women. Moreton-Robinson has written that Indigenous women want stricter controls over abortions and sterilization because they have been "practiced on our bodies without our consent." She details how Aboriginal medical services in the 1970s and 1980s were using Depo-Provera, a contraceptive injection not approved in Australia until 1994. "It did not work and many Indigenous women became pregnant and suffered spontaneous abortions," Moreton-Robinson wrote. A 2020 study of factors influencing contraceptive use or non-use among Aboriginal and Torres Strait Islander people found the post-colonization history of contraceptive abuse enforced upon these women still impacted their decisions. These included the use of Depo-Provera without informed consent as a form of short-term infertility, sterilization for unexplained reasons or without consent, prevention of reproduction through forced removal of children, and the criminalization of having children with other members of Aboriginal and Torres Strait Islander communities.

Academics Boni Robertson, Catherine Demosthenous, and Hellene Demosthenous wrote a 2005 paper based on stories collected from a yarning circle of Indigenous women, including children of the Stolen Generation, in which the question "Why can't I be a mother?" was repeated. The authors point out that debates in Australia about "reproduction and the national future" questioned the capacity of poor, white women to reproduce, but for Aboriginal women, their right to reproduce and mother their own children was "completely out of the question." Aboriginal women have always been accepted as "fit to care for and rear the children of white women" while being denied the rights to mother their own children. The authors wrote that the agendas of so many white women's groups failed to address not only the rape and abuse of Aboriginal women at the hands of white men but the denial of their right to be mothers and theft of their children by the state. "[Advocates] seemed to have ignored the fact that while others had a choice to reproduce and mother their own children, Aboriginal people were being controlled by the state and told what to do as women and as mothers," they wrote.

Moreton-Robinson noted that for many Indigenous women in Australia, "motherhood meant having their children forcibly removed from their care" and radical feminists have failed to take that into account. It is not just that white feminists have failed to secure the same rights for Indigenous women—white women in Australia were given the vote in 1902 and Indigenous women were not granted this right until sixty years later—it is that they often colluded with institutions who denied them these rights. "As beneficiaries of colonization, white feminists have been able to challenge and remake themselves as white women through the state and other institutions," Moreton-Robinson wrote. While white women have been gathering power, aspiring for the same lives as white men, "Indigenous women assert that by working to improve the conditions of impoverished women in Australia, the status of all women will be enhanced."

The right to fall pregnant, to safely carry that pregnancy to term, and to parent free of discrimination and coercion is as important as the right to prevent and terminate a pregnancy without discrimination and coercion. These rights are not valued as they should be by the patriarchy under which we all live, nor by the mainstream feminism that is failing to resist it for all women. Moreton-Robinson detailed decades ago that if Indigenous women's lives, needs, and experiences were ever going to be valued, white feminists would need to let go of power and only then could feminist practice "contribute to changing the racial order."

The year Queensland decriminalized abortion the state's ombudsman found one in six Indigenous children did not have a birth certificate, which would potentially prevent them from enrolling in school, accessing government benefits or getting a driver's license. In New South Wales, the legislative pushes to decriminalize abortion and make it more private were underway at the same time adoption without parental consent was legalized, despite the landmark "Bringing Them Home" report released two decades earlier recommending that statutory adoption be a last resort for Aboriginal and Torres Strait Islander children. A 2020 report found 40 percent of children in out-of-home care were Aboriginal, nearly ten times the rate of non-Indigenous children.

The campaign to decriminalize abortion in the Northern Territory gained momentum in the year Australians watched horrifying footage of young people in the Don Dale Youth Detention Centre outside Darwin being stripped down, physically held down, abused, hooded, and bound in a manner the prime minister himself likened to Abu Ghraib and Guantanamo Bay. The following year, abortion was decriminalized in the region while a toothless Royal Commission into the Protection and Detention of Children in the Northern Territory failed to bring criminal charges against anyone responsible for the violations perpetrated against these children, and its recommendation to raise the age of criminal responsibility from ten to twelve is yet to be implemented. Data released the next year showed every single child in youth detention in the Northern Territory was Aboriginal.

These contrasts aren't about priorities—ideally, we would live in a country in which people have control over and safety within their own bodies and children are not criminalized, unsafe, and removed from their families—but they tell us something about which community campaigns politicians and lawmakers will eventually respond to. They tell us when and for whom the patriarchy might bend.

White middle-class feminists have long used the state to achieve safety and autonomy. As I write, there is momentum around criminalizing coercive control in domestic relationships. As many abolitionist feminists have pointed out, these approaches, while intended to support survivors seeking justice, rely on a faith in policing and the criminal justice system that many victims can't afford to have. Almost five hundred Indigenous people have died in custody, five in the month I write, in the thirty years since a Royal Commission into Aboriginal deaths in custody made a series of recommendations. Many of the suggestions are yet to be acted on while others were done so in a piecemeal way and in some cases only after years of campaigning and activism led by grieving families. "Mass incarceration and criminalization of Aboriginal people has been ongoing in this state since colonization," Dr. Hannah McGlade said during a Black Lives Matter rally in June 2020. "There is racial profiling and discrimination at every stage of the criminal justice process." A feminism that pushes toward greater engagement with any system of violence and discrimination is never going to bring the survivors of that violence and discrimination with it.

Gomeroi academic and author Amy Thunig felt undermined by medical professionals even as a teenager. When she was sixteen, all of her friends were going on the contraceptive pill so they could skip their periods and so she asked her doctor if she could do the same. He refused until she had done a pregnancy test even though she was not sexually active. "Being made to do a pregnancy test in exchange for the script, even when I explained I had never had sex, made me feel frustrated and not believed," she says. "Not being heard within medical systems became an ongoing thing. It drains you of time, energy, everything. In my late twenties I developed a mix of pretty severe symptoms, but I ended up having to fight to access a pretty basic diagnosis. It always comes down to not being believed and having your physical pain treated as psychosomatic." Amy was finally diagnosed with endometriosis and fibromyalgia when she was thirty-two, even though she'd had years of pain so debilitating it made her vomit and had been hospitalized for anemia from the heavy bleeding that accompanies endometriosis.

"After seeing white male doctor after white male doctor for three years and still having no diagnosis I said, 'I'm so sick of seeing stale, pale, and male, who can I see next?'" She sought out a female gynecologist. "I will never forget that first appointment," Amy continues, her voice breaking. "She looked at me and said, 'I have been through all the notes on your file and I want to know if you've ever read them.'" The doctor explained that the first specialist Amy had seen about her pain wrote down that she was just stressed and that her symptoms were psychological. The next specialist was going off these notes, as was the next one. After years of delay, Amy was booked in for surgery and the endometriosis tissue was lasered off. The gynecologist also referred her to a rheumatologist who diagnosed Amy with fibromyalgia.

Amy chose to start having children at age twenty-two in part because Indigenous people have a lower life expectancy and she wanted her children to know their Elders. "I wanted them to grow up with the strong Aboriginal people who raised me up, especially my Grandfather Malcolm," she says. "[Parenting is] like a lot of things for Indigenous people—the violence and the rage is always going to be there in the systems we are forced to navigate, but simultaneously there is great joy and great abundance in our community when it comes to support and love and guidance and I couldn't do anything without the support of my Elders and community." Amy also wanted to give herself time to build professional and financial stability, so by the time her children were school-aged she could give them more opportunities. "It was a conscious choice to have my children young, and while I was studying, because I didn't have any generational wealth or access or anything to fall back on and I have been financially independent since I was fifteen," she says. "I knew that to build myself any stability or career and the kind of empowerment I knew I wanted long-term as a parent and a woman would take a long time."

In Australia, Indigenous mothers are more than twice as likely to die in association with pregnancy and childbirth as non-Indigenous mothers. They are almost twice as likely to have a baby with a low birth weight and they are less likely to attend an antenatal visit in the first trimester.

When Amy arrived at the hospital to give birth to her first child, she had already been in labor for two days, but was ignored and dismissed by the staff. A midwife rebuked her for using a high-pitched voice during contractions and denied her access to the pain medication she requested, instead telling her to soften her shoulders and "relax." "It was an ordeal, things only improved when I'd labored for so long in hospital that there was a shift change and I got a new midwife. The trauma of that birth experience was so full-on that for three years, I said I wouldn't have any more children," she says. "I was so scared to be in that vulnerable state and to be completely not listened to, not supported and to have no control. It should have been a magical experience and it was traumatic." For her second birth, Amy chose to birth at a different hospital, an additional forty minute drive away, and paid for a birthing doula to be in the room—"not because I wanted someone to rub my feet but I wanted a bulldog" to advocate for her.

I am suspicious of motherhood, but few people would be suspicious of me as a mother. Not doctors, not police, not bystanders. In that way I have more freedom than many women. I still expect that motherhood would be laden with guilt and judgment but most likely from people I know, not institutions through which I need safety, justice, support, or care.

For some women, motherhood can be a shield, where for others, it makes them a target. In an attack claimed by the Islamic State in 2016, a man drove a truck into crowds celebrating Bastille Day in Nice, France. Hundreds of people were injured and eighty-six died. In the wake of the attack, Australian breakfast television host Sonia Kruger said that she would ban Muslim migration if she had the power. After she was criticized, she tweeted that "as a mother" she believed it was vital to be able to have these discussions without being labeled a racist. In our newsroom, "as a mother" became a kind of cheeky shorthand for the ways in which usually rich, white women with platforms used the fact they had offspring to defend their bigotry. For white women, motherhood can come with an assumed valor, eliciting forgiveness and care.

The number of Indigenous children being removed and placed into child protection systems is still escalating, and the number of Indigenous children in out-of-home care is expected to double by 2029. Aboriginal and Torres Strait Islander children make up only 6 percent of the child population in Australia, but 37 percent of the out-of-home care population. Amy refers to a tweet by an Indigenous journalist who, on her son's eighteenth birthday, announced that she was finally able to throw away the journals she'd kept since he was born detailing how she had cared for him in case anyone ever took him away.

Amy says the risk of a healthcare professional contacting child services makes every interaction with staff more stressful. "It impacts everything. It impacts your autonomy as a parent." Amy knows that refusing a treatment or wanting a second opinion can be taken as neglect. "I tend to be over-the-top with being risk-averse because I am aware if my child has hurt themself and it turns out it's worse than it looks, I know how easy it would be to be labeled that negligent Aboriginal mother who didn't seek support, who wasn't looking after their child," she says. "There is so much less grace for Indigenous parents when it comes to how we treat our children and what we offer our children and what we see as an emergency and what we see as a bump or a scrape." A healthcare worker threatened to contact child services when Amy did not take the immediate medical route they had suggested for her child. "What was really frustrating about that was I was going to agree to it anyway," she tells me. "They were so ready and so quick to pull out that 'you will do this' and 'you will do this today' and 'you will give your permission to this or I will contact Services and report.' I didn't even get to take a minute or ask questions about what the treatment looked like or what happens if we do it, what happens if we do nothing, what are the risks, what are the possibilities. I didn't even get to have that conversation."

Amy has driven the two hours each way to access specialist medical services in the city because she knows there are services nearby that are racially unsafe, which she acknowledges is a privilege. She recently took a risk on one of these public specialist services after assurance from her GP that she did not need to go private. "The very first phone call with them was so violent and aggressive and when I said to them 'thank you very much but I won't be using your service,' they sent a letter to my GP alleging that I had decided to not have my child looked after at all and claiming that they had tried to refer me to private providers, but that I had declined as I didn't want to pay for things. Which wasn't true at all," she says. "I have the means to go elsewhere, and had been going elsewhere, [but] that is a privilege five years ago I wouldn't have been able to afford."

Medical institutions that might represent safety or support for non-Indigenous mothers are still sites of hyper-surveillance and racism for Amy. "As a parent and as an Indigenous mother, I am constantly aware that they don't exist as a neutral system that you can access and that will always work for you." Amy sighs before continuing. "It is always a risk. You're always walking that line of wanting to advocate for your child, but also not wanting to be taken as an aggressive resistant parent." Amy states that the system is violent and it is not built for her. "We have made our best attempts to retrofit, to carve out some space, to make adjustments so you might be culturally understood and safe."

Sexuality, pregnancy, and motherhood are "deeply racialized experiences," writer Caroline McFadden insists in *Radical Reproductive Justice* and we should look at the privileges we have through them that rest on the disempowerment of other women. "Those interconnections are not always pretty or palatable, but often laden with racism, colonialism, imperialism, and privilege," she writes, proposing her own approach to begin asking questions that she states are critical to white feminism. In the case of reproductive justice, this would mean we stop assuming our experiences are universal and common, stop pretending there is nothing to interrogate, encourage communication between women, help de-marginalize women of color, secure racism as a priority issue, look back on what we have prioritized and ask which women it benefits, and include mothers and would-be mothers. "A true self is not an isolated self that engages in self-reflection without cognition of others; instead, a true self interprets itself in relation to others by comparing and contrasting similarities and differences, not as a stimulant for fear and uncertainty, but as an act of human solidarity," McFadden writes.

I want to reorient myself away from circumscribed victimhood and toward a collective responsibility. When you redefine reproductive oppression it allows you to reinterpret reproductive liberty as sociologist Dorothy E. Roberts has. Roberts wrote in *Killing the Black Body* that these rights have for too long been translated as negative—pushing against state interference rather than a positive right—getting the resources we all need to prevent pregnancy or have and parent a child. "This view recognizes the violation in a statute that bans a white, middle-class woman from taking the procreative option she wishes," Roberts writes. "But it disregards how poverty, racism, sexism, and other systems of power—often facilitated by government action—also impair many people's decisions about procreation."

A person's autonomy against oppressive government power is important, but as Roberts noted, "liberalism has failed to deliver on its promise of freedom for all citizens."

After decades of panels about a post-Roe world, Roberts was with her daughter and her daughter's friends, all in their thirties, when the recent *Roe v. Wade* decision came down. Roberts realized these women would have fewer rights to autonomy than she did at their age. "At the same time, though, there's a reproductive justice movement that is so much stronger than it was when I was their age," she told *Vox*. "We are in a contradictory time because with the fight for justice, it seems like we're going backward while at the same time building movements that are so much further than we were when we were growing up."

Any genuine effort to improve reproductive healthcare for everyone will value social justice as much as personal liberty. The right to parent your child without fear that they will be taken away from you, the right to parent your child with enough support should you need it, the right to safe healthcare from pregnancy to birth and beyond. These rights must be equally important as the rights to prevent or terminate pregnancy.

Embedded within my misgivings about motherhood was an awareness of mother as a political category, even if it began as a blinkered fear of becoming politically irrelevant. I am asking how I accumulated the power I felt fearful of losing. I am asking how my body and the ones I could help create move through the world. I am evaluating the organizations I encounter along the way, in my work, in my relations, in a potential pregnancy or parenthood. In critical white motherhood, we would be vigilant in asking and asking again where we assist, benefit from, and partake in white supremacy.

I know this will involve, as sociology professor Erika Derkas writes in *Radical Reproductive Justice*, contesting "unearned, stolen, socially constructed, and assumed privileges built off the lives of others." We would ask questions: How are our families upholding structures of oppression or how we are helping to make them safer? How are we voting and participating in our communities? How are we redirecting our resources to communities where it is not appropriate for us to involve ourselves but to help them accommodate their most vulnerable? Where are we living and sending our children to school? Where are we donating and volunteering? What history are we teaching or not teaching our children and why? How are we paying rent while living on stolen land?

The violence, the suffering, the inequity any person suffers is real, but for too long for white middle-class women our experiences of gender have been the main lens through which we are willing to understand and organize when it comes to family planning and parenting. The question of parenthood is a prompt to ask more questions about our politics. It is a chance to ask what we want to reproduce in ourselves and in the world we know, whether or not we physically reproduce.

Shame and guilt can be paralyzingly self-involved emotions, but we can do better than acknowledging that our struggles are not as marginalized as those of other women.

Koa Beck writes that acknowledging privilege has become an avoidant transparency disclaimer for white feminists rather than what it should be—a "perforation." It should be painful. It should tear us open, open us up. It should lay bare what the priorities, goals, and strategies of "personalized autonomy, individual wealth, perpetual self-optimization and supremacy" have actually done for other women. Understanding the smallness of our world should not make us retreat further into the confines of our experience; it should encourage us to learn the history, needs, and struggles of people beyond it.

This connection can mean stepping up, stepping back, or stepping down. It can mean using resources to decenter yourself and demarginalize others. At the bare minimum it can mean being honest about the rationality of your own fear. Uncomfortably, for a group of women practiced at personalizing before politicizing growth, it can also mean understanding that progress will not be measured by your own individual experience of pregnancy, motherhood, healthcare, and justice. "The revolution will not be you alone, despite what white feminism has told you," Beck writes. "There are only the resistance movements that you will build with other people."

3

Work

LOVE HAS ALWAYS BEEN A verb to me. It is something you do. An expression, an action, an exertion. I am a husk filled mostly with all I want to do for the people I love. It would be chic to quietly emanate love like moonlight—a coy glow settling on the rooftops of your dearest as they fall asleep, a comforting presence they know to be there if they look for it out the window. But my love is hot and garish like sunlight—I want to help you photosynthesize, I want to dry your laundry, I want my kisses to leave constellations of freckles across your cheeks. I can't stay still long enough to suspend myself in love as a noun—a state, a feeling, a passive reality, a fact once established, never tested, a framed photograph collecting dust on a mantelpiece.

When I learned about love languages, I felt for the first time fluent in something—speaking with my time, words, body, energy, and trinkets—and simultaneously nervous that my love might seem like a performance. But the displaying *is* the loving. And I love loving. Without the work, the love remains a presumption, distant, rarely visited, hanging silently above us in the night sky. The problem with accepting labor as a function of love is that it is a prerequisite for buying into most exploitative folklore about both motherhood and paid employment. The idea that unpaid domestic labor and caring work isn't work at all, it is love and so need not be recognized or compensated, is ancient propaganda while the notion that you must "do what you love" has become a misleading ethos for working millennials. The problem with interrogating a motherhood built on the myth of love as labor or questioning a paid job that requires labor as love is that it complicates the question of what to devote yourself to and where you might find meaning in your life. The problem with finding a ready answer for a readily asked question—*if not kids, then what?*—is that I am running out of time.

A career felt like a complete answer to me until it didn't. A woman whose entire life revolved around her job was enviable until she wasn't. Yet, even if it was financially viable, I can't imagine ever completely abandoning paid employment.

People have always been aware of how parenthood would interrupt their career trajectory and for those who have invested their selfhood into their jobs, as many of us have, a child threatens to disrupt not just our earning capacity but our identity. Parental leave isn't only a drop in hours but a voluntary, even if often temporary, desertion of a central place of meaning-making. Now I find myself considering how dramatically my love and labor would be divided in parenthood and all that I would need to abandon about how I value myself and how I would expect others to, particularly those holding political and industrial power. I now need to consider for whom I toil—work, family, both, neither—and how I would do so.

The only things more tedious than conversations about "having it all" are the conditions that necessitate them. Stubborn statistics show women continue to arrive home from full-time work to perform a second shift of unpaid labor—globally, women and girls still perform trillions of dollars' worth of unpaid labor every year. Most workplaces are still fundamentally not set up to support primary carers. We know one in two mothers and one in four fathers in Australia have reported experiencing discrimination in the workplace at some point during pregnancy, parental leave, or on their return to work—one in five mothers in the United States say they have experienced pregnancy discrimination. We know mothers who went back to work before they were ready to, anxious about the growing gap in their resume. We know mothers who retired with half as much superannuation as their partners. We know working mothers who said, as did the research, that home-schooling fell to them during the pandemic. We know mothers who felt self-conscious about their choice to have kids ahead of their careers. "We're contemptuous of 'lazy' poor mothers. We're contemptuous of 'distracted' working mothers. We're contemptuous of 'selfish' rich mothers," journalist and author Kim Brooks writes. "We're contemptuous of mothers who have no choice but to work, but also of mothers who don't need to work and still fail to fulfill an impossible ideal of selfless motherhood." To consider how you might ration your love and labor for the rest of your life is to consider how you might be perceived for that allocation.

A friend of mine who has a toddler is the first and, she believes, the last, to have a child in her friendship group as her peers are prioritizing their careers. "I feel like a bumpkin sometimes," she admits. My instinct is to remind her how amazing she is at her job, how well-read she is, how her career will progress as the group's has once her kid is older and she is back at work, but I stop myself. She shouldn't have to feel valued as a paid worker while her shift as an unpaid worker never ends. She is a working mother as all mothers are. The next time we speak, she is exhausted because her kid hasn't been sleeping and she feels like she can't ask more care of her partner, who is still working full-time. He says he will "take" the kid for a few hours, that he will "mind" him. I tell her this is just parenting. Later she says, "Sometimes I just think, 'What has feminism done for me lately?'"

I am in the generation of goal-setting, opportunity-seizing, yes-saying professionally starving women who, as writer and journalist Lisa Miller writes, are now realizing they have been sold another "bullshit promise"— that the workplace would provide total fulfillment as their mothers and grandmothers were promised the home would. "The men in charge are still in charge," she writes. "It is impossible for women to continue to have faith in a vision of their own empowerment, when that empowerment is, in fact, a pose." Don't turn to the workplace, as previous generations of women were encouraged to turn to their husbands, to answer the big questions about your life, Miller implores.

My newfound disillusionment with a life built only around a career has not made a life structured around a child more appealing. "The days with the baby felt long but there was nothing expansive about them," the protagonist in author Jenny Offill's *Dept. of Speculation* ponders. "Caring for [my baby] required me to repeat a series of tasks that had the peculiar quality of seeming both urgent and tedious." My working life has been nothing if not a series of urgent and tedious tasks—rushing to report on breaking news, transcribing hours of interviews, jumping in a cab to a press conference, making fruitless inquiry after fruitless inquiry, fact-checking once, twice, thrice. And yet my labor is waged, it is visible, and it is valorized because historically it has been done by men. I was indeed sold a bullshit promise and yet at least in full-time work without children, I have some predictability, the promise of a linear path to something that looks like success, a series of problems to be solved with resources to solve them and little treats when I do so, some respect within the places I've learned to seek it.

When I was a cadet journalist, a man who held a senior columnist position at the newspaper politely approached me to talk about a then topical debate on whether politicians should be allowed to breastfeed at work. "How is that any different from a male politician asking to masturbate in the chamber?" he asked in complete seriousness. I didn't know how to respond to someone who thought feeding a child should be as private an act as sexual gratification. I understood then that the sight of employed women was less offensive to some men than having to witness the obscenity, the sheer work of mothering.

I am considering motherhood after spending a decade committed to the idea that women find their freedom in the workplace, glamorizing what is paid and sympathizing with or ignoring what is not. I am reconsidering where employment belongs in a life well lived and how I came to understand it as the foundation. I have inconveniently stopped believing in many of the fairy tales that informed my plans for where I would find meaning in my life just as my career ascends and my fertility declines. For any potential parent there are practical negotiations to be made with partners, employers, and themselves about the division of paid and unpaid labor in households that are probably, but not necessarily, dependent on two incomes. Even for people whose sense of self is healthily unattached from the demands of their job, all of us poised on the threshold of this decision have questions to answer about work and family, the answers to which will follow us into parenthood, should we choose it.

Before the ambivalence, there was something that felt like ambition. I realized it was a scam to pretend producing progeny wasn't actual work long before I understood the grift of profit-producing as progress. The women in my family had been homemakers and I resented the notion that I needed to construct my identity in the home because of my gender. This was fostered by the first kind of feminism I was exposed to. It was a hunger embodied by the child-free characters, though they were few and far between, I saw represented on television—the hedonistic Samantha Jones, the imperfect Elaine Benes, the tragic Liz Lemon, the ambitious Jessica Pearson, and of course the impervious Cristina Yang—"I choose medicine, I choose me, I choose that over the remote possibility that I might one day regret not having a child."

I allowed motherhood and its domestic labor to be degraded by the logic of a corporate feminism that fetishized the enlightening, empowering, and stimulating potential of paid work. Alicia Florrick, the main character on the TV show *The Good Wife*, smiles as her son says, "Sometimes I think of you as Mom, and other times just as this interesting person who lives in our house." There was a time when it would have been a status symbol for a woman not to have to work, but now that the workplace is understood as a site of intellectual growth and weight, camaraderie, and creativity, paid employment is a sign you have made it. I wanted to be the interesting person who lived in the house before I considered populating it with children.

Mainstream feminism feels increasingly out of step with social ideals of equality, rights, and justice and, as American studies professor Catherine Rottenberg points out, more often compatible with political and economic agendas of free-market capitalism, consumerism, and privatization. When I began university, feminism was not only socially acceptable but marketable. This was radical for an eighteen-year-old who wasn't raised a feminist. I felt part of something that validated my experiences of womanhood so far. It was learning what consent was and wasn't, it was body positivity on Instagram, it was girls in my university tutorials growing their underarm hair, it was encountering intersectionality and privilege and then failing to do anything meaningful with it, it was realizing there was a gender pay gap, it was freeing your nipples, it was fugly "fuck the patriarchy" tote bags and enamel pins, it was wanting to be a #girlboss in the #workplace, it was a messy introduction to the most self-interested and least self-aware form of neoliberal white feminism you could imagine.

I began my first job in journalism at a newspaper staffed mostly by graying conservative men. I felt completely out of my depth and I was grateful that there was a journalist looking out for me. She didn't have children but she had a lot of front-page stories. She gave me a copy of Sheryl Sandberg's *Lean In* to help me survive. I was at an age where a lot of my friends were in and out of relationships with men who behaved appallingly and then responded to their girlfriend's distress by telling her things she could alter about herself if she wanted the relationship to work. It was her reaction to his behavior that was disrupting the relationship. That's how I felt reading *Lean In*. The conditions need not change; I just had to become less sensitive to them. "We can reignite the revolution by internalizing the revolution," Sandberg told me. Find a way to make sure you were in an office higher up in the building, but don't damage any infrastructure on the way up.

The newspaper was a hierarchical workplace where stress pressed downward, hard, and I was at the very bottom, so was told: "failure is not an option," "if you don't find the right case study today, we don't have a front page," and "don't take a sick day again—if your leg falls off, bring it in with you." The culture of bullying, the sexism and harassment, the glee taken in watching newcomers learn by suffering—it was my problem, and I was ready to be a good feminist and turn it all inward, at least for long enough, I told myself, to get a job at a publication where I could do work that felt meaningful. I saw the advancement of my own career as liberation from the expectations of womanhood. All of this work, even in my self-interest, could be a feminist act. If I worked hard enough, if I made myself useful enough, if I mimicked men in the workplace for long enough, I would eventually have the freedom they did to pursue the stories I wanted to.

This attitude didn't last long. One day I was out on a job with a middle-aged straight-talking photographer I looked up to. Over the preceding weeks we had been sent out to pursue several impossible stories during which the chief-of-staff or editor would call almost hourly to ask gruffly whether we'd been successful yet in securing a front-page photo. It was jarring to hear her shift from her natural bluntness to an almost slavish tone as she responded to the hounding requests of men we'd usually spent all day slandering. At that time, newspapers had all but scrapped their photography departments and this freelancer was on a random roster sometimes decided on by the day. As we drove to the next location, I told her it was unreasonable that someone with her experience and talent should have to be routinely spoken to like that. I think I secretly wanted her to talk back, to stop apologizing and start asserting her needs as a man would, as Sheryl Sandberg might.

As she hauled her big clunky van around a corner, her hands pulling at the wheel, she said, "Gina, in this business, a lot of the time you've just gotta bend over, grab your ankles, and take it." I was shocked, not by the lewdness of the metaphor, but by the honest resignation, the antithesis of putting your hand up and asking for a seat at the table. This photographer was telling me how to survive and, in the end, she was right—I found far less friction bending over than leaning in.

I left the newspaper and fell in love with my new job, reporting primarily on sexual and reproductive rights for *BuzzFeed News*. I was writing about something so sparsely covered in Australia that I was able to break new ground each week with ongoing legislative pushes and political debates on abortion that kept the momentum going. I had the kind of freedom and autonomy unheard of for reporters my age and I was working with a team of people who felt more like friends than colleagues. The difficult and boring moments in the job were irrelevant in between the genuine fulfilment. I had no interest in climbing an editorial ladder. I didn't need career progression, I had meaning. I had arrived at where I wanted to stay.

Our 9 a.m. news meeting was my favorite part of the day, when I got to sit and listen to talented smart people pitch stories that I cared about—revealing the unending brutality of Australia's offshore and onshore detention regime, covering fascinating court cases, and exposing how climate denialists, anti-vaxxers and white supremacists were using social media to network and spread misinformation. Our colleagues abroad were dropping high-profile global investigations into fraud, corruption, sexual assault and harassment, torture and murder, as well as the US government and the president's finances. I was a person who used the phrase *dream job*. The question of motherhood was answered. I wanted only to bear fruit in service of journalism. I loved my editors, I loved my readers, I loved my interviewees, I loved my work. I was enamored in a way that was so consuming it is embarrassing now. "If caring work is familial love, based in the all-sacrificing love of the mother, creative work is romantic love, based in a different kind of self-sacrifice and voluntary commitment that is expected, on some level, to love you back," labor journalist Sarah Jaffe writes. "Yet work never, ever loves you back."

In mid-2020, our entire reporting team was laid off as the economic impact rippled through the already contracting news media industry. I had been working seven years full-time and in the wake of my redundancy, I felt incapable of saying no to any freelance opportunity and found myself working most days to meet competing deadlines. I was anxious to make rent but above all, I knew I was frantically trying to maintain my identity as a journalist. I just wanted to keep doing what I loved.

"Where on earth did you get this Protestant work ethic?" my mother's bemused voice echoed over the phone line. *Actually, it is Catholic guilt, and I got it from you*, I thought to myself bitterly. This was untrue. I had not inherited my inability to extricate my identity and sense of self-worth from my job from my mother, who had been a schoolteacher for most of my life and had always worked to live, not lived to work. Work has become if not the one, then certainly a central place of meaning-making for many people my age. Even those who loathe their employment feel somewhat defined by it and often complain not just of the long hours, shitty pay, and lack of security but also of the monotony, the futility, and lack of creativity required.

Australian essayist Eda Günaydin writes that it is a "millennial rite of passage" to convert our passions into jobs or at least side hustles. "The advice to Westerners, and middle or upper-middle classes, is that we should follow our bliss, start businesses that mean something to us or—if we are employed in impersonal work—that we personalise it: invest real emotions, or our individual flair," she writes. The cult of productivity cares not for hobbies, so you should either pursue meaning by monetizing your hobby or else find a way to make your job feel as personal as your hobby. The neoliberal project has moved beyond promoting the joy that can be found in the material benefits of capitalism to reimagining work as "a source of joy in and of itself," says art historian and commentator Miya Tokumitsu. "Seductive slogans about work as self-actualisation and images of blissful labour are ubiquitous," she writes. The virtue in work changed from suffering to pleasure with the Baby Boomer generation, Tokumitsu claims, when a "culture of self" arose and people were thinking more about their own improvement and fulfilment. This "do what you love" (DWYL) rhetoric has helped sell overwork and sleep deprivation as fulfilling, she says. It has helped rebrand exhaustion as a status symbol that tells the world that you are needed, you are skilled, and you are special. The devotion must be unwavering. "After all, ideal love is nothing if not constant," Tokumitsu writes.

For a few years, I felt I was a journalist before I was anything else. I could not see a future in which it wasn't the main source of connection, community, and fulfillment in my life. It was where I felt I offered the most value to the world. It was where I felt useful, smart, capable, creative, impactful, and resilient. It was only when I became less naive about the limits of journalism, and by that I mean less naive about the limits of truth, that I began seeking out other ways to become a more useful citizen, strategizing about where I put my time and money and why. My redundancy story wasn't special—at least 150 newsrooms in Australia closed during 2020. The same week I was laid off, a Pulitzer Prize winner was put on unpaid furlough—and yet it felt personal. I hadn't just lost a job, I'd lost what I thought made me, me. I felt worth less without it.

The chance to be consumed by and compensated for this kind of work is of course attainable to very few people. "Polite society may prefer to pretend otherwise, but the kind of jobs that provide public visibility, ready-made identities, and the promise of self-fulfillment are strictly cordoned off by class boundaries," Tokumitsu writes. "DWYL provides cover for beguiling ourselves that work and class float free from each other, that the work one does is a function of personal choice rather than class membership and that class membership is a function of nebulous other facts, often implying strength (or frailty) or moral character." Those who choose to overwork are lauded and those who have to overwork or who want adequate hours to get by are ignored.

However, it is wrong to assume the desire for meaningful work is always the product of affluence, that once we have attained our physical and economic security, we are able to reach up the shelves of Maslow's hierarchy of human needs, fumbling around for love and belonging, esteem and self-actualization in our employment. But as sociology professor Jamie McCallum writes, it is the opposite. Workers' demands for edifying work emerged from the boring monotony of factory work in the 1970s and gained momentum as the economic rewards for work declined. This isn't just a preference—some people caring more about social or emotional benefits than monetary ones—but a seismic societal shift, a reconstruction of our "cultural scaffolding" in which meaning becomes supplementary rather than complementary to the wages and benefits of a work package, McCallum says. "The worse work gets and the less we are paid to do it, the more meaningful we are told it should be." I highlight the passage and make a note: Like motherhood?

Everything we used to value outside of paid employment has been braided into it and companies are investing in company "culture" faster than you can say "minimum wage." I loved it. For four years I believed work was a place I would always be excited to go to and that there were decades of fun and novelty to come. I didn't care about the job's most alienating attributes, I didn't need wage growth—I had subsidized exercise classes, work drinks, catered lunch twice a week, free avocado toast on Fridays, unlimited protein balls, and a kombucha machine. Working for an organization headquartered in the United States felt like a preview into where all employers who were investing heavily in non-monetary perks were headed. In December, the chief executive would wear a tacky Christmas sweater and reveal what this year's present would be. One year, it was wireless headphones. We had a "culture club"—in lieu of proper HR—to ensure we had fun ways to recognize people's work and events to look forward to. They once gave us a massage voucher to apologize for how long it had taken to subsidize private health insurance, a perk I didn't use because, and I'm not sure if they were aware of this, we have universal healthcare in Australia.

When I spent a week working from my former employer's New York office, I sat at my desk, enjoying the free bagels and unlimited complimentary froyo and, for the first time in my life, I felt like a misanthrope. I peered around, quietly marveling at the unceasing extraversion, the high-fiving, the unrelenting niceness to each other, someone chirping, "neat!" and another, "awesome!", one person telling another they'd love to take them bouldering. They still wore the grinning cynicism reporters all don to cope in a job that requires you to consume news all day, but it couldn't compete with this springy camaraderie that felt foreign, as it didn't seem to be built on a foundation of making fun of each other.

Jasmine, an Australian working for Seattle-based tech company Amazon, laughs knowingly. "I am so careful at work about what I joke about and I really have to tone down my sarcasm," she says. It is not just the earnestness but the blinkered emphasis on work that Jasmine finds bewildering. "It is this American psyche of your purpose in life being linked to work," she says. Jasmine wholeheartedly bought into it for eighteen months until she was so burned out, she had to acknowledge her values just didn't align with the premise. "You do feel a sense of achievement and I get excited about work and the stuff we do at scale, but we have these tag lines like 'work hard, have fun, make history' and I have my fun in other ways," she says. "Work isn't the highlight of my year when I look back." Jasmine explains a common practice where managers tell people they are earmarked for a promotion but wait a year to give it to them. "It drives people to work extra hard for a long period of time and then they eventually get rewarded for it."

Amazon's owner, Jeff Bezos, calls the hard work a "bias for action," but former employees have described it as "a drug that we could get self-worth from." As one of the company's HR goals declares: "Employees come to Amazon to do meaningful work."

Jasmine works hard and long hours, but now stops once she has closed her laptop for the day. "I don't feel guilt," she says. When a woman on her team seemed to be having a bad day and eventually admitted she was struggling to steady herself during the hormonal fluctuations that accompany the weeks of injections needed for egg retrieval, Jasmine learned that Amazon pays for egg freezing as a company benefit. In Australia, egg freezing costs around £3,350 per cycle and six months' storage. Jasmine knew she wanted children one day but hadn't met the right person. For a few weeks, she injected herself twice a day with a syringe to stimulate her hormones, her eggs were then collected and they are now sitting in a freezer somewhere in Seattle. "I was surprised at how much of a difference it made to how I was feeling," Jasmine says. "I felt free." She finally feels like she can take her time with dating and find someone who she is compatible with long-term instead of settling for a partner who wasn't right for her. "That would be a far worse outcome than not having a family."

The rise of corporate egg-freezing subsidies—nearly one in five major US firms offer it and UK firms like NatWest and Centrica have followed suit—points to the fact that companies would rather buy more time with an unencumbered worker before investing in a workplace that might better suit mothers or others with caring commitments. But, as with all company benefits, they primarily benefit the company. "In the short-term, they will get a lot more out of me because I will remain unmarried without children," she says. Amazon pays for the egg storage as long as she is an employee. I thought about Jack Donaghy, the comically cold-blooded executive on the TV show *30 Rock*, saying, "Our healthcare costs are way down since we started putting something in the coffee to keep women from getting pregnant."

In 2019, almost two thousand of Amazon's working mothers, who called themselves The Momazonians, claimed the company discriminated against parents, particularly mothers, and called for Amazon to provide back-up childcare options so they could meet their work demands. It was only temporarily granted during the pandemic. Jasmine's future options seem to be either delay parenthood which was supported by the company, balance parenthood with very little support from the company, or become a mother and leave the company for somewhere that is more amenable to parenthood. "No career ambition is worth sacrificing myself and my family not being able to see me."

"All the women in my mothers' group have been made redundant." Rosalind Bragg remembers hearing the phrase from clients more than once when

Maternity Action UK was established in 2008 in the midst of a global financial crisis. "We were seeing extraordinarily large numbers of pregnant women and new mothers who were being made redundant, often in circumstances which were manifestly unfair," Rosalind, the organization's director, says. "[I]n a pandemic we're seeing it again." While the Equality Act prohibits discrimination on the grounds of maternity and pregnancy, Rosalind says it is difficult to exercise those rights. Even if it is understood someone has been fired because they became pregnant, it is almost impossible to disprove the alleged rationale given for the redundancy. Many women can't afford the time and formidable cost to take a claim to a tribunal so many never begin the process of holding their employers to account.

Eight years before we spoke, Edith had a miscarriage. The pregnancy was not planned but it was wanted. Edith works in film and television in London and the cramping came during her morning meeting with the production team. By the time she arrived at an afternoon shoot, Edith felt the blood and was grateful to be wearing black jeans. She left work half an hour early, which her boss made her feel guilty about. Edith did not take a sick day—"you don't really have them in the arts"—and told no one but her partner that she had lost the pregnancy. "The last thing I wanted to do was to let anyone know I wanted kids one day," she says. "I had quite big career ambitions."

When Edith fell pregnant again two years later, she had just accepted a promotion she had been working toward her entire career. Edith has spent "too much time" trying to figure out how her boss found out, obsessing over when and where she could have been spotted at medical appointments or taking pregnancy vitamins. "I was called into his office and told that they had reconsidered the promotion and it was going to go to a man who was almost qualified, but had a resume about half as long as mine," Edith remembers. "I pleaded for a reason and he couldn't look me in the eye. I asked for some sort of rationale in writing, but they wouldn't give me one. They just said they had re-evaluated the position and thought his skillset was more appropriate." The rest of the staff were confused but as the pregnancy continued, her bump protruded from her blazer, an unspoken explanation. "I felt revolting . . . I was so hormonal and angry and I felt so powerless and humiliated because everyone knew why this had happened," she says.

The workplace does not accommodate the pregnant body. Edith found herself working longer hours and continuing the most physically demanding parts of her role in an effort to prove her boss was wrong to rescind the promotion. Rosalind says there are very few routes for women to challenge an employer who has deemed a workplace safe—if they are forced to pursue an employment tribunal claim they could be waiting more than a year for a hearing. "If you're on a low income the tribunal award will be significantly low and you're not pregnant anymore, you may have even left your job already because it is unsafe," Rosalind says. "Four percent of pregnant women leave their jobs because of health and safety concerns and they are overwhelmingly women on lower incomes in lower skilled jobs."

Edith didn't want to be known as a squeaky wheel when she was ready to re-enter the workforce, but a friend encouraged her to explore her options about the withdrawn promotion. She spoke to the union, who connected her to a lawyer. "I'm not from a posh family, so it was almost impossible to get a job in this field and harder still to keep it on the shitty salary," she explains. "I explored the legal cost of pursuing action, but for me it was more about reputation. There aren't many women in this industry and I felt like I was doing myself a disservice by ruining my own reputation when I'd fought so hard to get here."

Rosalind and Edith repeat the same phrase almost word for word: "There is always a business case to be made" for fewer shifts, for changing working conditions, for demotions, for redundancies. The real reason can remain unspoken. The ideal worker does not need to be reimagined as someone with people to love and toil for outside of the workplace. Recently Edith was interviewing for a deputy and found herself reconsidering the most qualified candidate because she was thirty and might be considering parenthood. She knew differences in the resumes could be explained away and had a suspicion the men on the interview panel also wouldn't want to be filling the position again in a few years. "There is always a business case to be made," she repeated sheepishly. "The worst thing is there was a man who applied and he had a child and could very well have planned to have more, but it didn't even *occur* to me that his wife wouldn't take on that burden should the time come," she said. "I was so ashamed of myself for trying to repeat the same discrimination I had faced all because I didn't want to be inconvenienced."

Rosalind says there are employers making a genuine attempt to support parents to balance work and caring responsibilities "but we also get calls from some of those employers who have discriminated against pregnant staff." The gap between policies and their implementation can be vast as good policies don't make good line managers, she says. "Policies facilitate good practice but they don't compel it," she says. The data is also incomplete as gender pay gap reporting does not include maternity retention rates to document the proportion of women who remain in work a year after returning from maternity leave. "This would reveal the less flattering picture of companies who are unsafe or discriminatory workplaces for pregnant workers and mothers," Rosalind says. "Workplaces are designed around employees who have no caring responsibilities." Time with family is compromised by the boundless nature of work as we now know it, while progression in the workplace is hindered by having anyone to care for but yourself.

It didn't have to be this way. In the 1970s in Padua, Italy, a radical campaign refused to put the workplace over the home as the most important site of women's liberation. Wages for Housework began drawing attention to the unpaid work women were doing—cooking, cleaning, rearing children, caring for the elderly—that kept paid workers fed and clothed. These physical, repetitive, skilled vital tasks were made visible not as acts of devotion but for what they were: labor. The movement's pamphlet, *Wages Against Housework* (1975), authored by Silvia Federici, opens: "They say it is love. We say it is unwaged work." She challenged the notion that housework was an aspiration "coming from the depth of [their] female character," an innately womanly desire. "Capital had to convince us that it is a natural, unavoidable and even fulfilling activity to make us accept our unwaged work," it reads. Nurturing is natural, housework is inevitable, mothering is purpose.

On some of the pamphlets, an exhausted mother steadies herself with a broom as a flock of children tug at her skirt. In her other hand, she holds a wad of cash. The dollar sign is a tiny scribble, but it makes the image feel radical even almost half a century later. The crass audacity to put a price on something you have been socialized to believe is as fulfilling as it is fated. You only have to look at the wages of childcare workers, teachers, and aged care workers to see how this lingering presumption complements a "do what you love" ethos to devalue work that is traditionally gendered female. Care work in the home has been denigrated for so long that it still fails to be compensated fairly outside of it. Wages for Housework made exploitation a starting point. It was not an attempt to degrade or institutionalize love, nor an attempt to make husbands pay their housewives salaries; it was an attempt to dismantle the default inequitable organization of the home by demanding wages. It was not discouraging women seeking work outside the home, but sought to ensure they did so not out of desperation for a skerrick of financial independence but with genuine agency and autonomy. As Federici wrote, contraceptives are "the only true labour-saving devices"—how else to seize the means of (re)production?

"No one's work will be done until the work of being a woman with no money is undone," reads the *Black Women for Wages for Housework Bulletin* of Autumn 1977. These campaigners warned with eerie prescience that the first site of resistance should not be the workplace but the home. Paid employment was not going to free anyone until the enormous problem of unpaid work was dealt with. Neither the family nor the firm was going to liberate women. "They wanted, instead, time for themselves, freedom to discover what love and sexuality might look like outside of relations of power and labor," Jaffe observes of Federici and her peers in her book, *Work Won't Love You Back*. Women were entering the workforce as unions were losing power and employment became more precarious, or "at the moment in which the roof of the factory was falling down" as Federici puts it. "Women were expected to pick up the slack by taking up paid work while not reducing the amount of work they did in the home," Jaffe writes. "The new social conservatives, hand in hand with the ascendant neoliberals, aimed to reinforce the traditional nuclear family at the same time as policies were being put in place to wring more work out of everyone, reinstituting the Protestant work ethic by law if not by choice."

Just as many of the material benefits of work are being supplemented by meaning, material benefits can be withheld if assigned "meaning" is not fulfilled. In late 2020, the Australian government announced it will extend a punitive scheme mostly targeting low-income single mothers with children under six, docking welfare payments for parents who fail to attend "story time" sessions, and demanding domestic violence survivors retell their stories with their children present to keep payments. "It should come as no surprise that, just as the scrutiny of mothers reaches new heights, the welfare nets that once provided material support for families are assiduously dismantled," authors Camilla Nelson and Rachel Robertson write in *Dangerous Ideas About Mothers*. "What the scrutiny of mothers conceals is the reality of a world in which every woman is defined through the ideal of maternal care work, regardless of whether she is—or even wants to be—a mother." Nelson and Robertson argue that blaming mothers for social ills makes inequality a matter of individual will and allows real material causes like poverty to go unaddressed.

As critic Anwen Crawford has written in *Meanjin*, the financial hardship created by a disciplinary conception of welfare "as the last resort of the least deserving" exacerbates gender inequality for single mothers. "How, as a society, should we recognize and compensate for the labor of child-rearing and domestic work, which has almost always gone unpaid?" she writes. "Is full-time wage labor the only means of measuring social contribution that we are prepared to endorse?" Parenthood can sometimes feel like a path we are supposed to consider if we have cleared some undefined state of financial stability. We might not expect other people to do so—I don't judge my parents for having a child as penniless teenagers—but it is a standard I know many of us hold ourselves to. The notion that we should delay falling pregnant until we don't need welfare, have a stable career or adequate savings is, as Connor Kilpatrick points out in a piece for *Jacobin*, just the inverse of previous commands for women to stay at home and procreate. Both, he writes, ask women to defer to something beyond their desires. "How can we ever win a program that socializes the costs of bringing children into the world if so many liberals still see the desire to have kids as something like a timeshare in Vegas—a costly, foolish, and tacky investment mostly for the rubes?" Kilpatrick writes. There is a personal and political cost to deciding parenthood is an indulgence.

The child poverty rate in the United States is around 17 percent while eight in every thirty children, the size of most classrooms, in the UK live in poverty. Since 2017, the government's two-child limit, which the Child Poverty Action Group maintains is a major driver of rising child poverty, has restricted some benefit payments to the first two kids born to the poorest households, unless they were born before the policy came into force. Research by York and Oxford academics found the policy was "creating an almost impossible context for affected families" and risking long-term harm for millions of children whose parents struggle to pay for basic necessities. One in twelve children in the UK lives in families impacted by the policy, which Alison Garnham, the chief executive of CPAG, describes as "utterly disgraceful." "There wasn't a problem with the birth rate they were addressing, it is clearly about punishing poor families," she says. "It was a money-saving measure they thought would play well with the public because if you say to people 'if you can't afford to have children you shouldn't have them' everyone nods along; but that doesn't pay any regard to reality." Data showed the policy was irrelevant in pushing so-called "benefit scroungers" into employment because the majority (59 percent) of families hit by the limit were already working. "It's not the feckless poor sitting at home, it is actually people who are working and who made decisions about their family and then things have taken a turn for the worse and for whatever reason they need a top up," Garnham says.

Almost two thousand mothers were exempt from the limit as their third child was born as a result of "non-consensual conception," also known as rape. The message is plain: If you are not wealthy and you choose to have more kids, you will be punished. Graham says the policy is "clearly discriminatory" against populations who are more likely to have larger families. "We're not even replacing ourselves," she says. She emphasizes that the UK's falling birth rate, "will not be helped by continued austerity." Adding the growing need for food banks in Britain is not surprising considering the "massive retrenchment" of social security before the pandemic and the current cost of living crisis. "We need decent maternity, childcare, and child benefit provisions that don't pass on all the costs to parents."

I am trying to understand the obstacles faced along a single route to civic worth that leads out of the home and through the workplace. I see clearly now how equating my paid labor with my own value in society was not just foolish, but in direct opposition with how I value other people. It does not square with how I value the time and effort of my brother, an unemployed person living in social housing, nor how I value my mother's domestic care on the days she wasn't teaching. Any progress, particularly for women, that confines itself to the workplace feels to me now not just incomplete but exclusionary. In overvaluing paid employment, we devalue what is under-paid or unpaid and allow the state to continue shifting the burdens of social reproduction onto families.

Just as the emphasis on all the rewarding but priceless qualities of care distract from the fight to make parenting affordable, an obsession with the noneconomic benefits of hard labor slows the fight for more good jobs—ones that might even feel compatible with parenthood. Even before the pandemic hit, wage growth in Australia had fallen short of the government's official forecasts for eight consecutive federal budgets and business elites blamed this on a lack of productivity. Our own former prime minister said, "Once you see that sustained productivity and that sustained profit, then that should flow through to wages." As though if the average worker was producing a little more, they would be paid a little more. As though the lack of real wage increases has nothing to do with employers holding the balance of industrial power. As though profits had always trickled down to workers' pay packets in the most productive of our industries. As though bosses are loving par-ents, stuffing each of their children's Christmas stockings with extra treats at the end of a fruitful year.

Workplaces aren't family units but, in writing her book *Work Won't Love You Back*, Sarah Jaffe says she came across workers who told her their bosses defined them as such. "With little time for a personal life anyway, we are even more likely to try to make work more pleasurable, even to seek in it a replacement for the love we lack elsewhere," Jaffe writes. I invested my love and care into my team as though it was a family but ultimately, it was the union that exemplified what family means to me—a bunch of people who keep in irregular contact but sometimes show up for each other in a crisis. My mum turning up at midnight to collect me and my suitcase after an ugly breakup. It was the union who checked in, who answered my questions, who helped me understand my rights and made sure I wasn't screwed over with my severance package. This family should be bound by loyal ties that allow for collective imagination and action, not just reaction. A weaker workers' rights movement means there is less of a counterweight to business to fight for good conditions just when a generation of potential parents might need it most.

The question of having both children and a full-time career is fraught, not only because it is hard to imagine love divided but because the problem of unpaid labor can be solved for some via delegation. Many households now rely on two incomes and with little time for housework and child-rearing, having it all seems a feat only possible if you have a partner who is a primary carer or if you are earning enough to outsource some domestic tasks. I have watched older women I know, particularly those without extended family networks like myself, give up on begging their husbands to contribute equally at home and instead hire babysitters, nannies, and cleaners so they can keep their careers.

As Koa Beck writes in her book, *White Feminism*, domestic workers are essential to white feminists' "self-interested and often capitalistic, ascension to gender equality—either within their homes, their workplaces or within their own families." Whether it is a joint decision the couple makes together or not, a whole cohort of women is in fact getting a wage for housework—not to tend to her own family, but to take on the load of more highly paid white-collar workers. Even when pay and conditions are good for these workers, their efforts are still undervalued and the roles offer little progression or recognition of experience—care is care. As journalist Kimberly Seals Allers writes in *Slate*, the labor of some women is used to allow other women to pursue their corporate and civic dreams. The conversation about work-life balance often ignores the "simple economics" of how we ended up here—"White women had money but wanted more time. Black and brown women needed more money." As activist Angela Davis wrote in 1981 in *Women, Race, and Class*, "women of color—and especially Black women—have been receiving wages for housework for untold decades." And yet, as she points out, we have been reticent about the fact that our ability to excuse ourselves from the home has relied on this labor. A #girlboss narrative relies on a single heroine who has scaled a corporate ladder unaided and alone.

Catherine Rottenberg has stated this situation only further solidifies market rationality while also "creating new and reinforcing old class-based and racialized gender stratification." The endgame, as Rottenberg sees it, will be a total economization of reproduction. "Once certain women are able to freeze their eggs successfully, rent a womb, as well as hire various caregivers, new and intensified forms of racialized and classed gender exploitation will occur," she writes in *The Rise of Neoliberal Feminism*. "Indeed, this trajectory of powerful women is bound to produce new populations of dispensable 'service' providers, the vast majority of whom will be women." I don't think Rottenberg is diminishing the place of assisted reproductive technology or surrogacy in many families, but highlighting that neoliberal feminism does not service all women. As Kim Brooks writes, equality won't come from women foisting their exploitation onto less privileged women. Instead, she calls for women to collectively say: "From now on, they have to pay us, because as women we do not guarantee anything any longer." What kind of work-life balance relies on maintaining the invisible, devalued, and gendered nature of reproduction and care work? One that seems unsustainable for everyone involved.

Emma Goldman, an anarchist imprisoned in 1893 for inciting a riot with a speech to unemployed workers and later for disseminating birth control information, wrote of the "narrowness" of the existing conception of woman's independence and emancipation. "The dread of love for a man who is not her social equal; the fear that love will rob her of her freedom and independence; the horror that love or the joy of motherhood will only hinder her in the full exercise of her profession," Goldman wrote in *Anarchism and Other Essays*. "All these together make of the emancipated modern woman a compulsory vestal, before whom life, with its great clarifying sorrows and its deep, entrancing joys, rolls on without touching or gripping her soul."

A century later, this conception prevails. I find myself unmoored, soul neither touched nor gripped, between the work of mothering and the work of reporting, a binary that says either, or, both, but never neither. How long left do I have to consider a life in which the most important thing isn't a job nor parenting but something else entirely? What is the sum that accounts for the labor I want to give my friends, my community, myself? How can I make space for that calculus and still pay rent? "How do I create a fulfilling life for myself that isn't only work-focused?" a childless friend asks. "What if you're not a careerist?"

Matresence, the anthropological concept which describes the identity transformation involved in becoming a mother, captures the friction between fantasy and reality, the guilt and the shame, the way you were mothered and the way you want to mother and the ambivalence, psychologist Dr. Alexandra Sacks writes about in the *New York Times*. "Even those who don't experience [postpartum depression] are undergoing a significant transformation," Sacks notes. I read about how slowly scholarship on mothers and their subjectivity has developed, but I find writing on whatever the opposite of matresence is sparser still. I read about people who tried but could not have the family they wanted, those who devoted themselves to a job or cause, but find little on those who never wanted either. I can't find a template for an ambivalent woman.

I call Judy, a family friend. I was obsessed with her as a child because she was a glamorous architect who toasted nuts before she put them on salads and had dinner parties with friends who stayed for days. She painted flowers and was the only adult I knew in a physically affectionate relationship. I idolized her because she did not have her own children. I could see how she had the luxury to tend to many things I imagined my mum might have time for if she didn't have four kids. Her partner was the first man his age I had encountered who was not in some way demented by the model of masculinity he had grown up with. He was gentle, affectionate, expressive, creative and not self-conscious about these facts. Now in their seventies, Judy confirms their life is as rich as I fantasized. As a child I thought she was a woman who chose architecture over children but I see now she chose many things instead. She is surrounded by friends, their children, their grandchildren. She still travels, she still paints. She is still deeply in love with her partner of four decades. Together they built the beautiful life they wanted. I didn't expect Judy to admit that underneath their decision not to have children, which was made many times, was a lot of fear. The financial cost of children, the toll it might take on their relationship, but specifically, the lack of control over who her children might be and the bad choices they might make. She lists parents and grandparents she knows whose children's decisions have caused them grief.

"The risk is just enormous," she cackles. "Maybe I'm a coward."

How does categorically deciding you will not have children and then experiencing not having children transform you? Are the tensions the same? Who would I be without children? Who would I be without children and a career? Why does it still feel radical to admit I might want a life in which I am not preoccupied by either? I entertain notions of being an especially involved community member, an unbelievable cook, a more present auntie, a better friend to more people, enviably fit, the most well-read and well-traveled person you've ever met. In every scenario, I see myself endlessly producing. How would I protect any of these pursuits from the cult of productivity? "In a situation where every waking moment has become the time in which we make our living . . . time becomes an economic resource that we can no longer justify spending on 'nothing,'" writes Jenny Odell in *How to Do Nothing*. Is my disenchantment with the prospect of motherhood instead of, or, worse, alongside another four decades of journalism just early fatigue with the compulsion to prove I am devoted to doing *something*?

I had never considered I might not be consumed by something; for the first time I pictured myself consuming. I might want to sleep in, to stay at the pub for a few more rounds, to miss both the sunrise and the sunset devouring two books per year that I'd never post a picture of, to enjoy more of my partner, to go for long walks, steps uncounted, to watch movies that won't make me a better person, to never grow a vegetable, to be free any night you are, to stay in the bath for longer and listen to my podcasts about D-grade celebrities. I might want to do this more often for the rest of my life. Even typing it out, my fingers feel sticky with something indulgent. But what if more idleness isn't self-interest but survival? What if from the ashes of the #girlboss rises what author Gabrielle Moss calls the girlloser? A feminism that doesn't see unorganized people as "deadweight," that doesn't confuse "focus, ambition, and organization with a celebration of womanhood," that doesn't instruct us to be "painfully responsible," that doesn't paste hard worker over mother as the complete female identity. "Everything is chaos, and being a boss can't protect you," she writes on *Medium*. "So you might as well give being a loser a shot." If respite is not defeat and rest is not death and being average at something is permissible, the choices we make in an imperfect structure feel a little lighter.

After taking my job very seriously I was, ironically, made redundant by the very publisher of culture writer Anne Helen Petersen's ultra-viral essay about the burnout generation. Millions of millennials shared the article that summarized their situation—a generation with less savings, more debt, waning union protection, and who couldn't take stable employment at the same company for granted but instead must keep self-optimizing. "Never too sick to work, never too sad, never too besieged by familial obligations, never heartsick, never traumatized by the images that surround them, never existentially fearful for the future of the planet, but endlessly resilient, endlessly striving, endlessly motivated by more money because somehow, no matter how much you have of it, you never feel secure enough," Petersen writes. Even in trying and failing to fulfill this role as an ideal worker, "you only solidify it as an ideal."

I want to deconstruct myself as any kind of worker, regardless of whether I am eventually made into a mother or a woman without children. I am apprehensive now about the relentless, goal-oriented, outcome-obsessed, self-interested texture of paid employment, as most of us know it, folding into any part of my future. Sorry to the women who dreamed of taking their aprons off to go to university *just* so I could imagine staying in my dressing gown a little longer each day, pursuing mediocrity in each part of my life.

In love, we find who we are, in devotion we express it. Love can mean recognizing all mothers as working mothers. Love can mean solidarity, organizing for security and conditions or valuing care work. Love can mean regarding a human as more than a speck of capital whose interests will rarely align with anyone who seeks to exploit them as such. Love does not begin as labor, and it exists beyond it.

4.

Emotional Labor

A FRIEND DISCOVERS SINGLE WOMEN using donor sperm are the fastest growing segment of the assisted reproduction market and tweets: "I'm assuming this is because it is easier to raise one baby rather than two."

It feels like an uncool time to consider irreversibly and indefinitely tethering yourself to a straight man by creating a child together. If you spend enough time online, writes academic Yuhe Faye Wang for the *Outline*, you get the sense that heterosexuality is on the way out. "Among a particular set (woke social justice warriors), it is a truth universally acknowledged that heterosexuality is a prison, a form of Stockholm syndrome for women cursed to date men," Wang writes. The Internet is rife with what Asa Seresin calls heteropessimism—"performative disaffiliations with heterosexuality, usually expressed in the form of regret, embarrassment, or hopelessness about straight experience."

No one in good faith is claiming alignment with the most normalized sexual orientation is inconvenient, particularly when it comes to family-making. Nor are they in good faith claiming it is oppressive to pass as straight courtesy of your relationship, rather it's that heterosexuality as an institution is looking a bit worse for wear. Unlike those spouting vile homophobia and transphobia online, people who have turned the question "are straight people okay?" into a catchphrase, have good reason to be concerned. A news story about a woman whose husband told her to "shush" while she was in labor. Are straight people okay? A gender reveal party firework that sparked a wildfire, forcing hundreds of people to flee their homes. Are straight people okay? A *New York Times* article titled "How I Trained My Husband to Be a Dad." Are straight people okay? A T-shirt that says "My favorite Disney villain is my wife." Are straight people okay? An entire interior design article explaining to women which items in their home might be off-putting to men (cactuses are "unwelcoming" while art or vases featuring individual women might wrongly imply you're happier single). Are straight people okay?

Straight men bear the brunt of the bewilderment. There are endless posts ridiculing behaviors deemed to belong to them. They have loud cars and loud sneezes, they call each other by their last names, they wear long board shorts, they love to spit on the ground, they walk up the stairs two at a time, they lie about being six foot, their skincare regime is just soap, they believe they're not sexist because their girlfriend is a woman, they believe they're not sexist because their mother is a woman, they don't clean their fingernails, they're in leadership positions but can't cook a microwave meal, they do the bare minimum and receive unending praise from their partners and society at large.

In between the justifiable mockery of abusive men, incels, and trolls, there are infinite jokes in which straight men play teenage boys and the women dating them are patient mothers. They fit roughly into two cartoonish archetypes. The man who is hopelessly emotionally inexpressive, intent on adhering to bizarre codes of masculinity, clueless, lazy, out of touch with himself, and unable to connect with women. During the pandemic @blairsocci tweeted, "My heart goes out to men whom without sports are feeling their feelings for the first time instead of yelling at the screen: 'Welcome bitch, here's a white wine.'" He's the unromantic boyfriend, the doltish sitcom patriarch for whom patience is waning, the jock we now demand vulnerability from. The other broad category is a man who is more emotionally literate or at least has the vocabulary to appear so, but expresses too much, too soon and he is ridiculed in the same way women often are—for being needy, clingy, oversharing, sensitive, easily offended, at best delicate, at worst manipulative but importantly still selfish and unable to treat women well. Or as the satire site Reductress declared, "Clever! Man Co-Opting Social Justice Language to Emotionally Abuse You." These men and their variants blend into the same virtual portrait of a man who has unreasonable needs and an underripe ability to respect boundaries, to care, and to communicate. I was one of the 237,000 people who laughed and hit 'like' on this tweet by @kylieGjansen in 2020: "happy mother's day to every straight guy's first 3–4 girlfriends."

You can almost hear the chorus of snickering and knowing groans across keyboards, a virtual but genuine solidarity in the shared weariness and wariness of dating men. If this was a story about bad men or male entitlement, it would fit neatly into 240 characters.

I understand that parental love should be unconditional and that the care of a child can be unrelenting and unreciprocated and go unrecognized. You are there to catch your child's emotions when they come all at once and when they are withheld and hard to read. I expect a child needs you to communicate patiently and intuit their needs attentively. Your value is in what you do, not who you are because your primary function for them is to keep them safe and supported so they can grow in every way. What I want to understand is how this dynamic has been woven into our romantic relationships and why. I want to know why so many women feel obliged to be the main provider of emotional security for their partners. In patriarchal culture, love becomes a resource, something men should "receive without expending effort," wrote author bell hooks. "More often than not they do not want to do the work that love demands." Despite the reductive tweets, most women I know are not at risk of procreating with a grunting boofhead or manipulative man-child. They are instead depleted by the most traditional and tiring features in their otherwise progressive relationships and worry how bearable these patterns would be in parenthood.

Within many heterosexual relationships, this imbalance creates a simmering resentment. For better or worse, women can feel responsible for our own well-being and, since we've been encouraged to treat the self as an enterprise, our own personal growth. For many, our twenties were a process of maturing, introspecting, sharing our thoughts and feelings with each other, and sometimes a professional, and moving in and out of relationships with people who were yet to learn to do the same. We found the words, not just in snide tweets but in tired group chats, to describe the aftermath of what hooks says, in *All About Love*, is the first act of violence that patriarchy demands of men: "That they engage in acts of psychic self-mutilation, that they kill off the emotional parts of themselves." We begrudged the ministrations that fell to the person in a relationship who was not encouraged to amputate, but rather overwork and strengthen the emotional part of herself until it was muscular enough to carry another person. The one who had spent her adult life confronting, understanding, and improving the ability to communicate her own feelings and patterns of behavior, reckoning with past trauma, and practicing leaning on others for support. The partner who was already more likely to do the majority of the household labor became the partner more likely to take on the bulk of care and communication. The one who then not only became the human list, calendar, alarm, diary, schedule, reminder, booking system, archive, and point of contact for their partner (and any potential offspring), but also the person who must start and finish hard conversations.

"Managing your partner's emotions—anticipating needs, preempting displeasure, and keeping the peace—is something women are taught to accept as their duty from an early age," writes journalist Gemma Hartley in her book *Fed Up*. Many of my friends and I, most of whom are childless, have taken on unpaid organizing or caretaking and been made to feel this comes more "naturally" to us, until the assumption self-fulfills. A housemate once glanced up from playing FIFA on his PlayStation to encourage me to finally "write the book about mothering." He had not done a weekly chore in three months, but I smiled and thanked him for the encouragement as I walked up the stairs I had mopped earlier that day. I could fill pages about just physical unpaid domestic labor—of which women do nearly three times as much as men— but it is often the invisible, ill-defined emotional labor I want to understand. By the time we're nearing our thirties, my friends and I have been in rela- tionships, even fleeting ones, with men in which the division of care and communication was so asymmetrical that for most of our twenties we arrived at each other's houses lopsided, ready to vent until our spines were straight again. We've all been among the straight guy's first three to four girlfriends. I scroll past the same phrase on TikTok, Instagram, and Twitter in a single afternoon: "Dating a man is just microdosing motherhood."

A friend tells me her Italian family uses the phrase *mente fresca*, meaning a fresh mind, a clear-headedness you can default to. "Mente fresca, mente fresca," she repeats it like a directive. Since becoming a mother, she finds herself thinking about all of the men in her life who "get to be mente fresca" about most things. "They are only burdened by the things they allow themselves to be burdened by." She fantasizes about what would happen if she stopped taking mental responsibility for the laundry, the food, the sleep schedules, the appointments. "But it can't be more than a thought experiment because I have a baby that depends on me to keep him alive."

Sociologist Arlie Russell Hochschild, who coined the term *emotional labor* in the 1980s to describe the managing of one's own emotions expected of workers in certain professions, has said while the term can apply to relationships, it is being wrongly used for a range of household tasks or romantic functions. Modern usage of the term has drifted far from any recognition of class relations, but I think it was pinched because there weren't yet the words for what we now describe this way. I consider how we might keep these emotional tasks intact, attached to their genuinely loving origins while tearing them from their default association to women in relationships with men. It can be hard under capitalism to evaluate emotional labor without becoming a resentful ledger-keeper who sees love and care as commodities to be transacted. But there's an undeniable atmosphere in which, for many women in relationships with men, the thought of starting a family feels daunting because they are already depleted by the relationship, however loving. Not sometimes drained in the way networks of reciprocal love and care might ideally ebb and flow, but constantly at a loss. Motherhood does not promise to balance the sheet.

When I first turned up at a therapist as a teenager, I was there to figure out how to survive the mental illness and addiction that was destabilizing my home. This doctor had proven himself a wizard, magicking away my night terrors with a kind of hypnosis. He helped me learn a language with which I could articulate feelings to myself in times of paralyzing fear and fathomless depression. I trusted him completely. Although I knew by that age I no longer believed in God, I didn't mind that he was a Catholic; in fact, I secretly hoped, as if by osmosis, I might absorb something holy by being near him. I welcomed his belief in the sanctity of life, a bracingly simple and helpfully abrupt response to my suicidal ideation. "How lucky are we to be in this body, on this earth? Life is far too precious to give away in a moment," he said dismissively. But there was one appointment, the only one I remember clearly, in which his religiosity cemented my ideas about how I believed men and women should give and receive care. I have been trying to unlearn it ever since.

I knew even as a teenager that the feelings I described in this appointment were obvious and unoriginal. I told him I felt like I could never shine brightly enough or else make myself small and needless enough to be worthy of the same love and attention I felt my brothers had earned through their personal struggles. I described for the first time a cloak of unwanted anonymity within my family that only slipped off when I felt worthlessness. In other words, I only felt visible when I felt like I'd failed. I followed this disclosure up with a guilty rant about how I knew this wasn't actually important and that my mother, our primary carer, had enough on her plate with four kids and I was lucky not to need much consideration. I asked him how I might show my parents how clever and strong I was without inconveniencing them.

The psychologist did not dwell on either of my requests. Instead, he spoke for the rest of the session about the Virgin Mary. He spoke of her as Our Lady of Sorrows, or the Sorrowful Mother, depicted in Catholic imagery with seven daggers piercing her heart. Each sword, he explained to me, represented each of the sorrows she felt about her son, Jesus. "That is how mothers love their sons," he said. He seemed touched by the archetypal mother's pain, which he said was present on her face in every depiction of this Catholic devotion. British academic Jacqueline Rose describes the image of the tortured mother, particularly the Virgin Mary grieving her dead son, as a stable of maternal imagery. "With the suffering of the whole world etched on her face, she carries and assuages the burden of human misery on behalf of everyone," Rose writes in *Mothers*. The psychologist made explicit that the love a mother has for her son is unavoidably consuming and inherently painful—see the blood seeping from her wounded heart, see her grief-stricken gaze—and in this he made implicit what I'd already been socialized to believe for years: that a daughter should be forever self-reliant, a grown-up while growing up, a martyr-in-waiting, a rock in a river, and always unarmed—after all, there's nowhere on Mary's heart left to wound.

The psychologist encouraged me to find a church where I might find this image in a stained-glass window or a sculpture and to kneel before it and meditate on the fact that I can't change that I'm a daughter but that that was okay.

My housemate gets a package from her mother in her home country. The note reads: Thank you for taking such good care of yourself for me.

In *The Empathy Exams* essayist Leslie Jamison captures the danger in assuming that female pain is inevitable. "We risk transforming their suffering from an aspect of the female experience into an element of the female constitution—perhaps its finest, frailest consummation," she writes. I was uniquely primed to believe, as she describes, that suffering, particularly in service of men you love, is the "unending glue and prerequisite of female consciousness."

An ex-boyfriend told me that when he was about to get his tattoos, his mother, distraught about the idea, offered her own body up instead to be inked, wanting his skin to remain as unblemished as it was when she'd created him. Throughout our relationship, I told his mother repeatedly that I didn't want children, but she asked again and again and again in different ways when I might. "Do you love spending time with your gorgeous niece and nephew?" she asked pointedly. "Yes, so much, and I enjoy handing them back," I responded, smiling. I was a uterus; an invisible site of unfertilized potential.

She drove us to the airport after our visit. Bags out, trunk closed, time for goodbyes. She hugged me too tight and whispered, "Take *care* of him," slipping an invisible baton into my hand for the next leg of the relay. I didn't know it yet, but I would delight in this race then, somehow, resent it. I would fail miserably, eventually returning him back into her superior care with a broken heart. In every relationship with a man I learned that I am not infinite as I'd learned mothers must be. I discovered that my reluctance to cause men discomfort, to trust that they will survive my boundaries, to have my own needs and then express them clearly does not make for honest or equal relationships. Only a child thrives on care that is given out of obligation, and I want to believe that most men are not boys. But they once were.

Dr. Judy Y. Chu's research shows that conditioning men to be invulnerable starts very early. Her two-year study followed boys from pre-kindergarten through first grade and found many tenets of masculinity—emotional stoicism, aggression, inexpressiveness, or social ineptitude—aren't innate but a learned performance. These boys desired close relationships and were able to express their emotions as well as little girls, but by age five or six, they had learned to publicly discard these skills and reject or hide friendships with girls. "Both boys and girls are born with a capacity for and a fundamental desire for relationships—to be close and to be connected and if anything they find that boy babies need more help regulating themselves," Chu told the *Atlantic*. "When they are upset they need their primary caregiver to help them regulate and come back to a feeling of contentment." She points out that while infant studies show all kids seek connection to others, later studies show adolescent boys reporting fewer close relationships and lower levels of intimacy. "They start out wanting and thriving in relationships, and then they are moved away from those protective relationships, and there's a cost."

Psychologist and former president of the Society for the Psychological Study of Men and Masculinities Dr. Andrew Smiler says that because boys in Western English-speaking cultures are not taught to express their feelings, they are implicitly encouraged not to pay attention to them. "Why pay attention to something you are not going to address?" he asks. Smiler writes that the person in a partnership who is more knowledgeable about feelings and relationships will become "the relationship expert" who "invests more time and energy in strengthening the relationship and smoothing out its rough spots." The ideal of men as problem solvers encourages them to *do* instead of to be or to feel. "This is epitomized in our tendency to ask men, 'What are you going to do about it?' instead of 'How do you feel about it?'" I learned early on in journalism that you're more likely to get an interviewee who is a man to tell you how he feels about something by asking him what he thinks about it.

I want to understand the rules, but it was strange to read them and know my understanding of masculinity as a hard rock that has only recently softened enough to take new forms is ahistorical, according to Smiler. Unlike in the 1800s, when he says men were permitted to display passion and affection in their friendships with other men, our late twentieth-century version of masculinity, is more "explicitly toxic." He argues this masculinity specifically supports men's violence, aggression, and risk-taking and directs men to minimize certain aspects of human-functioning, such as emotional expression and connections with others. "Many of these men claim that it is better to be angry or aggressive than to express other feelings," he writes.

Social scientists Robert Brannon and Deborah David's "man box"—a definition of the evolved industrial model of masculinity that we have all encountered—consists of four principles. The first is "no sissy stuff," or avoid engaging in behaviors or displaying traits that are associated with femininity like displaying emotions or relying on others. The second is "be a big wheel"— use your ambition and competitiveness to strive for status and success. The third, "be a sturdy oak," instructs you to function independently from others and to speak through actions, not through feelings. The fourth is what they refer to as "damn the torpedoes, full speed ahead," which is the directive that men be decisive, take risks, and display aggression, adventurousness, and fearlessness.

It was strange to read these rules and know immediately how they applied to the men in my life while simultaneously seeing how they were also the basis of a kind of aggressive corporatized feminism, in which women are encouraged to adopt the most power-hungry and inhuman aspects of masculinity in order to access what men have. I can see how these traits, none of which are exclusively or consistently bad, are impossible to follow all the time as a member of a social species with emotional needs.

Associate professor Michael Flood, who researches men, masculinities, and violence prevention at Queensland University of Technology, used the man box in his research. He found that the belief in stereotypical masculine norms among men aged eighteen to thirty is around an astounding twenty times more important than demographic variables like education, occupation, and ethnicity in predicting the use of physical violence, sexual harassment, and online bullying. Endorsement of these masculine norms was eleven times more influential than other factors in predicting binge drinking and ten times more influential in predicting negative moods. Suicidal thoughts were associated most strongly with men's conformity to "hyper-sexuality" and "self-sufficiency" including agreement with the statement: "Men should figure out their personal problems on their own without asking others for help."

"One of the key lessons that is part of traditional masculine socialization is to repress emotions, particularly emotions that indicate vulnerability or weakness. So anger is legitimate and capable of being expressed, but more vulnerable emotions of fear or distress or hurt are punished and associated with femininity and one of the key lessons that boys and men still learn is that 'above all we should not be women,'" Flood tells me. "That then plays itself out in men's lack of emotional reflectiveness, lack of emotional skill, and in unequal divisions of emotional work."

Flood is quick to identify that women experience "frustration, dissatisfaction, emotional exhaustion, burnout" from these imbalances. I expect us to spend some time talking about the way these rules might disadvantage men in relationships with women, as his work so clearly shows these masculine norms don't benefit the men who abide by them. Instead, he only points out that men themselves might lose out if their partners have less relationship and sexual satisfaction, and if their partners eventually leave them.

"Of course, there are advantages and privileges for the person who is doing less in the same way [there would be] if they are doing less childcare and less housework," he tells me. "The benefits of time and space, and also the benefits of attention to your emotional needs and having your emotional needs looked after. If you're not spending time thinking about how the other partner is doing and what they are facing and how you can support them, then you have more time for your own leisure and paid work and your own emotional needs." Even as an academic who has spent years studying and thinking about masculinity, Flood says he is still discovering the ways in which his gender impacts the emotional health of his own relationship. "I have poorer emotional literacy than [my partner]," he admits. "I am poorer at recognizing my own emotions and expressing what is going on for me. In the past, I've often said I feel a bit flat and I've been pushed by her to come up with more adjectives, to come up with a richer and more diverse language than 'flat.' I've realized that 'flat' can be I'm angry or frustrated or despondent or sad or embarrassed or guilty or lonely. There are all kinds of emotions that flat can conceal."

Movember director and clinical psychologist Dr. Zac Seidler, who works mostly with men, says often patients come in and say they just broadly feel "shit." He gets out a big wheel with different colors and adjectives on it to figure out what kind of "shit" they might be feeling. I'm stunned by the simplicity of this. I want to ask if the men find this patronizing but I know it is the wrong question. "It sounds like they're learning a new language?" I offer instead. "It is exactly that," he says. "They have the adjectives, they would just never use them to describe their emotional experience, but I always say, 'I don't want you to talk in any way that is not comfortable for you' and 'I'm not going to get you to put words to things that don't make sense. I want you to describe it in a way that is useful to you.'" Seidler works with his clients to break down physical sensations like sweaty hands or a racing heart to help determine feelings like "anxious." "I'll pick up that there is clear discomfort in them saying, 'nervous' or 'blue' or whatever it may be and so I'll ask, 'Why does that feel so uncomfortable?' And they'll talk about stigma or they'll say I feel weak in saying that or guilty because people are worse off," he says. "It's called emotion coaching, and we do it with children and you do an adult version, I guess with guys who are really struggling."

I call a friend who has a one-year-old. She struggles to know what to do with her partner's emotions, which he can rarely name. Their communication always reaches "a natural dead-end" beyond which he can't be reflective or specific about his emotions, but now that they have a child there is even less time to find a way back to each other. "Now it is laid bare every day," she says. I think about emotions that aren't verbally expressed as what they are, how sadness, worry, and fear can look like anger, irritability, frustration, obsession, possessiveness, inertia. I think about how a child does not need to articulate their precise emotion for parents to identify there is a need. I think about what I would do if I was struggling to name an emotion and realize I do this regularly. I take time to diagnose anger. I feel like it is not an emotion that I am allowed to feel, much less express. It can take me some time to know it is there and I then usually take it to the only place it can be expressed without censorship or judgment—a group chat of women. I read through the flashes of anger in our messages. Brief flares that disappear between the videos of birds and cats and links to long-form articles we want to read, skanky tops we want to buy, and TikToks we want to laugh at. A voice memo that begins, "sorry but . . ." Are we also guilty of cleaving off parts of ourselves and sharing them in privacy away from our partners? Does it matter?

There's a reason when men have a gender preference when choosing a therapist, it is a woman, Seidler says. "If you only go to your mum to talk about your emotions, then you end up getting mothered by your partner and that is where it starts," he says. "You need to see your dad and grandpa talk and express emotions early on because this stuff gets locked in so quickly."

I ask Seidler about relationships where a man's girlfriend might be the only person he is vulnerable with. "I guess if she's got a therapist and a huge circle of friends she can talk to without shame it gives his vulnerability this kind of weight?" I ask.

"Exactly! You've got everyone to lean on and you have everyone to have those connections with," he says. But the heaviness of this responsibility doesn't make many women I know feel special; in fact, there is a sense of anonymity in relationships with men who need a lot of emotional caretaking. The speed and intensity at which he wants to be soothed or comforted doesn't track a genuine intimacy in which each person is learning about the other.

My friend Hayley has often observed, "This guy doesn't actually know me, so it isn't me he thinks he's falling in love with, he just likes how I make him feel." This sense that your value is in your output, not in your personhood, feeds the comparison to mothering—a child needs the care of his parents, but is rarely interested in their inner life. Hayley describes feeling like a kind of hybrid mother-therapist, "even in one-night stands" somehow. "I'm helping them to process their emotions, work out why they're feeling a certain way, or why they reacted a certain way, show them what they're suppressing or resenting me or other people for, teach them how to respond better in a situation of conflict with a workmate or something and often show them how they are unfairly judging their ex-girlfriend's side of the story," she says. "They'll say things like, 'you make me a better person,' 'you understand me,' 'you make me comfortable,' 'you make me realize things I've never realized before,' 'you've taught me so much,' 'you're the only person I can or have ever spoken to about these things.'"

The Australian Housewives' Manual (1883) said: "[Your husband] sleeps as securely as a child, simply because you have nourished him, soothed him, and driven away every trace of care and discomfort." Even though research shows men are just as likely as women to want emotional intimacy in their friendships, 25 percent of men aged thirty to sixty-four had no one outside of their immediate family they felt they could rely on. Heterosexual white men have the fewest friends of anyone in America, and this isolation worsens in early parenthood—an increasing number of fathers lose contact with close friends in the first year of welcoming a child, which worsens stress levels. Who meets your social and emotional needs when your family unit contracts around a child?

The responsibility to be the sole witness to your partner's emotion, once glorified as a gift—"it is only by quiet devotion that you will win his confidence and become the partaker of his innermost thoughts . . . his reliance on you will know no bounds" *The Housewives' Manual* claims—has become characterized as a burden, in many ways because it is presumed to not weigh anything at all. "[The effort of emotional work] has commonly been overlooked because [it has] tended to be characterized as reflections of interpersonal intimacy or love," sociology professor Rebecca Erickson writes in the conclusion of her research on the topic. "Caregiving, in whatever form, does not just emanate from within, but must be managed, focused, and directed so as to have the intended effect on the care recipient." Hayley's describing short-term dalliances with often subjectively insignificant others but in the moment she feels what any human being would: a responsibility to handle someone's feelings with tender attention. For years I've watched this play out in her encounters with guy after guy, and even though I know she doesn't want a boyfriend, as an outsider it seems as though in each situation the best parts of a fling—heat, spontaneity, independence, freedom from expectations and explanations—are eventually eclipsed by the one-way responsibility for someone else's emotional stability.

As a Reductress headline mocked: "'I'm Not Looking For Anything Serious,' Says Man Who Will Rely on You for All His Emotional Support." "There are also the small things, like reminding them to eat or get a good night's sleep or calming them down when they're angry or stressed and there is the constant, constant, constant listening to them rant about themselves or people who have wronged them," Hayley says. "It isn't a conversation, just a one-way monologue about themselves . . . it's not reciprocated, but I know they can't actually help me in the way I help them."

Hayley is one of the few friends I know who has rejected the idea that a partner must be a neat mosaic of what we seek in all our human relationships. Instead, she found emotional intimacy in her friends, romance in prose, intellectual stimulation in her study, financial stability in her work and in doing so managed to make it through her twenties without much heartbreak or regret. She has never been bothered by the fact that these people weren't right to build a life with, but now at thirty, she is considering what a future with one person might look like and whether that involves children. The only type of man she has been with all expect her to perform a role she would never sign up for long-term.

Erickson's study unsurprisingly found that men who held a more "traditional" gender ideology were more likely to perform less emotion work and their wives were more likely to perform more childcare. I don't often try things I'm unpracticed at either. Hayley embodies many "masculine" ideals, including stoicism and competitiveness, and she isn't someone I would describe as people-pleasing. Erickson's study found applying more feminine-expressive traits to oneself was associated with the performance of more emotion work among women, but even women who saw themselves in masculine terms were more likely to perform emotion work. In other words, no woman seemed immune to the far-reaching impacts of gender norms.

Hayley is remarkably independent and, since we were kids, I've watched her take complete responsibility for herself. She has read countless philosophy and psychology books, she has meditated and practiced yoga, she has thought deeply about how her family structure has shaped who she is, she has journaled, and she has contemplated how her own tendencies and behaviors will impact her needs in all of her relationships. Whenever I get indignant about how immaturely those men are behaving, Hayley will laugh and shake her head and say, in the voice of a patient mother, something like, "What can you do? They don't know any better." She sometimes feels like she has left these men better than she found them for the next woman. At the tail-end of every one of these encounters—at the outset of which the man, pre-empting that fabled feminine clinginess, has insisted there will be "no strings attached"—I find myself observing again that she is doing the work of the girlfriend without any of the perks. There is none of the two-way care one might expect in a stable monogamous relationship and instead a denial that anything exhausting is underway—how could it be after all? This isn't exclusive, you're not my girlfriend, you're not my wife. Hayley and I often talk about how avoidable this would be if the guy had been previously emotionally intimate with someone other than their mothers, or sometimes ex-girlfriends. If he had been encouraged to introspect before he was approaching, or in some cases surpassing, thirty, he wouldn't be having these epiphanies with a near stranger at 2 a.m. in his bed, on which hours before she had put the sheets—"I honestly don't think he knew how."

Seidler says there is no evidence boys are somehow innately unable to experience and express a full range of emotions. "You slowly watch this restriction and closing in boys' emotional experience to the point where they start to fully cut off a part of themselves, which is so terribly sad," he says. "If you don't have that ability and don't practice, you lose capacity and confidence . . . it is not condoned and the people around them are not asking for it and don't know how to respond to it." Romantic relationships "open up a man's emotional spectrum," Seidler says. "Which is shit scary. They feel things they haven't felt before and they can't name them and their partner is pushing them for descriptions of love which have been literally drilled out of them over time." Seidler describes a subclinical phenomenon called *alexithymia*, derived from Greek meaning having no words for emotions. A (lack)—lexis (word)—thymos (emotions). "Lots of the research suggests there is a thing called male normative alexithymia, as in it is the norm for guys to not be able to do this," he says. "What I tell lots of our male clients is that that restriction means they lose the potential to express and describe grief and sadness, but they also lose joy and they lose lightness and they lose fun."

He remembers a male patient who came in and was talking about his relationship problems and Seidler asked him what ran through his head during the conflict. "The man responded, 'What do you mean?' I said, 'What do you think to yourself? What comes to mind? What do you reflect on? Do you chastise yourself? Do you get angry with yourself, do you reflect in any way?' And he goes, 'I don't understand' and it became very clear very quickly that he does not have an internal voice. I could not comprehend how he never reflected on things." Seidler said although his relationship was in disrepair, the man was "mentally healthy." "He just hadn't honed that skill and so I talked him through that and he started to build it up over time."

While women are more likely to suffer from severe stress and anxiety, one in seven Australian men experiences depression or anxiety or both in any year, and Australian men are three times more likely to die by suicide than women. In the United States men died by suicide 3.88 times more than women in 2020, yet evidence indicates men are far less likely to seek help for mental health conditions. Despite this, Seidler says not enough clinicians are doing the hard yards early on in appointments to orient their male patients to a foreign system. He makes clear the practical outcomes of treatment and uses language that is about taking action and problem solving. "I empower him to change and understand his responsibility here and that's a way of leveraging masculinity by explaining that he is in control and he is the expert," he says. "I say it's going to be tough but that is what bravery is and that is what courage is." He uses the metaphor of a personal trainer—you might see him for an hour a week, but if you don't work out in between, you won't get results.

Seidler wants there to be more realistic depictions in media and art of men in therapy so men come in willingly. "It is always like Woody Allen lying on a couch being neurotic and talking about his mother," he says, laughing. "I see so many men that have been forced in by their partners and mothers and they don't want to be there and I need to give them a reason to connect, a reason to gain skills that is not doing it for someone else." Men are far less likely to seek professional help and are far less likely to lean on their friends for emotional support, so his partner might be trying to provide all the support a community should.

There was a flood of tweets about things men would rather do than see a mental health professional—"get a whole new girlfriend" instead of going to therapy, "unnecessarily reverse into a parking space" instead of going to therapy, "watch hours of James Gandolfini going to therapy on *The Sopranos*" instead of going to therapy, "start a new workout routine" instead of going to therapy, and "literally run for president" instead of going to therapy. "If there's one thing a girl with a bad boyfriend has, it's the moral upper hand in the religion of mental health," writes Kristin Dombek in *The Selfishness of Others*. This piousness can be useful when your friend has left a relationship with a man who has refused to take responsibility for himself—she can bubble with indignation like hot oil, frying any lingering crumbs of care or concern to a crisp. She can move on. But the upper hands of women with ostensibly good boyfriends, with whom they'd like to remain and maybe even procreate, are strained from overuse.

In 2020, US sociologists published a study surveying hundreds of same-sex and different-sex marriages that found providing "emotion work" in relationships reduces the psychological well-being of the person providing it, especially when the spouse and recipient of the care has elevated depressive symptoms and when one's spouse is a man. "There has to be something more than therapy," a friend says to me, rebuking the flood of online pleas from women for men to sort out their mental health instead of bringing it into the relationship. We talk about this imperative to pay for what we don't want to ask of others and what it might mean for our sense of community and accountability. I don't want someone else to have to outsource and privatize their mental health, as I've watched so many women do. I'd rather people of all genders grow up feeling comfortable enough to talk to their friends, partners, and a professional, if needed.

Seidler says men are ready to talk about their feelings but people aren't willing to listen. "We did this study at Movember where over 80 percent of guys are comfortable and wanting to open up about their emotions to someone in their life, 41 percent who had done so to a friend, family member, or doctor and had a really shit time were not going to do it again," he says. "We end up with this group of men who go, 'Alright, I was willing to, I gave it a go and they just didn't know what to do with it.'"

When describing her "work shame" researcher Brené Brown often describes shame itself as gendered—women's shame comes from not meeting multiple conflicting and unrealistic expectations, while men's shame comes from showing weakness. While the women I know want their partners to feel safe and supported when expressing difficult emotions, Brown believes we're failing at it. "The truth is that most women can't stomach it," she writes. "In those moments when real vulnerability happens in men, most of us recoil with fear, and that fear manifests as everything from disappointment to disgust."

This notion makes me bristle with a kind of defensiveness because I have tried and failed to recall feeling disgust or disappointment when a man has shown emotion and, with admittedly smug relief, I find that I can't relate to the feeling at all. This isn't to say I haven't internalized other unrealistic expectations of men or that I haven't been judgmental when a man has resorted to other coping mechanisms to deal with his emotions— minimization, substances, aggression, violence, denial, or avoidance. Just as I believe many men have accepted the narrative that women must be caring and are disappointed when their nurturers have needs, I know many women are following a script that casts men as unflinchingly stoic and can feel unequipped in the face of their emotionality.

When I think about the instances when my friends feel a kind of disappointment or disgust with their partners, it hasn't been a momentary recoiling from disclosures of emotion, which they understand as flashes of bravery. It has been a diffusion of their desire as it trickles down the very asymmetrical slope I am trying to understand. I recall a series of conversations I've had with many friends in relationships with men over the years about how assuming a caretaker role impacts the way you perceive your partner. It wasn't until our mid-twenties when we discovered and subsequently developed a parasocial relationship with Belgian psychotherapist Esther Perel that we found the language for it. Her work attempts to explain how the demands of modern monogamy—"we expect one person to give us what once an entire village used to provide, and we live twice as long"—is a series of tensions between security and space, surrender and autonomy, the domestic and the erotic. "Love likes to shrink the distance that exists between me and you, while desire is energized by it," she writes, or as she often puts it "fire needs air."

Perel believes balancing these contradictions is the central challenge of modern relationships at a point in history when individuals more often enter into marriage as a romantic rather than an economic partnership. "Caretaking is the most powerful anti-aphrodisiac for women," she says. "If I am in caretaking mode, I am in mothering mode, not lovemaking mode. I am in taking-care-of-others mode." Cue a series of "omg this" texts. This is part of the reason women can need more foreplay or time to transition into a state of mind compatible with sex. Perel says it takes a moment to reorient one's attention from meeting other people's needs to focusing on your own, and feeling selfish enough to have them met. This is a time-sensitive example, but it is helpful to speak of "modes" because the problem for many women is the structure of their relationship forces them into caretaker mode close to full-time, often before they even have kids. As Perel puts it, "It's hard to experience desire when you're weighted down by concern." The unabating if I don't do it, it won't get done because he won't think to or doesn't know how mantra means women can't frequently move in and out of caretaking mode as many husbands and fathers can. This isn't necessarily a problem of how much or what types of care someone is taking on in a heterosexual relationship—there are plenty of women who want to take on these types of tasks—it is about whether that care was deliberately divided by two adults or unthinkingly and silently assigned based on gender expectations.

Seidler has no time for the phrase *toxic masculinity*, a "media-invented term" that he says offers us nothing. There are parts of traditional or hegemonic masculinity that can be beneficial and protective, he argues. "Stoicism and silence and getting the fuck on with it sometimes is going to be really useful for you in an evolutionary perspective when there is a crisis happening as long as when you come out of the fire you can reflect on it and cry and talk to your wife about it and do the work," he says. "We need to have masculinities, plural, and embrace that they are contradictory and they coalesce and change over time between and within men. We need to be able to open up to masculinities moment to moment." He describes one of his patients, a towering, tattooed builder. "If I based my treatment plan on how he looked and spoke in the first fifteen minutes, I'd have locked into the idea that he was a traditional man. In fact, over time, he was the most emotionally in-tune man I'd ever met and it changed between sessions, he would go back to being rough as shit and then he would go into being lovely and soft and crying."

We are in the midst of a gender reckoning, says Seidler, and men are stuck, trying to straddle between new and old expectations of masculinity. "It is like, be vulnerable, be emotional, describe everything that is going on for you, be a better father, be soft, be caring, and then as well as that do all of the traditional things, don't lose them because we don't know how to get rid of patriarchy and masculinity," he says. "They feel like they're constantly failing at both." I think of my friend ranting, "I just want [my boyfriend] to communicate with me more often and not in these big bursts when he's really at a low or when he's drunk. Is that unreasonable?"

I find myself wondering. There aren't enough public examples of men who can comfortably move between these masculinities, Seidler says, which is why young men are buying up *12 Rules for Life: An Antidote to Chaos* by self-help guru Jordan Peterson, who believes "the masculine spirit is under assault" by social progress and that good women should be "conscientious and agreeable." "Peterson is selling a male doctrine for living and it plays into masculinity because it goes, 'here are the rules, just follow them you'll be sweet,'" Seidler says. Nor is it hard to see why comedian Joe Rogan, whose podcasts have almost millions of monthly downloads, is capturing this demographic. As writer for the *Atlantic*, Devin Gordon, who spent six weeks immersed in the world of Rogan put it, these men are aware of their privilege but are "sick of being reminded of it" and feel "thwarted and besieged and sentenced to an endless apology tour." Seidler says Rogan plays on the fact that his audience feels under siege, and that while they have the patriarchy behind them, they don't feel supported. "[A Rogan listener] doesn't feel powerful; he feels disenfranchised," Seidler says. "Right," I respond. "So it is kind of a situation where equality can feel like oppression if you're the person who stands to lose power?"

"Men are starting to go, 'Wait a minute, we are not being benefited by the patriarchy,' and sadly it has taken, and is going to continue to take, women to push for change," Seidler says. "The way out of this gender reckoning is for men to realize amongst each other that they need to do some of this work and women will prop them up, naturally, because they want to see it happen." I make another note at the end of the interview: Prop them up naturally. I slowly circle the word *naturally*.

A 2019 study examining the association of marital strain with psychological distress in gay, lesbian, and heterosexual marriages found that women in different-sex marriages reported the highest levels of psychological distress while men in same-sex marriages reported the lowest. Those outside of heterosexuality were asking whether straight people are okay long before the memes. "Not only for our own sake—because we fear homophobic violence or erasure of queer subculture—but also because straight culture's impact on straight women often elicits our confusion and distress," Jane Ward writes in *The Tragedy of Heterosexuality*. This isn't to say living under the cultural weight of heteronormativity isn't hard when you don't fit within it, Ward writes, nor is it to say queer people don't hurt each other. "But the key difference between straight culture and queer culture in this regard is that the latter does not attribute these destructive behaviors to a romantic story about a natural and inescapable gender binary."

What does parenthood look like beyond that fairy tale? "When it comes to parenting, the fact that same-sex parents can't slide into default gender patterns creates some striking differences," Stephanie Coontz, author of *Marriage: A History*, writes, noting that surveys consistently find that men married to women spend the least amount of total time and the lowest proportion of their non-work time engaged with their kids. A US survey from the Families and Work Institute of hundreds of dual earner couples, found same-sex couples tended to share more duties and assign various chores based on personal preference while straight couples slipped into traditional gender roles, with women, lower earners, and those with fewer work hours taking primary responsibility for stereotypical female chores like laundry. It found same-sex couples were twice as likely to share childcare duties.

This doesn't mean same-sex couples don't assign specialized roles based on relative (to their partner) socioeconomic factors; in fact, research shows they do so more often after they become parents. "Though the couples are still more equitable, one partner often has higher earnings, and one a greater share of household chores and childcare," journalist Claire Cain Miller writes in the *New York Times*. "It shows these roles are not just about gender." Research finds even when they don't divide labor equitably, gay and lesbian couples are more likely to find their division fair. A twelve-year comparison of how couples initiate and handle disagreements found that while overall relationship satisfaction and quality was roughly the same across all groups, when it came to conflict, gay and lesbian couples used fewer "controlling, hostile emotional tactics" and displayed "less belligerence, domineering, and fear" with each other than straight couples did. The Gottman Institute study found they used more affection and humor to resolve conflict and were better at soothing one another.

In a depressing op-ed for the *New York Times,* in which she encourages mothers to keep a "martyr log" of situations when they've gone to unreasonable lengths to make life easy for their family, perinatal psychiatrist Dr. Pooja Lakshmin says she sees women who are struggling to meet the demands of their roles at work and home. She calls on the work of sociologist Martha Beck, who believes modern women are trying to reconcile what is irreconcilable to someone with only twenty-four hours in a day: Women should self-sacrifice and women should pursue their dreams. Mothers feel like they are managing rather than participating in their families, which both spawns feelings of disconnection and fosters a "learned helplessness" in children and partners. "I meet mothers who lean into their guilt like it's a security blanket and hold up their self-sacrifice as a badge of honor." Is there any lesson about our gender that women internalize more than the idea that our selflessness and suffering are somehow redemptive? Is there any realm in which this sacrifice and self-negation is sold as so perpetually rewarding as it is in motherhood? That somehow a woman who gives unconditionally is never depleted because the act itself is so fulfilling? "On one hand, being a martyr is about experiencing pain and destroying yourself for the sake of others," Lakshmin writes. "On the other hand it's about seeking glory, and paradoxically, your glory is in your smallness."

It wasn't until I found myself in a relationship with a man who wanted but didn't need me that I had to admit how much glory I'd found in my smallness, how much value I'd placed on my expertise. I was wholly unprepared to give up a role that I might not have agreed to be cast in but now excelled at. It threw me off balance and made me feel confused and insecure. If he didn't need me, why did he want me? I had to learn how to trust that I was not defined by what I did for my partner, but for who I was—a scary proposition for a good listener with an arsenal of recipes but a fairly low reserve of self-esteem. A friend describes a series of relationships in her early twenties with men who had various mental health issues, but who had not accessed appropriate help. "I guess it was definitely nice to feel necessary and useful," she remembers.

Journalist Gemma Hartley says that emotional labor can be "women's bastion of control" in a world that otherwise limits their power. "But holding on to control for the sake of control is no way to live," she writes. "We're not benefiting from our perfectionism as much as we think we are and neither are men." Hartley says women create "an altruistic persona" by allowing themselves to be subsumed by the needs of others. It is humbling to learn the difference between a persona and a personality just as you approach thirty. I can see now how even devoted dishonesty in a relationship can cause harm. I try to be aware of when I am seeking the protection racket of what Professors Susan Fiske and Peter Glick call "benevolent sexism," in which I gain approval for displaying a quality, like nurturing or comforting, that I am supposedly better at by virtue of my gender. Sexism that endorses positive stereotypes, sexism that we occasionally benefit from, is after all, still sexism. I would be lying if I said I didn't still need to stop and distinguish between genuine and adequate care, concern and affection, and an inextinguishable predisposition to bleed myself dry for someone else. I no longer romanticize this limitless potential to toil for others nor do I condemn it as a pathetic compulsion to shore up my own worth by giving. Lakshmin writes that releasing oneself from a martyr mentality is like building a muscle that represents your own thoughts, feelings, and preferences. "It's not a luxury; it's a necessity," she writes. "And it is a gift only you can give yourself."

Lately, I find myself conducting a secondary check, just in case. As mainstream feminism pushes for women to catch up and associate themselves with "masculine" traits like competitiveness, self-interest, and self-reliance in pursuit of strength, control, and power there can be a blurring of lines in which caring and nurturing, particularly in an unpaid capacity, is seen as a crisis of self-worth, boundary-setting, or assertiveness. You can really rebrand any exertion of effort for another person as a failure to "put yourself first."

Mostly though, I just feel in myself and in my friends a genuine desire to have our time and effort valued. I think it is okay to feel indignant and taken for granted. I think it is okay to feel frustrated by a culture that funneled people into a binary where they were taught two very different lessons about how to care and communicate. I even think it is okay to feel pessimistic, but I agree with Seresin who says that heteropessimism can distract from the extent to which heterosexuality is trying to change and, in doing so, re-inscribes its worst features. "Heteropessimism reveals something about the way we can remain secretly attached to the continuity of the very things we (sincerely) decry as toxic, boring, broken," she writes. "Faced with the possibility of disappointment, anesthesia can feel like a balm." I just don't find resigned heteropessimism soothing anymore. Isn't so much of our frustration rooted in the feeling that things don't have to be this way? I don't want to recite the same story about preordained gender relations just so I can be pissed off about them. I want them to change.

Writer Shannon Keating says that like many lesbians, she has endured drunk straight women who insist their lives would be easier if they were queer. The moping flattens the queer experience into an uncomplicated utopia, devoid of danger or stigma, ignores the ways in which heterotypical gender roles are internalized within same-sex couples and, as Keating argues, it is also just unhelpful to "pit queerness and straightness against each other." It is tempting, she writes, for everyone to "disavow heteronormativity" and its associated institutions altogether. "But what if we instead used our heteropessimism to encourage each other to reach beyond the bounds of the self—and beyond the bounds of our romantic partnerships and nuclear families—to imagine a better world for us all?" There is optimism in the reaching, to extend yourself toward the possibility of relationships and families that don't follow the rules you had to. All this premature mothering has helped me to mother myself too. And mum says we're allowed a few sour tweets if we try to harvest something sweet with the people we love most.

5.

Climate Change

"WHY WOULD ANYONE HAVE KIDS?" my boyfriend muttered, looking down at his phone screen, smoldering tangerine with footage of flames tearing through our state, razing hundreds of homes. We were lying in front of a fan, learning of the destruction as we do all modern disasters: incrementally, pulling down to refresh feeds while news outlets kept pushing articles onto our home screens.

Months before the coronavirus outbreak reached Australia, in the summer of 2019, we were already acclimatizing to a kind of dystopia in which face masks were selling out as people rushed to protect their lungs from the smoke billowing through much of the country. Fire and emergency chiefs agreed that bushfire season, which killed nine people and destroyed more than three thousand homes, was made longer and deadlier by climate change.

The years of my childhood in the 1990s were divided between delighting in summer and waiting for it to begin. When I learned the seasons were reversed in each hemisphere, I imagined the kids on the other side of the world feeling in May how I would in November—giddy with impatience for months of running around at the beach, picking frangipanis to put in bowls of water and behind ears, collecting seashells and threading my brother's fishing wire through them to make necklaces, eating yellow nectarines, and shaking the sand out of my library books before returning them. I was unbothered by the sweat, the mosquitos, or the sunburn. The bushfires and extreme temperatures seemed to me as isolated and infrequent as any other horror flashing across the 6 p.m. news bulletin. The days were long with daylight and possibilities and still I wanted these months to stretch on indefinitely. I vowed that when I was an adult I would hop between hemispheres, chasing summer so I would never have to wear a cardigan again. I would have wished for what is now our reality—Australia's summers have become twice as long as our winters. Now that I have experienced heat as oppressive, I feel only a sheepish trepidation for December.

On December 30, 2019, volunteer firefighter Samuel McPaul died when extreme winds lifted the back of the ten-ton truck he was traveling in, encasing it in a tornado of fire. His wife was pregnant with their first child. Two days later, a couple of hours into the new decade, Dr. Steve Robson drove through Australia's capital city, Canberra, as it recorded its worst air quality on record. The air quality index reading peaked that morning at 7,700—more than twenty-three times the hazardous AQI of 300. His headlights barreled through the smoke as he made his way to the hospital to deliver a baby. When he flicked on his spotlight to examine his patient, he noticed this beam of light was also cloudy with smog. "This baby was born into bushfire smoke," he told me afterward. Robson reminisced about the deliveries two decades earlier, when he experienced an unadulterated joy in chaperoning new life into the world. It was a different time, when parents believed their children faced abundance and nothing was insurmountable. We had just survived the Y2K bug, he remembered, laughing. "There was a sense that people could solve big problems, but that sense seems to be very ephemeral, it has evaporated," he said. "Every single mother-to-be and every single dad-to-be I've seen today has expressed to me anxiety about what the future holds for the child they're carrying."

I interviewed Melbourne obstetrician Dr. Nisha Khot, who said pregnant patients close to their delivery date were asking about whether they should induce labor due to the bushfire smoke, which unbeknownst to either of us would a week later cause the worst air quality in the world. "They're asking,

'Is my baby safer inside or outside of me right now?,' they're asking, 'What does this mean for my baby's growth?' and 'Do I need extra ultrasounds?' and I have to say, 'I can ultrasound scan, but it won't pick up any effect of the bushfire smoke that may or may not occur because there isn't a test that picks that up.' Those are the difficult conversations."

People start families throughout wars, recessions, and ecological degradation, but millennials are statistically more likely than those who came before us to be anxious about climate change, perhaps because we can no longer deny it. A survey of thousands of millennials across thirteen countries at the end of 2020 showed even a global health and economic crisis couldn't shift climate change and protecting the environment as their top concern, above unemployment, healthcare and disease prevention, and income inequality. Half of all millennials and Gen Z interviewed said they believed society had reached a point of no return and that it was too late to repair the damage caused by climate change, and when asked if current and future efforts to protect the planet's health will be successful, only 40 percent of millennials expressed optimism, a number that had dropped eight whole percentage points from 2019, in a single calendar year.

"Maybe it's the case that every generation has felt themselves at the end of the earth, on the brink of disaster, though I suspect never with as much evidence as we have now," writer Léa Antigny considers in an essay in *The Lifted Brow*. She describes a "fundamentally physical, bordering on erotic desire to feel pregnant," to sense new life growing inside of her even at a time when rising temperatures will affect the timing and seasons of our natural world. "I want to be reduced by love to just bodies and to grow a family from it. But what comes after that?" Antigny realizes that she might be "rich enough to shield her descendants," as the *New York Times* put it, from the incoming impacts of climate change. "Is the fact of my privilege reason enough to forge on? I want to be able to answer why beyond simply saying, I want to, and I can."

I am still deciding, but if the answer was yes, could I find and hold my *why* or would I allow it to become eclipsed by a *how*? How on earth? How on *this* Earth?

. . .

My friend Alex says that he has always imagined himself as a father but climate change has become the biggest factor in deciding whether or not he and his wife will have kids. "Some days I'm really hopeful, like at the start of spring I sit in the backyard with Mary and we're surrounded by flowers in bloom in a garden that cannot be stopped and the bees are thriving and everything smells glorious and hopeful and I think we are going to have a dream life," he says. "And then the bushfire season starts." Their simmering worry always boils down to the question of whether existence is a gift or a curse. "Are we leaving behind a world that is better or are we kind of cursing someone to deal with the impacts of whatever it is we have done, or if not done, been mildly complicit in?"

In *The Birth of Tragedy* Friedrich Nietzsche described how Silenus, friend of the god Dionysus, declared the best thing for men is "not to have been born, not to exist, to be nothing." At a picnic, my friend with a toddler says to me, "No one regrets being born." It is this tension, strung with guilt, that hangs above me and other people I know who are undecided about having children. Although I do feel it in waves, it is hard for me to authentically buy into the deep-throated anti-natalism that has captured many of my peers. Even in my darkest moments, I can't bring myself to accept the period between birth and death is so perpetually painful and sparingly joyous that I'd never have jumped aboard.

It is hard to predict precisely how the cataclysmic shifts in our climate will cause pain and steal joy from the next generation, and so when Alex and his wife do let themselves imagine a life with kids, they feel ill-equipped. "How do you prepare? How do you prepare for having children and then how do you prepare children for whatever the world is going to be next?"

I want to know how I might temper the ambient dread about the climate for long enough to evaluate whether I wanted to foist another carbon footprint onto the aching earth and, I believe more significantly, foist these increasingly untenable conditions onto another human. If I choose not to have children and the climate becomes the biggest feature in that decision, I need to be able to explain to myself why I believed the prospect was too much to bear even on the days where I am not concerned with rising tides and blanketing smoke. If I choose to have children I need to have a justification that feels less fragile than the fetus growing inside of me. And so, I sought out people who were forced to stare directly into the future of the climate crisis. I found them swinging, just as I was, between hope and fear.

Joëlle Gergis is an award-winning climate scientist. She is a lead author on the Sixth Assessment Report by the United Nations Intergovernmental Panel on Climate Change (IPCC), a body that assesses the scientific basis of climate change so governments around the world can develop climate policies. "I'm watching the things we talk about theoretically actually unfold on a planetary scale, that is the stuff that freaks me out," she tells me. "There is no analogue in the geologic record for where we are. We are kind of off the map. We have never had 7.6 billion people on the planet altering the earth's surface and the chemistry of the atmosphere and the ocean on this scale." When we speak, Joëlle has just worked through the weekend to meet an IPCC deadline and she's exhausted. The workload is grueling, but Joëlle wants to know that at this "important juncture" for turning emissions around, she did what she could. Joëlle is an expert in Southern Hemisphere climate variability and, I soon notice, an expert in loss—the potential, the inevitable and the irretrievable. "Kids that are alive today are going to see the Great Barrier Reef deteriorate and die, and kids that come after that are going to learn about it in the same way we watched grainy archival footage to learn about [extinct] Tasmanian tigers," she says.

I went to the Great Barrier Reef as a child with my dad. It was surreal, borderline unreal: the tiny tiger-striped clownfish weaving in and out of translucent anemones, the manta rays soaring down steep coral shelves, the dopey green sea turtles, most of whom were at least twice my age, disinterestedly drifting past as I gasped into my snorkel. The tanned skipper, a marine biology student, explained that the noise pollution and disruption the boat was wreaking on the coral atoll was a small price for the reef to pay if everyone on the boat developed an appreciation of and desire to protect it. At that age, my understanding of environmental catastrophe was a series of disjointed incidents in which criminal corporations or careless citizens harmed innocent animals—dolphins starving to death, their noses caught in plastic bottle rings, harpooned whales bleeding out on the deck of a ship, seabirds black and greasy from petroleum oil spills. These individual battles to save distinguishable species were sad but tractable. I didn't understand how changes in the ocean temperature, runoff and pollution and overexposure to sunlight would stress, bleach, and eventually kill this dreamlike ecosystem.

There have been five mass global bleaching events of the Great Barrier Reef since I was born. If I had children, they would never experience the beauty of what should have been guarded as a national treasure but the loss feels bigger than the reef itself; after all, most generations enjoy something the next do not, even if coral hosts a quarter of all marine fish. It feels like defeat. We didn't preserve this UNESCO World Heritage site from rising sea temperatures, we didn't guard a 46,000-year-old sacred Indigenous site from mining companies, we didn't protect the 250 hectares of tropical rainforest (previously thought to be nonflammable) from the flames. There is so much to lose and not enough political will to save it in time. Joëlle uses the word "planetary" eight times in our conversation to describe the scale of the climate crisis. Each time, I feel my stomach drop.

As Joëlle watched flames destroy more than 20 percent of Australia's forests in a single bushfire season, she felt as she had when her father died—a deep awareness that something so loved was now gone. Grief. "The planet has always been able to cope with us, hasn't it?" Joëlle ponders. "We had that 'Save the Whales' iconic species type conservation, but now we are talking about the planetary system really starting to buckle and that to me is completely different. Climate change is taking the worst, most extreme aspects of Australian climate variability and just amplifying it." Joëlle says that the 2019–2020 bushfire season will be average by 2040 and cool by 2060. "This will absolutely barrel through everyone's life, whether you're holed up in your home from regular fifty-degree summer temperatures or your property becomes flood-prone and uninsurable because you live on the eastern seaboard or you're paying AUD $13 a kilo for bananas because the farmers who grow our food keep having crops devastated."

Joëlle does not have children, but she does not judge anyone making this decision and says self-flagellation is unproductive. "I'm not sure if it is helpful for people to feel even worse about something that is already a very fraught and deeply personal question because then the issue becomes very heavy. I think if you are bringing kids into the world, you just have to go into it eyes wide open knowing that they are not going to have the life you had," she says. "I think it needs to be really firmly grounded in the reality that it's going to be a more dangerous world, particularly if we don't turn things around."

When I did my first round of bushfire media training as a junior reporter at a newspaper, the instructor explained that a fire front could move faster than any of us could run. Once you got close enough, you could die before the flames even touched your skin. If you got out of the car and tried to run, there was a 100 percent chance of dying, but if you lay down in the backseat and covered yourself with a heat-proof blanket, you had a less than 10 percent chance of surviving, albeit with burns all over your body. I knew I would run. I knew in the moment I would believe I had a chance of surviving it and that this conviction would be the certain death of me. When I get off the phone to Joëlle I think about how I might keep my eyes wide open as she suggested. I think about how I might actually ground myself in a terrain that will always be as rickety as politicians and executives allow it to be. For days I read as much as I can about everything we discussed: unbearable heat, emissions timelines, planetary boundaries, cascade of dominoes, king tides, coral bleaching, devastating crops, rainforest loss, tipping points. I softly place my forehead next to my keyboard and close my eyes.

As the summer approached in 2020, Rebecca, a general physician in a regional town, discovered babies born to her patients who were pregnant the previous bushfire season were coming early and underweight. The placenta is normally pink and healthy and comes away easily during birth, but these were gray and grainy, as they are in pack-a-day smokers, requiring an operation to remove them. "One patient brought in photos and I know what placentas look like, I've seen a lot of births during my obstetrics training, and this one was just horrifying," Rebecca tells me. "The placenta is a magic filter that feeds our next generation and we have these smoke particles lodging in there." She explains that drugs in Australia are grouped into categories (A, B1, B2, B3, C, and D) based on how safe they are to take during pregnancy and there is an extra category (X) for drugs that have such a high risk of causing permanent damage to the fetus that they should not be used in pregnancy or when there is a possibility of pregnancy. "A pregnant woman during these summer bushfires, breathing in that toxic smoke, is effectively breathing in a category X and that is alarming to me," she says.

Rebecca lives on the property she grew up on. The dam that supplied the farm with water for sixty years is completely dry and the summer berries now come in spring. Fires burned the farm out a few seasons ago and she has since had to evacuate twice with the kids and dogs while her husband stayed to defend it from flames. "I have been in that position holding a six-week-old baby and racing out of the house while a bushfire comes over the hill," she says. "For three months of the year, actually now six months of the year, we have generators ready, we have fuel ready, we have bags packed ready to go at any moment." Rebecca is passionate about preventative health—she speaks in factories and at pubs to men in lower socioeconomic demographics about reducing alcohol, smoking, and blood pressure. "Sometimes I wake up in the middle of the night and think what is the point of doing all this work every day to save people from having heart attacks if we're all going to be living in a world that is two degrees hotter by 2050?"

Air pollutants have been linked to premature birth, low birthrate, and miscarriage in the first trimester. One study showed that a 20 microgram per cubic meter increase in nitrogen dioxide (NO_2) resulted in a 16 percent risk of miscarriage. In Sydney, where I live, the NO_2 increased by 122 micrograms per cubic meter during the 2019–2020 bushfire season.

A friend and I sit at a café, estimating the ideal month someone would conceive to avoid smoke damage to a fetus. It is disorienting to imagine the dangers of climate change reaching a baby when they are yet to feel the safety of their parents' touch.

I lost all sense of time when I spoke to Chris, an evolutionary and conservation biologist in his thirties, about his deep desire to start a family despite witnessing devastating biodiversity loss every day. There is an urgency to his work—mapping the consequences of rapid environmental change for native animals—but he logs it on a fathomless timescale that makes most species, including humans, look like an imperceptible last-minute arrival on Earth. "Do I think about climate change? Constantly, because I study any rapid changes or novel scenarios that shift the playing field and totally disrupt species," he tells me. Chris is currently helping to develop a model that can better calculate and predict what proportion of animals die under different fire scenarios, a project that came about when scientists realized they didn't have a way to accurately guess the animal death toll in that 2019–2020 bushfire season. The latest imperfect estimation is that three billion animals were present in the areas that burned. "A lot of the animals in Australia are actually adapted to fire and they have a whole lot of responses to deal with it and so if you suppress fire, you change the distribution, abundance and composition of species in the landscape, which had all been maintained by Indigenous Australians for thousands of years [before colonization interrupted it]."

These animals long ago learned to burrow lower or climb higher when they sense fire, then a carefully managed phenomenon, but scientists are wondering how native species will cope with the increased severity and frequency of Australia's new fire regime. Any significant environmental change discharges a starting pistol in a race between adaptation and extinction. "Extinction will win if the change is too quick, and the problem is changes are happening at a rate that is unprecedented," Chris says, before correcting himself. "Well, there have been multiple global extinctions across the planet."

As we talk, I fleetingly group humans in with our treasured marsupials and reptiles for their ingenuity and resilience—a comforting comparison—until I remember that we, settlers, are both the perpetrator and the victim, the invading and the endangered species; we are lighting the match and then fleeing the fire. Over the past twenty years, Indigenous community–based landowner groups in Australia's very fire-prone north have used traditional fire management practices—burning early in the dry season instead of suppressing fires that ignite late in the dry season, which is a post-colonial practice that creates bigger and more severe fires. I wonder how these practices will be maintained in unprecedented heat and aridity. "I am currently living in a place that is on the edge of what humans can tolerate in terms of climate," Chris says. "It is insanely hot here and any level of warming will make an already intolerable place beyond tolerable."

Chris doesn't think people should deny themselves a family because of climate change. "It is like when people can't really appreciate evolutionary change because it happens on a scale that is incomprehensible to us," he says. "This problem is incomprehensibly big and it is more than any individual can take on and, while I think people should live responsibly, I don't think they should be racked with guilt for choosing to have a child which is a totally natural decision to make." His desire to be a father feels more than biological. "I can't really describe it, but there is an innate desire in me to have [fatherhood] as an experience and I don't know how I know this or why I feel this way, but I feel like I could make a child's life happy and fulfilled and good," he says, his voice changing in a way I can't understand in the moment. "This is ridiculous, but you're the first person that's going to hear this . . . this has become much more, ah, practical than theoretical because we just found out that [my wife's] pregnant."

Just as Chris finds it hard to articulate the scale of fathomless evolutionary timeframes, I struggle to capture in words the bolt of celebratory joy that crackled through the phone line. In between his peals of laughter and my blaring exclamations and repeated congratulations, I later hear him on the tape in stoked disbelief say quietly, almost to himself, "Yeah so . . . I *am* going to be a father." Hope itself needed to become more practical than theoretical. "My feeling is even when things are difficult, it is better to be alive than not to be."

In 2017, Dr. Sophie Lewis was expecting her first daughter and working on an academic paper examining when current record-breaking extreme temperatures in Australia would not be considered exceptional but average and eventually cool. She was emailing back and forth with another author on the paper, who was also pregnant. "One of the sentences I had written in this really dense, verbose scientific language was that by 2035, it was going to be far hotter and [the other author] wrote back a comment in the Word document just saying 'oh fuck.' It just cut through this great excitement we were experiencing personally for these long-fought-for girls who were about to join our families because in 2035, they would be in high school. Everything just collapsed into one. There was no scientific research and babies on the side. It was just this one thing and I knew this wasn't some time period in the future that was separable from our kids." Two years later, Sophie became the

Australian Capital Territory Scientist of the Year and the bushfires hit, fill-ing her home with toxic smoke. "I find the air quality indescribable, but it is incomprehensibly bad," she remembers. "It feels immediately horrifically bad for your physical health. There is something powerful psychologically about smoke that sends your body into a panic that this isn't safe and you shouldn't be here." Smoke was rolling into Canberra from the east coast of Australia where fires cremated the first place Sophie took her daughter on vacations. "The homes of friends and the homes of animals were burning and that smoke was blowing into our home and I couldn't keep my daughter safe from that."

As the New Year ticked over, Sophie left her partner in Canberra and took their daughter across state to give her fresh air. Each night, Sophie would put her daughter to bed and cry. "I think it was a deep grief for what was going on environmentally and it was a period of deep reflection on what I was doing, and where I was putting my time and energy. I felt like my scientific work was really of little value, you know? Decades of clear and consistent science has not prevented [the bushfires] from happening and there was no sign that any of that was going to change," she says. "Why do I leave my kid to go to conferences to talk about this? Why do I work sixty hours a week when I get paid twenty-eight hours a week for something that is not having any impact on the world?" When Sophie returned to Canberra at the end of January, 80 percent of Namadgi National Park, some 60 kilometers from their home, was consumed by another fire. Her family watched gigantic smoke clouds rise by day and roaring flames crest over the mountains at nightfall. This was the eighth consecutive month Australia had been fighting fires. "I think my discomfort was turning into a feeling of betrayal of our lives and my daughter's future because we have done nothing to prevent this in terms of climate mitigation and adaptation."

Sophie, in her mid-thirties, has always known that she wanted kids. She says she would have twenty-five if it was possible for her and the planet, but she has just one and another on the way when we speak. The family has endured three consecutive miscarriages. "We had all of those concerns regarding what [the decision to have children] meant for those kids and also for the world and being so aware that there is an enormous environmental cost to having kids in the life that we live," she says. The decision was made repeatedly. "When you don't have the core biological components to create a child, it is a very active decision and there is so much thought that goes into how you will do that and the practicalities and that prompts, all those decisions around what are you doing and why?" she says. "Because we had immense difficulty having our children we were revisiting that time and time again and affirming that was what we wanted when we had those natural exit points we could have had." Sophie describes her fear around climate change as relentless but her hope as stronger and more stable. She spends a lot of time working in schools with children and is impressed by how capable and knowledgeable they seem. "I feel more consistently hopeful and invested in that optimism. And then I guess I have these big waves of worry and dread and all those negative emotions which are quite oscillatory," she says. "There is such hope and joy in babies and young children. It isn't particularly fair to rely on them to generate those feelings."

In his book *Notes from an Apocalypse*, writer Mark O'Connell reflected on this burden, one his small children are now carrying, to be a beacon in a dark world. He wondered whether he had selfishly acquired a new sense of optimism about the world at the expense of his son, whom he protected from the news cycle. "But there are times when it seems that we are protecting him, and protecting ourselves, from a much deeper and more troubling truth: That the world is no place for a child, no place to have taken an innocent person against their will," he writes. "Given the world, given the situation, the question that remains is whether having children is a statement of hope, an insistence on the beauty and meaningfulness and basic worth of being here, or an act of human sacrifice. Or is it perhaps some convoluted entanglement of both, a sacrifice of the child—by means of incurring its birth—to the ideal of hope? You want to believe that it is you who have done your children a favour by 'giving' them life, but the reverse is at least as true, and probably more so."

It is uncomfortable to admit, but in those moments when I see the appeal of early motherhood, I am drawn toward this eternal presentness of children. This is out of self-interest—I'm reaching back to a time before I could see any rottenness in the world, before I was aware of my own fallibility, before I lay awake at night obsessing over my collisions with all that I found painful in the universe and in myself, pressing my fingers into these bruises, mauve with shame and fear. A proximity to children tugs your gaze beyond your own navel and into the present moment—following their eyeline and experiencing with them the novelty of things you take for granted, answering the disarmingly specific questions about how things work, lunging to prevent bumps and falls, and the sheer relentlessness of cleaning and feeding. I can't hear my own neuroses above the noisy *nowness* of children.

Artist and author Jenny Odell believes that we live in a culture that puts novelty and a cancerous rate of unchecked growth before all that is cyclical and regenerative. "Our very idea of productivity is premised on the idea of producing something new, whereas we do not tend to see maintenance and care as productive in the same way," she writes in *How to Do Nothing*. Is it fair to produce, primarily for myself, a human object of hope to live on a planet I have done little to care for and maintain? Am I drawn not just to their nowness but the sparkle of their *newness*? Somehow, this impulse toward the immediacy of children sits adjacent to an anxiety about what the world will look like when they are adults. I know that to have a child involves extending yourself into a hypothetical future, where they will have to survive in a world you have left. In 2021, a global survey of thousands of sixteen- to twenty-five-year-olds found "eco-anxiety" was fueled by the feeling that governments weren't doing enough to avoid a climate catastrophe.

Each year, millions of children around the world go on strike from school, demanding action on climate change. There Is No Planet B their signs, replete with wonky crayon globes, remind us. Their yelling, chanting, laughing, uncompromising belief in the most basic of human rights. I let myself believe these tiny marchers will save us, even though our fear, not our hope, was what they were demanding. "Adults keep saying, 'We owe it to the young people to give them hope.' But I don't want your hope. I don't want you to be hopeful. I want you to panic. I want you to feel the fear I feel every day," activist Greta Thunberg told those gathered at the World Economic Forum in Davos, Switzerland, in 2019. "And then I want you to act. I want you to act as you would in a crisis. I want you to act as if our house is on fire. Because it is." Yet, as philosopher Thomas Whyman has pointed out, Thunberg was addressing the business and political elite gathered in the Swiss Alps, not us. "Their hope, she is suggesting, is toxic—like bad air, choking out the stuff that we can breathe," he writes in his book *Infinitely Full of Hope*. "We need, as Thunberg points out, to found an almost entirely new world—just in order to survive. But they, who benefit from the existing order of things in such disproportionate magnitude that they might realistically expect to survive a massive crisis in the provision of basic resources, have a vested interest in our never doing so." Our hope is rooted in the potential of transforming our world, Whyman insists. The hope of the very elite is founded on the likelihood that we cannot.

When two volunteer firefighters, both fathers aged in their thirties, were killed after their vehicle hit a tree while on duty, it was revealed the Australian prime minister at the time was not in the country. A photo emerged of Scott Morrison secretly holidaying in Hawaii while the country burned during Australia's Black Summer. He smiled while the sun set softly behind him. His left hand made the shaka sign—hang loose, chill out, no worries, mate—while his right hand was locked into a firm bro shake with a grinning tourist. He would offer that same hand a few weeks later to an exhausted firefighter who had just lost his house to flames. He responded, "I don't really want to shake your hand." Morrison nonetheless awkwardly picked up the man's limp left hand before walking away.

When he was quizzed about why he had taken a holiday while the country was on fire, he compared his decision to that of a plumber who had to decide between seeing his kids or taking on an extra plumbing contract. "These are things you juggle as a parent," he offered. Morrison, who earns 7.5 times that of most plumbers, then said he wasn't going to give in to people who wanted Australia to do better on climate action. "I never panic," he said. "The urge to panic . . . is not something I'm ever intimidated by or distracted by."

In the winter of 2021, while millions of his constituents froze without electricity in a power crisis, Senator Ted Cruz fled with his family to a luxury resort in balmy Cancún. Two days earlier he warned that one hundred people could lose their lives as the weather worsened. He had delivered this message to Texans: "So don't risk it. Keep your family safe and just stay home and hug your kids."

Dr. Lara Stevens, a Melbourne Sustainable Society Institute research fellow, lay awake, anxious, after finding out she was pregnant with a girl. "I just started thinking about how she will navigate the world and what kind of world there was going to be for her at the other end of it all," she tells me. "I was watching Greta Thunberg's speeches at that time and feeling like 'what an inspirational figure,' but also the gravity of what she was saying . . . It was a personal crisis and a planetary crisis hitting me at the same time."

Lara wrote a one-woman live art piece *Not Now, Not Ever* on one of these panicked nights while pregnant. She later performed it on stage, breastfeeding her newborn daughter and reciting philosopher Georg Wilhelm Friedrich Hegel who stereotyped men as animals and women as "peaceful" plants unfit for political action.

I tell Lara that I have often thought about whether we would perceive the natural world as needless, infinitely giving, a bountiful enigma to meet our limitless material needs, if we had imagined Mother as a Father Nature instead. "By casting nature as feminine, it means the natural world is always a second-class citizen," Lara tells me. "It is there to be raped, to be beaten, to be eaten, abused, or otherwise manicured or beautified for our pleasure." These ideas can be found in ecofeminism, which emerged in the mid-1970s alongside second-wave feminism and environmental activism to make connections between the domination, degradation, and exploitation of nature and that of women. "Ecofeminism challenges the narrative that we are above the natural world, that we are its masters and we have to control it and use it for our gain, that it is there for us and our pleasure and it is going to feed us and clothe us . . . ecofeminists have been saying we come of the earth and we're interdependent with it and if we don't start addressing that mistreatment it will bounce back on us," Lara, who has written extensively about the movement, says. "The attitudes we have towards nature have a common ground with the way we treat women, but also other marginalized communities like poor communities, Indigenous communities, and LGBT communities."

This is not just metaphor-making. Every week a new study emerges that shows the dangers of global warming are disproportionately shouldered by minorities and disadvantaged communities. An examination of more than 32 million births in the United States found pregnant women exposed to high temperatures or air pollution are more likely to have premature, underweight, or stillborn children—one study found high exposure to air pollution in the final trimester of pregnancy was linked to a 42 percent increase in stillbirth risk. These risks were higher for African-American mothers, who the authors said were more likely to live close to power plants and other sources of air pollution and less likely to have air-conditioning in their homes or live in neighborhoods with green spaces that might keep temperatures down.

Lara believes we need to make a "wholesale change" as a species from an atomized, individualistic, and consumer-driven way of living to something that considers the interests of the community and the planet. The question of whether or not to have kids changes across borders, she says. "I think it is really important to bring race and class and nationality into the discussion and recognize that if we are having a child in the US and Australia they are going to use on average fifteen times more resources during their life compared to a child of the developing world," she says. "That is going to impact the decisions we make about how many children we have and how we live. A lot of people, and myself included as a privileged subject, are not going to like how our lives are upended in some of those changes that we are going to make, but we can't keep growing at the level of affluence we have."

In 2016, helicopter crewman David Key was awarded a bravery award for his rescue role in Australia's 2009 Black Saturday bushfires, in which 450,000 hectares burned and 173 people were killed. I interviewed him at the time about the day he put the lives of four strangers, a couple of horses, and a dog named Poncho ahead of his own when he descended into the hellish flames enveloping their property. He disconnected himself from the chopper to save his two colleagues hovering above and bundled the family into a car. One of the children held her horse's reins out the window as it galloped alongside them. "It was amazing the other animals that were running along with us: deer, wombats, and kangaroos," David remembered. He told me that the family and the Noah's Ark worth of wildlife that followed them all made it out of the flames and to the safety of a paddock. I absorbed this image as some kind of poetic proof of the democratizing function of disaster, that we are all just animals running toward a field. But we are not.

The burden of climate change has and will continue to fall unevenly. And yet, somehow, the allocation of responsibility has been skewed when it comes to the question of family planning.

In November 2019, more than 11,000 scientists from around the world declared a "climate emergency" and outlined six policy goals to address it, the last of which was to stabilize or ideally gradually reduce the population, in part by making "family planning services available to all people." Alongside fossil fuel replacement and ecosystem restoration, helping people family plan can seem like a benign notion, but even after writing hundreds of stories about how dangerous limiting abortion and contraception access is, it made me deeply uncomfortable. I don't think there is a way to set population control as a "goal" without emboldening people who have an opinion on which populations should be controlled. Unlike more familiar factions of the political far-right, ecofascists acknowledge the climate crisis is underway but offer genocidal solutions—rarely designated for countries with higher per capita emissions like Australia—to what they see as the scourge of overpopulation, industrialization, and immigration. In March 2019, a few months before the scientists announced their policy goal, fifty-one people at two mosques in Christchurch, New Zealand, were murdered by an Australian man and self-identified "ecofascist" who was a direct inspiration for another mass shooting three months later by a man in Texas who wanted to "get rid of enough people" to make our way of life "more sustainable." Environmentalism has long been misappropriated by white supremacists.

"Historically, population growth alarmism coupled with eugenic ideas about who is worthy of reproducing has led to a painful global legacy of coercion and abuse," writes social and behavioral scientist Kelsey Holt. In 2019, I had met with a global reproductive healthcare provider, MSI Reproductive Choices, the backbone of abortion provision in Australia and in much of the world. Each year, they prevent millions of unintended pregnancies and unsafe abortions and avert tens of thousands of maternal deaths. At this lunch, they told me about how their expansion of family planning services in Asia and the Pacific was helping girls into education, addressing teenage pregnancy, and reducing maternal mortality rates. A Cambodian employee explained the immeasurable impact this has had for women in her country. Then, the two white women talked about how women and girls in these regions were most vulnerable to the impacts of climate change, but could be "empowered" through reproductive healthcare with "solutions."

They gave me a pamphlet about their work in the Asia-Pacific that explained how family planning programs were an incredibly cost-effective "climate-change mitigation strategy" by slowing population growth and therefore lowering emissions. Whether in an innocuous brochure or a horrifying manifesto, the issue of population control ends with a proportioning of responsibility. If it was really a conversation about emissions, family planning organizations would focus almost entirely on increasing the contraceptive uptake of women in high- and upper-middle-income countries, where 86 percent of CO_2 is emitted globally. The research team for Our World in Data, based at the University of Oxford, found even if we added several billion additional people in low-income countries, where fertility rates and population growth are already the highest, global emissions would remain relatively unchanged. This is not to shift the burden of one uterus to another, but to acknowledge that it has ended up entangled in our reproductive choices at all.

The childless woman has long been a symbol of selfishness, an uncaring wench incapable of putting someone else first. The climate crisis has created the conditions for a new kind of shame to grow, in which self-sacrifice looks like a family with no or very few children. It isn't just spread by extreme groups like the Voluntary Human Extinction Movement, which calls for humans to stop breeding so the Earth's biosphere can return to good health, or the BirthStrikers, who refuse to procreate until the climate crisis is addressed. Most mainstream outlets have published multiple articles reminding us that the worst thing you can do when it comes to carbon emissions is to have a child. It is worse than having a car, boarding a plane, eating meat, or failing to recycle, we are told. An acquaintance posted a photo of his newborn baby on Twitter and below my "congratulations" someone replied,

"It's an inescapable fact that Earth is overpopulated. When are we going to stop saying 'congratulations' to those who had a choice, and start asking, 'How dare you?'"

We know that more than one-third of all greenhouse gas emissions since 1965 can be traced to just twenty fossil fuel companies. The idea that we should abridge our desires for the size of our families and communities before transforming our energy systems is peculiar. And yet, I know if I were to have a child, I would be scrambling to shrink its footprint before its feet even hit the ground.

In the 1950s, the packaging industry in the United States conspired with beverage brands like Coca-Cola to move the problem of litter from themselves, the creators of disposable packages, to the consumer via what became a wildly popular "environmental" campaign, "Keep America Beautiful." Americans stopped asking where these disposable goods came from and began policing themselves and each other for where and how these unsustainable materials were being disposed. The litterbug, not the litter producer, became the antagonist. This kind of corporate greenwashing, in which the individual is responsible for cleaning up a structural mess, is well underway when it comes to greenhouse gas emissions and it has worked on me. What does resistance look like when you see yourself as a single consumer rather than a citizen in a collective?

Veronica Milsom's voice is recognizable to most people my age in Australia as the former host of our youth radio station's rush hour program. It was strange hearing her in the middle of the night, raspy from lack of sleep as she tended to her baby's leaking cloth diaper, a reusable and more environmentally friendly alternative to the disposable plastic version. "She's wet her onesie all the way through because of these stupid fucking nappies that don't work," Veronica croaked on her podcast Zero Waste Baby, in which she tries to raise her second daughter to have as little impact on the environment as possible. A few episodes in, after months of endlessly changing and washing cloth nappies, Veronica learned it might have all been for nothing. Cloth nappies reduce waste because you're reusing them, but because Australia is so addicted to coal for power—it accounts for more than 70 percent of our electricity generation—that another environmental burden was created by the washing and potentially drying of so much laundry. If you washed with hot water and tumble-dried it might be even worse for the environment than disposable diapers.

"No!" I exclaimed stupidly to no one. I had caught Veronica's infectious enthusiasm and forgotten the systems within which she was making these decisions weren't aligned with her wish for a cleaner planet.

"I think it is important for us all to take personal responsibility for the part we play in helping the planet, but I would love it if our federal government showed any sort of leadership when it comes to implementing big changes towards a future of renewables," Veronica tells me. "The current state of politics is abysmal and embarrassing." The emissions gap—the difference between what countries have individually pledged to do to reduce greenhouse gas emissions and what they need to do collectively to meet the Paris Agreement goals—has widened four times in the past decade, my most fertile years. We need to act faster to achieve the same reductions.

The podcast reaches its natural conclusion—Veronica considers whether having no baby at all is better than having a "zero waste baby" in an interview with a prolific vasectomist. I ask Veronica about hope, considering even the most ambitious of personal commitments to reduce a new child's waste ended with a contemplation of the child not existing at all. "It only really hits hard on days when I'm feeling pessimistic about the future of the environment and the idea that humans aren't doing enough to steer this ship around to avoid complete disaster," she tells me. "I also think it'd be hypocritical for me to think like that because I was armed with all the same information to make my decision about having kids and I chose yes, and I absolutely don't regret it. Having kids is the single best thing I have and ever will achieve. They make me happier than I could possibly imagine and they make me want to be a better person and take care of our planet."

Ketan Joshi, a clean energy analyst, is defrosting when we speak. He has just cycled home through Oslo's icy sleet after dropping his toddler to childcare. When he arrived in Norway from Australia, he had never cycled, but the city had bike lanes allowing him to zoom past car traffic and he fell into the habit easily. "I'm incredibly unfit and I'm a bit scared of cars, but these bike lanes are really great. And because someone else fought in this collective action in the past, I made this easy individual decision," he says.

The term *carbon footprint* was popularized almost twenty years ago by British Petroleum when the oil behemoth unveiled a calculator so individuals could see how their daily activities contributed to global warming. On October 23, 2019, as Australia's bushfires were well underway, BP tweeted: "The first step to reducing your emissions is to know where you stand. Find out your #carbonfootprint with our new calculator & share your pledge today!" Ketan responded, pointing out BP was the eleventh in the world for industrial greenhouse gas emissions and included a graph showing the company's carbon footprint from 1988 to 2015 as similar to that of domestic emissions of the entire country of Australia. If BP was a country, he pointed out, its per capita emissions would be more than five thousand times that of any other nation in the world. "Just so you know where you stand," he wrote to @BP_PLC, adding a winking emoji.

In his book *Windfall: Unlocking a Fossil-free Future*, Ketan makes the point that the average Australian could live in a gigantic house, each of the eight bedrooms permanently air-conditioned, drive two 4WDs, and live a wasteful life and still you would never negatively impact the future of our planet as much as a single politician blocking action on climate change or an executive at a company that extracts or burns fossil fuels. It is the realization of this exact fact where Ketan feels the most fear and, unlike most people I talk to, he is not worried about a distant date linked to a sea level rise or a degree of warming. He believes it will come before his daughter even reaches high school. "In the next five to ten years, very novel changes to the biosphere will probably trigger a really violent moment of realization," he says calmly. "This is something that I hold to be a bit inevitable in that there is very little we can do to prepare for it." The realization, he predicts, will be a fundamental reconfiguration of how we allocate blame and therefore responsibility. And, he predicts reluctantly, it will be bloody.

"I think the bushfires that happened in Australia made people far more aware of climate change as a threat, but it has had absolutely no impact on making people link it back to decisions and behaviors from fleshy beings," he says. "You never end up back at the root cause, which is that a bunch of people knew the consequences and they went and did it anyway, and that is what caused the novelty and the intensity of Australia's bushfires. If you were to ask someone, 'Hey, what is causing climate change?' they would say, 'I think it's fossil fuels,' they wouldn't say, 'I think it's decisions made by a collection of politicians, corporate leaders, and individuals all contributing to this.'"

I think of everyone I know who has stopped using things that produce emissions and reduced the use of things that use emissions to be created. My housemates carefully sorting the recycling into different piles, the vegans, cyclists and reluctant thrift-shoppers. I think about Veronica folding dozens of cloth nappies every night, preparing for another day of mess, I think of all the reading I've done about lifestyle choices—having or not having children, raising them in a wasteful or not wasteful way. Apart from a few cowardly politicians, I have never really thought seriously about the individuals in government or corporations as making lifestyle choices, even though they will have far more impact on the style of life we will all have to adapt to.

Ketan says people will understand this didn't start with atmospheric physics or climate science, but with people who made decisions and that these decisions will be described as ecoterrorism and geoengineering. "It is geoengineering when a company like Shell says we are going to discover an oil field, extract it, and sell it because they are making a conscious decision fully aware of what the consequences will be on human life," he says. "When people get that and when that is widely realized as a consequence of disasters that hit with such frequency and intensity that people realize that could only have been done by people, it probably will be perceived as an aggression and reacted to with aggression." Ketan says this scares him because he has never lived through war, he's only read about it. "It is probably going to happen between countries and companies and people who remain wedded to the burning of fossil fuels in spite of this wider realization of this causal chain behind disaster and the people who want that to change."

While Ketan talks I have been speechlessly transcribing for fifteen minutes, my fingers tapping while my brain conjures images of widespread civil unrest. I am thinking about the IPCC report which described how a breakdown in food systems would aggravate poverty and hunger and increase "the risks of violent conflict."

"I know I sound a bit fatalist," he says almost apologetically. "But this is the only thing I keep in my doom bucket because I think this realization is inevitable, but then this anger will fuel not just a youth climate movement but an everybody movement."

Ketan describes his attitude toward solving the climate crisis as "infuriated optimism." His optimism seems to be rooted in potential. "Australia's potential to contribute to a resolution of this problem is far greater than other countries if it started to export renewables and use zero-carbon energy instead of fossil fuels. It is hard to overstate how much of a positive impact that would have," he says. Australia's variable environment leaves it particularly vulnerable to the impacts of climate change, but we are also uniquely placed to step up to help mitigate them. While 2.8 million petajoules of fossil fuel reserves lie underneath us, above us every year shines 58 million petajoules of the sun's energy, making us a perfect candidate for widespread solar panel use, he explains. His fury is about squandered opportunities to decarbonize and failure to close old coal-fired power stations in Australia when there are zero carbon, zero air pollution replacement options. "The frustration comes not from a lack of effort, but from seeing so many easily avoidable losses become losses anyway." Ketan shows me a photo of his daughter dressed up in a Christmas costume before we get off the call.

Anger felt like the necessary bridge between delusion and defeat. It took my hand from my brow, where it rested in despair, and off my heart, where it could no longer feel hope, and curled it into a fist. This might seem like useless tinkering, fine-tuning a coping mechanism, cognitive behavioral therapy in the face of an inoperable tumor that will only continue to metastasize your entire life, but I have to believe there is something with more teeth than faith. We won't be sustained by a crippling guilt, curled over seeking redemption in a handful of consumer choices. Unlike guilt, which folds us into ourselves, anger has an object, an other to be held accountable. This should always have been the case in a crisis that was made by humans with power and will only be unmade by humans with power, even if only in numbers. Optimism, after all, might be a luxury good—hope is harder to find when you are trying to protect your family from fire or flood—but resignation, too, can be an indulgence, enjoyed by the luckiest.

• • •

I was once pitched a very Silicon Valley story about a start-up that allowed parents to invest in a fund to pay for their adult children's IVF. It was framed as a cheeky way to buy yourself grandchildren. My first thought, an idea that would charm no shark nor secure any capital, was that I would think more seriously about having children if my parents' generation could instead prove they had converted their financial luck or political power into political will to address climate change. As writer J.R. Hennessy has argued, older generations living in the developed world are members of history's most under-appreciated death cult. "The loudest and most powerful voices when it comes to the future of the planet—the ones with their hands on the levers of power—have a strong tactical advantage: They will be dead before the shit really hits the fan," he writes for the *Outline*. Your contribution to a debate depreciates alongside your stake in it. "The kids want to win it," he writes. "Boomers just want to die before we get to the closing arguments."

In August 2021, the United Nations issued a "code red for humanity" as the IPCC delivered their starkest warning yet on the widespread, rapid, and intensifying climate emergency. There is an argument often put forward by columnists at right-wing publications that those on the left are deceiving prophets of doom who are inventing the irreversible impact of human-made climate change because they love the drama of it. In 2017 Australia's former prime minister, then treasurer, once mocked progressives by bringing a huge lump of coal into parliament, provided by lobby group the Minerals Council of Australia. "This is coal," he said, brandishing it as his colleagues chuckled behind him. "Don't be afraid, don't be scared." Fear itself has become politicized. Environmentalism is not apocalypticism and there is irrefutable evidence that the climate system is warming. It is appropriate to use language like "emergency," "crisis," "collapse," and "tipping point." I do, however reluctantly, agree with the idea that millenarianism—the belief that there is an incoming collapse of society as we know it—is spreading across the political spectrum and there are some people who take pleasure and purpose in it. It stretches beyond the threat of environmental disrepair and into civilizational Armageddon—you can see it on the feverish faces of preppers, high on their own self-sufficiency, preparing for, in their words, when SHTF (Shit Hits The Fan) at which time they can finally assert their unhinged machismo and protect their families. Writer Mary Annaïse Heglar saw it in all the "doomer dudes" she met while working at an independent left-wing newspaper as a twenty-three-year-old. These "climate de-nihilists" were almost always tall white men—"only white men can afford to be lazy enough to quit on themselves"—in cargo pants, who gleefully declared humans were done for.

I can see the tempting clarity in the doom. Catharsis, the purging and relief from negative emotions, has the same etymological root as Catharism, a medieval Christian religious sect opposed to procreation, a morally evil act as it perpetuated the chain of human suffering in the material world. Both words derive from the Greek *katharos*, meaning pure. I sense it in myself some days, the feeling that there is nothing to be done, and that feeling, no matter how fleeting, feels completely incompatible with having a child. In the same way that I don't fear death like I do dying, I am far more comfortable with the world's mortality than its morbidity, probably because it requires less from me, including the tiresome work of hope-making.

I received a news update that Australia's first satellite to detect bushfires within a minute of their ignition would soon launch. I wondered if that was where we were heading in lieu of treatment. The automated surveillance of our planet's terminal condition. *I guess we'll just get a bit faster at watching the world burn*, I thought, retreating into the horror.

The idea of an apocalypse is tempting because it allows us, as Irish journalist Mark O'Connell describes, to vault over the chasm of the future and all that we might do to change it and straight to the end of all things. "Out of the murk of time emerges the clear shape of a vision, a revelation, and you can see at least where the whole mess is headed," he writes in *Notes From an Apocalypse*. "All of it—history, politics, struggle, life—is near to an end, and the relief is palpable."

There is comfort in certainty, even in certain demise as it releases us from the responsibility to answer many of the questions we ask each day. How can I help mitigate this catastrophe? Too late. Should I have a child? Don't bother.

But I don't want to be a doomer dude, the kind who, with their "joyful nihilism," unknowingly convinced Heglar that environmentalism was inaccessible for years until she realized that because warming happens in degrees, there was always something to be done. "We, quite literally, have no time for nihilism," she writes on *Medium*. "I've never seen a perfect world. I never will. But, I know that a world warmed by two degrees Celsius (35.6 Fahrenheit) is far preferable to one warmed by three degrees, or six. And that I'm willing to fight for it, with everything I have, because it is everything I have." Heglar doesn't need a guarantee of success and neither should we. "Even if I can only save a sliver of what is precious to me, that will be my sliver and I will cherish it," she writes. "If I can salvage just one blade of grass, I will do it. I will make a world out of it. And I will live in it and for it."

In *The Selfishness of Others*, her book about narcissism, Kristin Dombek says to endure the selfishness of others is to witness your independence laid bare as a myth while watching their gaze turn away. "The selfishness of others is the feeling of time moving past you; what history feels like. The selfishness of others is the feeling of the center shifting, the knowledge it was never under you," she writes. It is learning the history of the complicity of governments and corporations in the chaos we will continue to witness in our natural world.

Dombek feels her own selfishness as absence. "The absence from my life of the trash I leave behind, which becomes the structures into which others must live, the broken hearts, the warmer air, the slower fish, the rising ocean: Whatever I do not feel, that to others becomes the shape of their world." She discards a cigarette into a snowbank. "There is time, still, to move backwards into the future of others, gazing at the disasters we are leaving behind and trying to mend," she writes. "My selfishness will be invisible until spring, when the world warms, the snow melts, and someone else turns the corner to find this littered street."

I read about a landscape architect, Kate Orff, who will use oyster reefs to mitigate the storm surges and tidal flooding caused by climate change by slowing the movement of water. "There's no more natural nature," she tells the *New Yorker*. "Now it's a matter of design."

It isn't our ideas that make us optimists or pessimists, but our optimism or pessimism that makes our ideas, according to the Spanish philosopher Miguel de Unamuno. If the scientists I spoke to didn't believe that we could, that we had to, avoid the iceberg, they wouldn't be toiling in the bowels of the ship, keeping the boilers at steam. They wouldn't be recording, mapping, fighting, and convincing. Regardless of whether or not I become a parent, I do not want to be absent. If I remain childless, I will use my anger and hope more meaningfully, beyond the random donations and the second-hand shopping and the infrequent rallies. If I did become a parent, I would pledge not to absorb the guilt and shame of the institutions who should feel crippled by it, nor assume my kids would pick up the slack of political action as our parents have done.

I will be here for summer, no matter how endless it feels.

6.

Fertility

THIS SHARD OF PLASTIC RELEASING progestin is my prayer, my promise, my postponement. The wishbone stationed in my uterus has given me time. Time to love and leave the wrong-at-the-right-time people, the right-at-the-wrong-time people, the wrong-at-the-wrong time people with nothing created together but fond or faulty memories and flimsy flat-packed furniture. Time to understand that you could feast on only friendship until the end of time. Time to learn together, women talking into the night, saving even more time by sharing the signs—if he is possessive; if he bares his teeth at your strength; if he tells you what to wear, who you can see, and how to eat.

"Gina, I'm telling you, if he polices your choices and refuses to look at you from the neck up when you have your hair tied back because you look prettier with it down, it is time, it is time, it is time." Time to make an escape plan. Time to know that if someone wants forever and you only want today, you need to let them give all of their tomorrows to someone else. Time to study, time to read, time to be self-sufficient, time to work, time to be itinerant, living with stranger after stranger until you are familiar with yourself. Time to know you can be alone. Time to write thousands of words making a case for and against motherhood.

We insert fragments of polyethylene into our arms and through our cervixes that make us cramp, we take injections and swallow pills until our heads and breasts ache, until our emotions, our weight, our skin and our libido feel beyond our control. Contraception is ultimately safer than pregnancy and childbirth, but our bodies pay a price. For years I was on a pill that has killed multiple women because it increased your risk of blood clots. Soon after I got my IUD, which has been linked to a higher risk of ovarian cysts, ectopic pregnancy, and intracranial hypertension, I wrote about a trial for a male contraceptive that was cut short because participants were pulling out. The men in the study found the side effects too burdensome.

My friends and I talk about where we would be without contraception. If we bore children before we knew whether we wanted to, before we had found in ourselves the knowledge or esteem we needed to survive. Women who were figuring out who they are, permanently tied to men who were doing the same. We shudder, we shiver with relief. We marvel at how much we have changed in more than a decade, as if we're sure we have arrived at who we are. As if the sun and rain won't force us to grow anymore. As if the seventeen-year-old who marched into the general physician's office for a prescription for the pill didn't think she was fully grown. As if I haven't wondered whether my ideas and values will shift by the time this book even makes it to print.

A friend goes off her contraception to try to conceive. I can't imagine what that would feel like, to withdraw your weapon after years of defending, to dream of what would have been a nightmare at a different time, with a different person. I wonder what all this time has done to my imagination, whether all the years have convinced me of my ability to control my own fertility. Each year I have achieved the desired outcome: not pregnant. I wonder whether all this time has allowed me to dawdle, refusing to engage in the math, the blunt ranking of what and when I would sacrifice physically, emotionally, and financially for a child.

The asking, the wanting, the choosing, the trying. Are these single steps that come in a universal sequence? What does each process do to the other? How long should we allow for each one? For years I interviewed women who did everything they could to prevent pregnancies and still ended up pregnant.

I had almost forgotten that it can be a deliberate choice and for many people one they need to choose again and again before they have a child that is theirs, whether by blood or law. I found people who showed me how "should we?" can come before and after and before and after and before and after "can we?," the two questions charging and depleting each other.

Contraception has long protected my "no" to motherhood by preventing pregnancy but it has also guarded my "yes" without my knowing by alleviating endometriosis, a condition that will probably impact my fertility. My IUD has not only shielded me from much of the bleeding and debilitating pain that comes with endometriosis by disrupting my menstruation and ovulation but it can slow the growth of endometrial tissue and prevent new tissue from forming. Tissue like that which usually lines the inside of a uterus will continue to embroider itself beyond it, across my ovaries, along my fallopian tubes or around pelvic organs, possibly scarring them. It could affect my egg quality, it could disrupt egg implantation, it could cause my immune system to attack an embryo. It might raise my chances of miscarriage and stillbirth.

Before I was born, when my mother wasn't much older than I am now, she miscarried. She kept the lost pregnancy in the freezer for a few weeks. I think about this a lot. I think about how her life caring for three young children would have gone on at a rapid pace while her grief was frozen still. When I imagine the moment she decided to take it out of the freezer, I am sure that I have never experienced real loss. I don't know if I could open myself up to it even once. I can't imagine deciding that I might want to conceive, finding out I can and then the grief, then the loss, then, maybe, nothing.

Grace and her husband always wanted children, but life—study, work, family, health—got in the way, as did a series of medical professionals who told Grace she needed to lose weight before trying. When she was thirty-nine, Grace found a clinic that was happy to accept her as a patient. She fell pregnant on the first IVF cycle. "We just couldn't believe that we had been so lucky," Grace says. "Until it happened, I hadn't realized this is what I had been waiting for so long." She knew immediately how she wanted to raise her child. "I knew I didn't want to necessarily enforce the way I live my life, but just to truly see them for who they are," she says. "There was something so powerful about thinking about raising them with unconditional love." Grace tells me there was some cultural pressure to have children, so her parents, who had always been gentle with her, were thrilled about the pregnancy. The global pandemic was just beginning, but Grace felt invincible. "It felt really blissful," she says. "It was one of the few times that I have felt completely content and at peace."

At ten weeks, she experienced light bleeding, at twelve weeks she was told there had been delayed growth, at fourteen weeks her obstetrician told Grace there was not enough amniotic fluid and her placenta was not looking like it should this far into a pregnancy. By fifteen weeks she was referred to a maternal-fetal medicine specialist who told her, "this is not going to be a good outcome," but that "where there is a heartbeat, there is hope." She was told her only option was to induce the pregnancy and give birth. "I couldn't decide to induce and watch my baby die." So Grace waited. Week after week passed. "I always thought I could be pragmatic when it came to things like this and that I could look at the facts, take on the advice, and make a decision, but when they were asking me to bring forward the labor and be induced . . . I just said, 'I need to know more. I need time.'"

For the next ten weeks, Grace underwent devastating scan after devastating scan. At twenty-three weeks, they told her that her membranes had ruptured and there was now no amniotic fluid around the fetus. At twenty-six weeks, her case was presented to a roundtable of doctors and she was told they unanimously agreed there was no hope. But, there was a heartbeat. "And where there was a heartbeat, there was hope," Grace repeated. She played "Here Comes the Sun" by Nina Simone during IVF, she played it during pregnancy, and she played it when she went into spontaneous labor at twenty-eight weeks and had to give birth once her baby's heartbeat had stopped. "I wasn't scared," she says. "I just really wanted to meet my baby, even though I knew she wasn't going to be alive." Orla was placed in Grace's arms. "She was so tiny, but so beautifully formed," she says, sobbing. "Everything felt right. The three of us together even though she wasn't moving." It wasn't just sadness, Grace insists. "In any relationship where there is love there is also grief." When Grace arrived home there were bouquets of flowers sent from friends. They were all white, the color of sympathy. "I don't want people to be sorry for our loss. I don't know how to say it was joyful without looking like I have lost my marbles." Now she buys brightly colored flowers every week in honor of her daughter.

Grace has done two more cycles of IVF. "I want another baby," she says. "I am happy to keep going until my body says 'no more.'"

When Sally and Jay began trying to have a baby, they expected to conceive quickly. "I was twenty-nine and I was ready," Sally remembers. By the time we speak, they have together endured ten rounds of IVF and four miscarriages over five years. It is hard to believe, watching them turning to one another and then to me, openly explaining the toll of the hope and exhaustion, that there were first times for everything—the first time they realized they might not be able to conceive easily, the first time they borrowed USD $7,200 for the first round of IVF, the first pregnancy loss, the first wave of judgment from their loved ones. "I remember being by myself and up in stirrups, waiting for them to do this for me. And I was just weeping because I knew this wasn't going to work. I was by myself under these bright lights and you're so open and vulnerable, and they are sticking things up inside of you and it's all a waste," Sally says.

She can't accept that she might not have kids. Not at thirty-three-years old, not with so many eggs, not when the doctors haven't been able to find a reason why. Jay has a low sperm count, but it does not explain why IVF has been unsuccessful. "It should be working and it's not, which is so hard to reconcile with. How do you stop when you don't know what is wrong?" The couple are now considering donor eggs or surrogacy. "If we end up in a situation where we stop trying and we don't end up with kids, it will be that we have found a way to live our lives without kids rather than consciously deciding we don't need to have children," Jay says.

They have learned how much they didn't know about the process: "How it often doesn't work, how you can pay (USD $6,700) and end up with nothing or end up in the situation we are in now and pay (USD $67,000) and end up with absolutely nothing."

The cost of these procedures makes them completely inaccessible for many people—between £1,500 and £5,000 per cycle of retrieval and transfer

in the UK or $15,000 and $20,000 in the United States. I can't help but consider the economics of delay. Are the same people delaying starting a family
until they achieve financial stability in fact increasing their chance of future
debt through IVF? Is this kind of consideration unthinkable to anyone but
the ambivalent? In between the numbers, Sally and Jay have learned how they
can both express grief differently while still wanting a child just as much as
each other. Early on in the IVF process, Sally responded with open expres-
sions of sadness and Jay did not. "I just completely shutdown so I wouldn't
have to deal with it and that was my way of trying to cope," he says. Now they
are together fighting for the family they want. "I don't want to think about a
life without children because that is so deeply not my choice," Sally says.
"We have really shown ourselves that we really do want a child somehow."

Sally and Jay seem to chart their position in the world by proximity to
their life as parents. They're living in "the almost." "We have been in a holding pattern for like five years, not living our full lives," she says this while
looking at Jay. The two of them are in tender suspension, orbiting the life they
want, waiting to descend.

Writer Alexandra Kimball writes in her book *The Seed: Infertility Is a
Feminist Issue* that her grief about not conceiving made her feel like a stack
of multiple identical women, "a chain of paper dolls that had been cut but
not yet pulled apart." Each of these dolls were living separate lives, some still
childless, some as mothers. "It's less about the loss of a potential child than
it is about the endless possibility that there may yet be an actual child."

Sally talks about the idea of the life she wants to lead and she looks
momentarily dazed before she says softly, "I get so lost thinking about all
that stuff." Jay says they have faced judgment. "It's like it is your fault for not
being able to do it and you should just give up on the process and adopt."
When Sally terminated a pregnancy in her early twenties, she felt there was
room in her friendships and in feminism to talk about it without shame, but
with infertility, she has found the smallest space, on a short lease. "When I
had my abortion I belonged somewhere and I had a place to understand that
time, but this," she sighs. "This, the biggest experience of my life and the
most traumatic, is totally absent from that discourse and it makes me pretty
fucking furious."

When I reported on stillbirth or miscarriage I would receive messages or tweets about my hypocrisy in interviewing people about these tragedies and also interviewing people about the lack of abortion access. I don't see a contradiction. I just see the reality—up to one in four women in the country I live in will terminate a pregnancy, up to one in five pregnancies will end in miscarriage, and one in every 135 pregnancies that reach twenty weeks will end with a stillbirth. Hundreds of thousands of people will, in their lifetime, have a pregnancy that is planned and a pregnancy that isn't. They will make choices again and again about what is right for them and their children. They will conceive, they will grieve. They will sit over toilets sobbing in pain as a pregnancy leaves them, whether spontaneously or with the help of two pills. Our bodies have long made space for complex truths.

Sally says while her favorite popular feminists are able to speak about abortion, the division of domestic labor, sexual politics, harassment and violence, and the workforce, they don't touch infertility. Feminism as we know it, drenched with a consumerist focus on choice, has done much to remove stigma around choosing contraception and abortion and little to support the plight of the infertile. This is partly because of the silhouette around which popular feminism still organizes as a privileged figure wanting to prevent or discontinue pregnancies. And so, as Kimball writes, resolving infertility is left by feminism to "passive faith" rather than political or material action. "In the language of hope, infertility is not a matter between women and the world, but one woman and fate."

When I think about every part of their bodies, every moment of their time, every reserve of the energy this couple has given to the administrative, financial, and emotional ordeal of trying to start a family, I understand why they want their loved ones to understand these numbers are a catalog of trying, not failing. We talk about the study that found the anxiety and depression levels of infertile women were equal to those living with cancer. Sally and Jay want recognition of this effort in a way feminism has failed to account for and, in doing so, reproduces the most ancient tropes of motherhood as natural and easy. "When maternity is the subject of effort, labor, and desire, it is unnatural and what does not happen naturally must be constructed,"

Kimball writes, summarizing where feminism has failed. "And what is constructed, especially under patriarchy, must be less valid."

In many parts of the world same-sex couples and single women are still categorized as socially rather than medically infertile and are excluded from support. Until mid-2022 only heterosexual couples experiencing infertility could access NHS-funded treatments. The persistent ideal of the young, fertile, cisgendered, heterosexual couple who are ready and determined to conceive in their twenties neglects the reality of family-making for most people and in doing so, erases their love and labor. Parenthood can begin long before you have a child.

Teacher Steve and his wife, both aged in their thirties, stopped using contraception on their honeymoon. "I thought in a couple of months we'd be pregnant," he says. "Clearly high school biology had failed me because I had so much to learn about the physiology of fertility periods." The next year, Steve's wife got pregnant and miscarried at six weeks. A few months later came another pregnancy followed by another miscarriage. "We were both suffering alone and it placed a lot of strain on our relationship because we didn't know how to talk about it and it was so uncommon to talk about it that it reinforced this feeling that we were doing something wrong," he says. "I didn't feel that I deserved to have feelings about it because I wasn't having the miscarriage." Steve says the entire process challenged his ideas about maintaining power and control over a situation. "I felt like I hadn't protected our unborn kid." When they didn't conceive, Steve was anxious it was his fault, that he was not "man enough" to produce a child, despite the fact that one-third of fertility problems originate with sperm.

Ovulation cycle after ovulation cycle passed without another positive pregnancy test. They decided to try IVF. They had appointments, underwent tests, and collected samples. Steve's wife began injecting herself with fertility medication and then a trigger injection when the time was right to collect her eggs. Then came the fertilization, embryo development, and embryo transfer and, eventually, a chemical pregnancy—a very early miscarriage that happens when an egg is fertilized but doesn't fully implant in the uterus.

When they went through IVF he felt he had no agency, that he was a passive patient in a medical process defined by chance. He wasn't sure who to talk to. "It made me reflect on who I actually talk to and what my friends and I actually speak about and how seemingly superficial a lot of guy friendships actually are, which is kind of sad," he reveals. Eventually, he went to a therapist and one by one spoke to his female colleagues, many of whom had themselves suffered pregnancy loss. "It was really nice to have people to talk to about it," he says. "We spend so much time talking about the end result of a pregnancy, a child, but don't talk about the struggle which gets you to that point where you have a baby in your hands if you're lucky to even get one. I think if I knew it was common and if I knew it might take longer, it would have helped when things didn't go right." When they fell pregnant again, a question mark punctuated every test and trimester until their son was in their arms.

Reporting on reproductive healthcare has overexposed me to all that can go wrong inside a uterus—interviewing women who have had devastating fetal anomalies, struggled to conceive, had stillbirths and miscarriages. It has all compromised the joy I feel when someone tells me they are pregnant, especially before twenty weeks. It is harder to gauge how rational that fear of grief and struggle is when people I know start experiencing miscarriage and infertility. I would never have started a conversation with Steve about pregnancy loss.

I felt nervous about public announcements, status updates excitedly posted, cribs pre-emptively purchased. But in mid-2019, I was scrolling through Instagram and saw Nayuka, a Gunai, Gunditjmara, Wiradjuri and Yorta Yorta writer, and their partner's smiling faces, squinting into the sunlight as they announced they were eight weeks pregnant with twins. "Was reticent about sharing because apparently you're not meant to share until second trimester, but the only reason for that is because we are scared to talk about death and grief and that seems really white to me, and in any case if we're grieving we would want our community to be there for us anyways," Nayuka wrote. It challenged my instinct to protect people by wishing their joy stays private so their pain might too. It made me question my participation in an online practice of sharing that was really a curation of withholding—in this case, tragedy and the fragility of the human body. It reminded me that I usually only found out about people's miscarriages well after the fact. It made me ask questions about hoping alone.

For the record, Nayuka does not think hope for the world is a prerequisite for creating or sustaining a family. "I am not particularly hopeful on a grand scale. I come from a people who, like, three members of the clan survived a massacre, so I don't think anyone should or shouldn't feel pressure to have children. But, for me the fact that the world is so brutal and still so racist and still a colonial mess that isn't enough for me to not have kids, because not having kids would be completion, in a way, of genocide," they say. When Nayuka and their partner began trying to conceive, they went to an IVF clinic. "They're driven by profit, but they're also driven by risk. So, they evaluate you based on risk, which no other population [trying to conceive] has to go through," they say. "You are subjected to a psych evaluation as a couple, individual, and group, and there was a police check. I was like 'my family, my great-grandmother was taken, my grandfather was taken, I'm going to have Black kids, the less state intervention the better. Why would I opt into it if I didn't have to?'"

Instead, the couple found a sperm donor and created a family at home. They now have a pair of happy, healthy twins. "I want people to know that you can do things without clinics and without state intervention," Nayuka says. Their donor was Enoch, an Indigenous and Polynesian screenwriter. "The whole idea of weighing up pros and cons for this felt really white," Enoch describes on a podcast about their donation as a favor for their queer Black family. "Sometimes when family need help, you just do and when asked for sperm, you bet I came." The dithering about whether it is ethical to bring children into the world—"over-population, fires, COVID, police just can't stop killing Black people"—feel to Enoch like "white projections of guilt."

"I can't help but feel that instead of policing Black bodies and what they should be doing with them, or whether they should be making kids, maybe we should start by telling the state to stop stealing kids or locking kids up," Enoch says. "Now I can't wait to see two young people experience play, community, and the ultimate beauty of what it means to be Black."

I ask Nayuka, "The way you did things by not involving a corporation . . . and I don't want to romanticize it, but did it feel like you were kind of solving fertility via community?" "No, that isn't romanticizing it at all. That is how we feel." Nayuka says another queer friend explained the insemination method. "I have been able to pass that queer transmission of knowledge on to other people and there is something really nice about that," they say. "I think about precolonial times and what families were and what motherhood was. We didn't have this nuclear family and this idea that it was just a mum and a dad and I don't see how a single woman today asking for sperm and then that kid being raised in the community is really any different to precolonial stuff." We talk about what is considered natural.

Kimball writes that it is clear whose pregnancies fall on the side of the arbitrary street where judgment lives despite the fact that the line between technology and nature has long blurred when it comes to making families. "Is the pregnancy of a couple who are together because they met online, who are both alive because of a lifetime of vaccines and antibiotics, that was bookended by hormonal contraception and elective sterilization, and which will be monitored by ultrasound and amniocentesis, really more 'natural' than say, that of an infertile couple who uses IVF to select a male embryo or a lesbian couple who uses donor sperm?"

When I mentioned to my family what I was setting out to do—write a book in an effort to figure out whether or not I wanted to have a child—the conversation turned into one about how women were choosing not to have children. Someone described it as an "interference," saying that by delaying pregnancy (presumably they knew through long-term contraception and not holy abstinence), women like me were meddling with our natural destiny as hatcheries. Yet I knew that if I had then used assisted reproductive technology to reproduce, they would pass the fruit of my loins around, cooing and pinching, no accusations of intervention.

News editor Rob is thirty-four and has always imagined himself as a dad. "Even though I'm gay, it had never really occurred to me to consider a life without kids," he says. "I guess I had never really thought about the mechanics of having kids myself until I were engaged. We thought 'Oh, we will adopt' or 'Oh, we'll have a surrogate.'"

The couple decided to go down the altruistic surrogacy route and chose Canada, where there is an established surrogacy network and where they wouldn't be taking a place in a small pool of potential surrogates and egg donors in Australia from someone who couldn't afford to go overseas. "Everyone told us this would be hard and they'd say, 'You have to understand things will go wrong, you'll get false leads, you'll begin the process with a potential surrogate and egg donor and she will pull out for various reasons.' And I thought, 'Yeah, but that won't happen to us, we'll be fine.' That is my natural disposition," he says. "Then the pandemic hit and things changed." Their plans to travel to Canada, go through altruistic surrogacy, and start their family were grounded along with international flights. Rob was thirty-two and his husband was thirty-seven. Rob's husband felt like the delays were pushing him into an "older dad" bracket.

When Rob received an email from the fertility clinic checking in on them in the first big wave of Australia's COVID-19 cases, he found himself poised above his keyboard, stiff with emotion, an anxious shell hardening for a moment around the soft tissue of what he wanted most. He discussed with his partner whether they wanted to continue trying. "He has less appetite for the ups and downs and didn't want to go through these false starts and heartbreak, and that was quite confronting for me because I had never considered life without kids," he says. "For the first time I had to assess what my purpose in life was if not kids and whether that was something I was comfortable or happy with." Rob sees parenthood as the probable end of his full-time career and he is okay with that. "I get a lot more fulfillment spending a day with a child and going to the park and reading them books than I do at work. I didn't really realize that until I was confronted with the possibility of not having children," he says. "It was the realization that none of it really matters that much and that my career has provided me with a stable enough financial life to have children more than it has anything else." He couldn't imagine himself building an entire life around work and even the perks—more disposable income, travel, freedom—didn't feel like they would sustain him into his old age. They decided to keep trying while in Australia.

Rob and his husband are two high earners with a company benefit that covers a chunk of the surrogacy costs, but still they had flights, accommodation, and legal fees to pay for and then, in the midst of a pandemic, they needed to organize getting a refrigerated box through customs into the country and their sperm back out through customs. Every step of the process was followed by an invoice, but Rob says the biggest drain was not financial but administrative. Making a family takes a lot of emails. They have a Canadian fertility clinic, a surrogacy agency, a lawyer in Australia, a lawyer in Canada, and a lawyer in the United Kingdom, where Rob's husband hails from. "The mental space taken up by the logistics alone is more than I ever imagined and it is exhausting," he says. "The surrogacy community is made up of people who have been through the process themselves and are trying to make it easier for others, but it can feel like an army of people are involved in a personal decision."

Every email, every bill, every sample of bodily fluid is a reminder of the extra burden they have to undertake to start a family. "I think when we get through this and if we are able to have a baby, not to suggest that we are going to love our child any more than a straight couple would, but I think there would be an appreciation of the amount of work and sacrifice that goes into it that makes it, if not sweeter or better, but . . . something." Rob pauses, trying to be diplomatic. "There have been a number of barriers placed in our way by all sorts of factors and it would be easier to stop and a lot of intended parents would. I guess what I am saying is, it is a real choice."

A real choice. Really choosing something that might end up being nothing, really choosing to pry yourself open enough to let life in and leaving just enough space for loss, really choosing something expensive, something invasive, something you might need to choose again. What does all that choosing do? What is the cost of not choosing? Or not choosing in time?

Sheree is thirty-three and was determined to stay single for a year when she was twenty-six. So, on a first date, she didn't waste energy trying to be the kind of chill girl we're led to believe men fall in love with. "I basically said I want kids one day and he said he was the same and then we didn't talk about it again for a long time," she tells me. Sheree just made it to the end of the year as a single woman, but by December she and her boyfriend were falling in love. They moved in together and three years later she raised the question of having children. He was avoidant, uninterested in the conversation, and never indicated that he might have changed his mind. "He knew I wanted kids and that I thought we would have kids and he never corrected me," she says.

When Sheree was thirty she went to the doctor about her irregular periods and requested a hormone test to get an idea of her ovarian reserve. The doctor told her to talk to her partner about whether they wanted kids before getting the test so they could face the results together. Her partner never gave her a clear answer, so she never got the test. She came to believe that asking for clarity was asking for too much.

For the next couple of years, she put his comfort over her long, unchanging desire to be a mother. Eventually she told him: "If you've changed your mind you have to tell me definitively because it is a deal breaker and I've spent so much time in this relationship. I obviously love you, but this is really important to me." He asked her for more time to think about it. Months passed, the bushfires raged on, the pandemic came, the city came out of a lockdown and she asked for his answer. "I haven't really thought about it," he admitted, a year later. When she broke up with him he was devastated. "I just told him that I didn't want to wait, even though I knew going out on my own the chances of this happening were low. I just knew it wasn't worth it to stay here with this uncertainty," she says.

Sheree had the test, which revealed she probably had a low number of eggs, and was told by her doctor to freeze her eggs immediately. During the egg harvesting process she had two failed egg retrievals, as the doctors could not get enough eggs to freeze. They told her she had the egg count of a woman more than a decade older. "My first reaction was vindication because my instinct about my fertility was right and then came regret that I hadn't done it sooner and then the anger," she says. The shapeless, deafening anger that echoed through the socially sanctioned silence about fertility, the indignant rage at her ex for not finding the words while her options were shrinking, and then a small, quiet frustration at herself for not trusting her intuition.

The first thing she mourned was the sequence—love, engagement, marriage, children—that she had always assumed she would follow as a child of two culturally traditional parents. But in the space where her expectations had been, she found the comforting conviction that motherhood was something she wanted with or without someone else. "I think I have a lot of value to give as a mother even if it is just me," she says. "The option that fills me with the most joy, calms me, and feels right is doing it alone and having a donor. It makes so much sense and if it doesn't work out that will be heartbreaking, but I can accept that as a reality more than I can hoping and holding out and waiting for someone else."

One of Sheree's friends mentioned seeing her ex's profile on a dating app shortly after the breakup. "Wants kids someday," it read.

"Oh my god, are you serious?" I gasp, shedding any pretense of professionalism.

"I know," she says, laughing.

"Wow. What a luxury to have that time to change your mind so much."

"Right!"

My mother told me when I came, ten years after her third child, she thought something would go wrong with the pregnancy because she was so old. She was thirty-four. I laughed at the time but now I know that if you conceive after the age of thirty-five it is referred to as a geriatric pregnancy.

Between 2014 and 2017, the number of egg freezing cycles in the United States increased by 79 percent. In 2020, the UK's fertility regulator recorded 2,377 egg freezing cycles in 2019, up 100 percent in five years. Between 2010 and 2018, the number of egg freezing cycles in Australia and New Zealand increased by 860 percent. Not every cycle will collect many eggs, not all eggs make embryos, not all embryos result in pregnancies, and not all pregnancies will give you a child. The reality is that if I decide I want to have a child in the next few years, I still don't know how stressed I should actually be about whether I could.

I call up Kate Stern, a fertility specialist who I have interviewed before, to talk to her about how valid fertility panic is for people in their late twenties. We talk about fertility diminishing with age, the limits of egg freezing, the distinction between the number of eggs and the quality of eggs you have, the fact egg quality actually improves in your early twenties before it declines. We talk about the ungenerous stereotype of the foolish careerist who couldn't hear her biological clock over her noisy ambition and left it too late.

Kate says most people seeking IVF just haven't found the right partner to make a family with. "A few people do egg freezing because they're ambivalent, but most people do it because they really want a child," she says. We talk about the sheer effort required of some patients—Kate has supported trans men who propel themselves into months of body dysmorphia by going off their testosterone to ovulate, collect, and freeze their eggs. I wonder if I have ever seriously yearned for anything. "It's important to be upfront about, the changes and the risks and benefits, even when it is hard for our patients to hear," Kate says. She will tell a patient what their chance of conception was when they first started IVF and then how it has changed. "So, I'll be saying to a forty-three-year-old woman, 'Right now your chance of conceiving is less than 5 percent and you have a 50 percent risk of miscarriage'. Do you think it is worth it?'" For many people, it is.

Once again, I am calling an expert not to hear explanations of her subject matter, but to hear how she manages the hope and despair, in this case other people's, involved in making a family. "You have to know when to call it, when there is no hope left, but we often stop well before that," Kate says. No hope, in this case, means zero hope, a 0 percent chance of pregnancy. "You have to be brutally honest and it would be great to be able to say there is a zero chance and that would be easy, but by that point often there is like a 5 percent chance."

Kate describes a patient who had been through two other fertility clinics by the time she reached her and eventually conceived. She reminded Kate afterward that they had discussed stopping. "She said, 'I have this beautiful baby' and I said, 'I know, but we had to make sure that you were clear about where you were.'" Kate says when she has to call it, she acknowledges that this is when a different kind of grief begins, whether that is considering an egg donor or whether there are no other available options and it is the end of the road. "One of the most important things we do is helping people finish."

Finish. For years I have used the word in writing about family planning, to talk about hysterectomies or vasectomies—the ends snipped off, a bow tied around a completed family. Finished. But how do you finish wanting? How do you finish trying? Do you only know your exhaustion point once you reach it? What if it stretches far beyond your finances? What if it doesn't match your partner's? What comes after? I am still listening, straining for the sound of a starting gun. If you don't know whether your desire has a beginning, how do you fathom its end?

Anna, forty-nine, always knew she did not want to bear a child but that if she ever did want to become a parent it would be "through a different route" like fostering or adoption.

"I'm a queer person, so it was never going to be 'have sex with my husband and have a baby,' I let go of those cultural assumptions long ago," she tells me.

In her midthirties Anna married Cal, who wanted to have biological children, so they tried fertility treatments and donor sperm.

"At a certain point we had run out of money," Anna tells me.

They looked into international adoption but found barriers for same-sex couples, especially in the Philippines, where Cal was born.

"I had a misplaced narrative, a saviorish approach, that a lot of Americans have about our adoption system," Anna says.

She attended a conference run by the Adoptive Parents Committee, the oldest group of its kind in North America, where she watched a speaker explain the reality of fostering to adopt. They admitted that "the easiest situation" for foster parents was when a mother was incarcerated. It was confronting to hear.

"You're really talking about destroying someone's life," Anna says, pausing before her voice could falter, "and I thought 'I don't want to start my family at the expense of someone else's.'"

The couple decided to pursue open adoption—where there is some interaction between the birth and adoptive parents and the child even if through an intermediary—as "all the adoption talking heads are basically in agreement that that's what's in the best interest of the child."

They did background checks and training and paid for a lawyer to remain on retainer. They were told how to present to potential birth parents—explain that you have a life a child would fit into, and above all "you do not say 'our baby, our baby, our baby' to the birth mom, as it is her baby."

We speak about the vulnerability in trusting a series of disconnected people—a lawyer, an agency, a birth parent—with securing your chances of a family.

"It is all very weird and vulnerable, which is common for a lot of aspects of queer parenting," Anna says.

She understood how exposed they are when they were finally connected to a birth mother who had a history of homelessness and addiction.

Potential adoptive parents are allowed to support the mother with expenses, which Anna and Cal continued to do, eventually against the advice of their lawyer when it became clear the money might not be used for its intended purpose.

"At a certain point I was like, 'I don't think there's a baby at the end of this anymore,'" she says.

They pulled out.

"You learn that there are a lot of really vulnerable people out there who are dealing with addiction or poverty and that in one way or another you become complicit in that," she says, her tone never accusatory or bitter, just frank. "It was really tricky."

They were still feeling vulnerable and raw when they got a call a month later.

A woman was about to give birth in a week and another set of adoptive parents had pulled out. Cal and Anna needed money, fast. They borrowed from siblings and parents and paid court expenses and filing fees and suddenly they were on a train heading to the hospital.

"Please don't flake out on me" was the plea from their son's birth mother. They didn't.

His birth mother didn't want an open adoption, and the communication can feel delicate and "one-sided," Anna admits, but she is committed to maintaining a relationship for "if and when those questions arise".

Their son is now four and the family feels secure and bonded. He knows he has a birth mother.

"Kids need to know who made them," Anna says.

Adoption has prepared them for the reality of parenting—it involves many other people.

"He goes to school, he has a babysitter, he goes to basketball . . . you're always kind of sharing with other people," she says. "Ultimately, the more people that love a child the better, and I think that is something, culturally, we don't recognize enough."

I began this period of writing nervous that I was spending so many words wondering if inside myself there hid something we learn is as unlabored and spontaneous as conception itself—"you just know." As if parenthood is first sown as an invisible, hermetic desire that precedes an effortless creation, as if the answer comes before any question. But in each interview, I saw an interrogation of self that needed to be so conclusive they could hear the clear, loud pulse of wanting by the end of it. The question was work; the answer was work. I was in awe of how each person braved the friction and the fight, opening themselves up to the vulnerability of creation. I felt my fear in presence of their courage. I no longer felt protected by my ambivalence, reassured I might not ever expose myself to loss. Instead, I noticed that in the time since I first decided to prevent motherhood, my relationship to desire itself had shifted.

Throughout my twenties my desire was incrementally defined in relation, but more often in reaction, to what I found I did not want. I did not want to live in fear. I did not want to live in this or that share house anymore. I did not want to use exercise, drugs, alcohol, or attention to avoid discomfort. I did not want to work at a job where men were encouraged to be vile. I did not want to be taken advantage of. I did not want to be defined by low expectations. I did not want unhealthy partnerships or fair-weather friendships. I did not want my friends to suffer. I did not want to play a victim. I did not want to choose dishonesty over discomfort. I did not want to enable anyone. I did not want to let anyone down.

I kept pushing off a wall of experiences I did not want to repeat, propelling myself toward something I had not yet defined. No after no after no . . . I scorched the earth and set a low bar above it. Each year, I learn new ways to hold the worst and best in others and in the world. I now understand the value of forgiving, repairing, maintaining. Now I find desire moves through me as hunger not evasion. I am finished building boundaries and find myself opening, wanting something not just for what it isn't but for what it is, for what it could be, a pursuit I once deemed as selfish but now necessary. I saw in these families a desire to create, to say yes again and again and again to something with all its risks and unknowns. I want to say yes, whether to parenthood or something else. I do not want to do that alone.

The protagonist in Sheila Heti's *Motherhood* rejected the identity "not a mother" because she wanted to protect her sense of self from becoming "the negative of someone else's positive identity." But that someone else is always a potential projection of yourself. Fertility forces us to sit with shades of perhaps, maybe, hopefully, hopefully not, overlapping at angles, a misshapen pile of photo negatives, the shadow and light of other lives unlived. On the gray ultrasound, I can see the white limbs of my IUD outstretched like the arms of a clock.

7

Inheritance

EVERYONE KNEW WHICH PARTS OF their history they wanted to rhyme, which stories they wanted to rewrite. It was an awareness of how a child could trace you like a stencil, even before you understood the template from which you came. It was not just that secretly drafted but rarely voiced curriculum vitae for the role of "parent"—it was a risk appraisal. It was a need to stop the past from living in the present, from living in the future. It was a fear of causing harm. It was both self-doubt and self-defense, and it surfaced in almost every conversation. A collection of people living through the positive and negative consequences of actions taken by those in decades past.

Perhaps that describes every generation, but millennials are more resentful and armed with an emotional literacy many of our predecessors did not have the latitude to develop before they were parents, or at all. We are all playing clairvoyant, psychoanalyst, weatherperson, theorizing about how our genetics, our trauma, our childhoods, our culture might live on in a child. They were considering not just how the darkest dynamics or brightest memories would shape their families, but whether the values, the experiences, the very air they inhaled throughout their childhood might expire out of their own children. What do we want to replicate? Can we sacrifice as readily as our ancestors? Are we destined to repeat their crooked patterns? Does the nervous father raise an anxious kid? Is the neglected daughter destined to smother her own? Or does this generation overcorrect and inflict an entirely new set of neuroses and painful experiences on their own offspring? How much control do we have over this?

Philip Larkin's legendary poem on the subject concludes with a directive to not reproduce, to stop the cascading misery and let it die out. That is the approach James, a policy analyst, is taking. He got in touch with me to talk about how his past had impacted his decision not to have children. "When I was a lot younger one of my main aspirations and dreams was to be a dad," the twenty-eight-year-old tells me. "I think because I had a complicated relationship with my dad I wanted to be a really good dad when I was older." James says his desire for a more present and engaged father left him especially vulnerable to his auntie's partner, who sexually abused him when he was ten. "He made himself out to be the cool uncle type figure, as is the case with a lot of these predators. They let children in on cool adult secret stuff like he let me watch horror movies," he says. "They give this illusion of treating kids as equals and also cast themselves as fulfilling that father role and then they exploit it." Around this age James began feeling too nauseous to go to school and the doctor could find no discernible cause for the sickness. After he watched a news report about child sexual abuse he realized that he needed to tell his parents. His mother and his grandmother both disclosed to James that they too had in their lifetimes been sexually abused by a family member. "I think they told me as a means to connect with me. I think there are times when my mother blames herself, not because she wasn't careful or whatever but because she wasn't [more of] a helicopter parent."

The first time I talk to James he tells me learning of the sexual trauma throughout generations made him feel, however irrationally, that his abuse was in some way inevitable. The second time we speak he is firm that he knows it wasn't fate. An adult made a decision to violate his trust and his body. "I don't think there is something in my personality that I took on from my mum who took it on from my grandmother, that made me more vulnerable to the abuse." By the time James was twelve he had been diagnosed with both a major depressive disorder and generalized anxiety disorder. "For many years afterwards I was very stubborn in not wanting to think about [the abuse]," he says. "It sat in a box that I would put aside." This ability, a natural response to trauma, has allowed James to function as safely as possible for many years. "One of the reasons that I can speak so candidly about this and don't consider myself a closed book is because of this defense mechanism that I developed over time, which is not to say I'm ever unfeeling when I talk about it, but I will feel both present and not present," he says. "I think that my biggest barrier to truly reckoning with my past is that I can't shake that aspect of being somewhat detached."

When James was younger and determined to one day be a father, he couldn't know how his trauma would echo through his life. He couldn't know his depression and anxiety would eventually become so much a part of his identity that he now finds it hard to distinguish his symptoms from his personality and his everyday experience of the world. He struggles to describe how his depression and anxiety first manifested because he can't remember a time without them. "I think [the idea of having kids] was a door that gradually shut for me and now it is for the most part closed," he says. "When I think about how that yearning for a father figure and the specter of my father played a role in my life, in throwing me off course in a lot of ways, it scares me and if I were to become a father that would be a burden I would take on and my child would take on." It is clear within minutes of speaking to James that he is resilient and perhaps realistic, but when I thought of his younger self longing for fatherhood, I hoped he was not being resigned. Author Sophie Mackintosh writes that she envisioned her life free of a child who she might raise badly, one who might inherit her "unpredictable brain" and who she might fail. "I had to study the narrative I'd built around myself, the narrative of who I was and what I deserved," she writes in the *Evening Standard*. "What if having a child wouldn't be a disaster? What if, actually, I was an imperfect person with a lot of love to give?"

At a time before the rights of the child were precious, before corporal punishment was so widely condemned, or emotional development so rigorously studied, psychoanalyst Alice Miller's ideas were revolutionary. "Experience has taught us that we have only one enduring weapon in our struggle against mental illness: the emotional discovery and emotional acceptance of the truth in the individual and unique history of our childhood," she wrote in her best-selling 1979 book *The Drama of the Gifted Child*. Miller upset a long-standing power dynamic in psychology by introducing the perspective of the child and granting people a voice, even if only behind the closed doors of a therapist's office, in their relationship with their parents. She excoriated parents for conventional child-rearing, which she called "poisonous pedagogy," condemning them for perpetuating cycles of trauma by reenacting the emotional neglect and violent discipline they had suffered. She told people to reckon with the mistakes made by their parents so they didn't in turn use their child's need for love and care to fulfill their own unmet needs. "Although the feelings of the abused child have been silenced at the point of origin, that is, in the presence of those who caused the pain, they find their voice when the battered child has children of his own," she wrote. Children who are not respected for who they are forgo their own emotional needs, adapting themselves to their parents' needs to develop a false self, which is unsustainable and is eventually riddled with psychic and somatic illness. "Our intellect can be deceived, our feelings manipulated, and conceptions confused, and our body tricked with medication," she wrote. "But someday our body will present its bill, for it is as incorruptible as a child, who, still whole in spirit, will accept no compromises or excuses, and it will not stop tormenting us until we stop evading the truth." You can't outrun your past, she yelled from the pages of her books, it would catch you eventually and haunt your children indefinitely.

Eight years after her death, Alice Miller's past came for her, just as it had come for her only child, Martin, who claimed she had subjected him to manipulative cruelty and astonishing neglect. In 2018 he published *The True "Drama of the Gifted Child,"* a devastating riposte to her bestseller in which he researched his mother's horrific personal history and tried to understand why she had perpetrated the emotional abuse she implored others not to in her work. "I became emotionally a part of my mother's Holocaust experience. I became a participant in a history of suffering, even though—or precisely because—it was unknown to me," Martin wrote. He learned that when his mother was in her early twenties she had to assume a Polish identity, changing her name from Alicjia to Alice, and kill a part of herself in order to survive and free her mother and sister from Warsaw.

Growing up, his mother had told him that his cruel and violent father had the same name as her Gestapo captor, but Martin discovered they were one and the same person. His mother, a bystander to the violence in their family, was able to disassociate from her surroundings and behave in a way he described as suspicious, short-tempered, insensitive, unreliable, tense, and anxious.

As a psychotherapist himself, Martin witnessed how war and other hardships could fray the connections a parent had to their child's needs, but just as his mother failed to apply her academic propositions to her own son, he could not see her as a product of her context, only as the mother who had failed him. Alice Miller was obsessed with how unresolved agony can ricochet through generations and yet she did not, or could not, protect her son from the shrapnel. She was either a perfect case study in her own theory—a parent who refused to face their own history to protect her family—or the ultimate contradiction—a parent who understood her own experiences and still could not stop the harm.

Once we account for physical and emotional abuse—which I agree with Miller, should be broadly defined—can we not release parents from the entire burden of psychic distress? How could a woman who survived the most brutal persecution under a regime constructed by strangers cast parents as the ultimate tyrants? (Miller even in part explained Hitler's atrocities, which claimed many of her family members including her father, by reference to his disciplinarian childhood.) Does becoming aware of your traumatic history actually release you from its lasting consequences, or do you just become bitter with rumination? In a passage addressed to his mother, Martin writes: "Today I am confronted with the paradoxical situation that you harmed me, almost killed me—but thanks to your radical ideas I found a way to save my own life."

In the end, it was Martin's correction of what he believed was an error in his mother's reasoning that really secured the closest he could come to peace. He learned as a therapist and as a son that when one critically appraises the way they have been raised as a child, it surfaces rage, hatred, mourning, pain, and fear about a story you are powerless to edit. Martin believed forgiveness and understanding had a limit when it came to the resentment people have for their parents, but his clients couldn't "become children again and start their lives over." The raging inner child is only comforted by offering oneself as an alternative to their parents and giving themselves the care they were denied, Martin writes. Establishing safety and stability you never had in a volatile home, listening to your needs if they were ignored, learning to accept yourself if perfection was demanded of you. It wasn't just tracing his mother's history, exposing himself to each of the horrifying chapters before integrating them, in his own words, into a book about her life, that saved Martin. It was the resultant understanding that he was not an unlovable child worthy of mistreatment, but a victim in a story that was being told long before he arrived and, crucially, one he would continue to write.

When thirty-year-old television producer Alexa found out she was pregnant with a boy, the flutter of anxiety she felt about having a child began to shake more noticeably inside her, unsettling the expectations of what her growing family might look like. "I was so convinced that it was a girl and I think that was probably my subconscious telling me so that I wouldn't freak out," Alexa, now five months pregnant, tells me. She thought to herself, *Everything you've worried about could actually happen now.* Alexa has never thought of herself as maternal—the first baby she will ever hold will be her own—but she felt confident about raising a girl. "I feel like I know how to teach her to navigate what will come her way and how you can be really strong in the face of all that shit, but I don't know how to teach a boy the balance between being strong and being aggressive or being forthright and being too angry. It feels so much harder."

Alexa's fear was not so much about having a son, but about having a son who might one day be a brother, an older brother like Mick. When Alexa started high school, he had a psychotic episode and jumped in front of a train. A few months later, once his bones had mended and he was discharged from the hospital with a diagnosis for schizophrenia and depression, the bullying and antagonism he had subjected her to throughout their childhood escalated into constant verbal abuse and intermittent physical violence until she eventually moved out of home, years later. He would barge into her room unannounced, smash her belongings, and stand over her, a full foot taller, yelling. "He would tell me I was an awful person every day of my life," she says. "He would call me a 'little slut,' particularly once I hit puberty."

Alexa could not stop herself projecting fear after fear onto her fetus: "What if my kid has really bad mental health issues and can't control them? What if they are a complete arsehole to everyone around them? What if they are just a toxic person?" When she first got in touch with me, I made a note next to her name as a potential interviewee: Alexa, in her thirties, pregnant, anxious about having a boy as brother schizophrenic. The note proved wrong. She wasn't preoccupied with the fact that her child's chances of having schizophrenia increased with Mick's diagnosis. In fact, Alexa only ever talked about her brother's disorder as something that might better equip her to recognize warning signs of poor mental health in her own children. She wasn't worried her kid might inherit her sibling's psychotic hallucinations or paranoid delusions; she was worried her kid might subject a sibling to aggression and misogyny. Alexa said she pictured having another child, a girl, and watching these same tensions play out between her imagined children. "It is irrational, but also it's not because my whole life has been dictated by that core relationship and that core relationship has permeated into every other relationship that I have with my family," she says. "Every single part of my life has been negatively impacted by it." It wasn't her son she was most concerned about. It was the possibility of a future daughter.

As Mick took up more of her parents' time and energy, Alexa expected less of them. When she achieved highly at school and then at university, they didn't want her to talk about it in case it made her brother insecure. "I took on the responsibility that I gave myself of always pretending that I was fine and everything was perfect," she says. Alexa's family home remains out of bounds to her as Mick, who she hasn't seen in four years, still lives there. The space between Alexa and her father, an already emotionally absent man, has grown while her mother walks on eggshells around Mick's feelings—she asked Alexa to move her wedding date to a day when he would be out of the country so she didn't feel guilty for attending. She suggested perhaps Alexa could write him a letter. "I said, 'No, Mum, I'm not the one that was ever a problem, I'm not the one who beat him up, I'm not the one who abused him every day of his life. If he thinks there is a gap to be bridged he needs to do it.'"

As we talk, Alexa's due date, a couple of days shy of her brother's birthday, looms like a prophecy. "What if he is even born on my brother's birthday?" she says. "Will Mum even come to the birth or will she not want to leave him on his birthday?"

Before she met her husband Jack, Alexa says she dated a series of "absolute losers." "I thought that was what all guys were like and it was totally normal for them to be low functioning babies that you had to help through life," she says. But Jack took responsibility for himself. He didn't need her to shrink so he could stretch. "His purpose on this earth is to grow a little human and help them form, and he is such a generous and loving and caring person," she says. "He will be such a great dad." When I thank her for her time, she returns the gratitude—"talking this through has made me realize I really need to process and can't keep avoiding it." Alexa has, for the first time, decided to see a mental health professional to support her in facing her dread before her child arrives. Alexa's confidence in her own ability to parent has wavered throughout her pregnancy, which has been plagued with nausea. She arrived at her last ultrasound anxious that her baby might not be getting enough nutrients as she hadn't gained enough weight. "I was scared I was already giving it a bad start as well as bringing it into a fucked-up family," she says. The doctor told Alexa her baby was active with a strong heartbeat.

Every day he grows bigger she pictures a new what if. "I am trying to picture what life might be like and it is a good picture. I can imagine loving that kid and I can imagine him loving me. I can imagine having another girl or another boy and them being great together as well. And I can see that in my future."

Whether in the womb or through our relationships, psychologist Mark Wolynn says life sends us forward with something unresolved from the past. "Traumas do not sleep, even with death, but rather continue to look for the fertile ground of resolution in the children of the following generations," he writes in It Didn't Start With You. Alexa unknowingly practiced what Wolynn asks his patients to: She allowed herself to be moved by an image strong enough to overshadow the horror she remembers from her past and that which she has projected into her future. On a neurophysiological level, Alexa is engaging not with her brain's trauma response center, but with her prefrontal cortex, where she can integrate the new image and, Wolynn says, neuroplastic change can occur. "Our minds have a vast capacity for healing through images whether we're imagining a scene of forgiveness, comfort, or letting go, or simply visualizing a loved one, images can profoundly settle into our bodies and sink into our minds," he writes. Life is rife with suffering, but Wolynn believes it is trauma that remains unaddressed and so unresolved that becomes a legacy for our children. "When the connection remains unconscious we can live imprisoned in feelings and sensations that belong to the past," he writes. "However, with our family history in view, the pathways that will set us free become illuminated."

I want to believe that the hardest moments in life tilt like a series of dominoes falling from one generation into the next, and if we try hard enough we can catch the falling tile before it hits another. I want to believe this even though I know the precursor cell of the egg I developed from was already in my mother's ovaries when she was a five-month old fetus, curled up in my grandmother's womb. Geneticist professor Robert Plomin believes DNA is the major systematic force that makes us who we are, and while parents provide "essential physical and psychological ingredients" for a child's development, the most significant element they give their kids is their genes. Plomin argues that for decades scientists have shown in studies using twins and adoptees that inherited DNA differences account for about half of the differences for all psychological traits, from personality to mental health to cognitive abilities. "The impact of our experiences is mostly unsystematic, unstable, and idiosyncratic—in a word, random," Plomin writes. "What look like systematic environmental effects, such as correlations between parenting and children's development, are mostly reflections of genetic influence. In the tumult of daily life, parents mostly respond to genetically driven differences in their children. We read to children who like us to read to them. We go along with their appetites and aptitudes."

Genetics can't account for everything, but research shows how they impact verbal skills, literacy, professional, cognitive and non-cognitive skills. The study of genes in human development usually defines genes as

independent predictors of some observable trait (phenotype) or consequence either independently, in the way they influence someone's likelihood
to smoke or be successful, or in how they interact with an environmental
condition like a stressful life event. Epigenetics is where nurture and nature
meet to offer a different flavor of fatalism on the journey to answer the
question of how much I will fuck up any potential offspring. It suggests you
can both pass on your genes and then adversely impact how those genes are
expressed. It is the study of how external modifications to DNA turn genes
"on and off." For a long time it was assumed that these switches were
complete after the embryological period, but now there are claims that a
person's exposure to environment or experience can actually influence their
genes and how they are expressed.

A gene responsible for some of the physiological response to stress was
turned off in newborn rat pups, who were licked and groomed a lot by their
mothers, making them calmer as they developed. One study showed children
of prisoners of war were more likely to die young than those of soldiers
who were not prisoners. Another showed girls born to women pregnant
during a severe famine in the 1940s had an above-average risk of developing
schizophrenia and the grandchildren of people who were undernourished at
age nine had better mental health.

Studies have shown the descendants of Holocaust survivors have a higher
risk of developing post-traumatic stress disorder, depression, and anxiety and
in 2015 Rachel Yehuda, a professor of psychiatry and neuroscience at Mount
Sinai school of medicine, published research claiming she had an epigenetic
explanation for the inheritance of trauma after studying the genes of Holocaust survivors who had been interned at Nazi concentration camps, forced
into hiding during World War II, or who had seen or experienced torture.
Yehuda was criticized for the small size of her sample and the preemptive
conclusions she drew before examining the great-grandchildren of these
survivors, as a pregnant woman already possesses the DNA of her grandchildren, but her field of genetics is compelling if contested.

One participant in Yehuda's controversial study, Josie Glausiusz, whose
father survived a concentration camp wrote: "I was troubled by a question:
How does one separate the impact of horrific stories heard in childhood

from the influence of epigenetics?" These kinds of distinctions seem impossible. Yehuda herself has said when she first established this clinic for Holocaust survivors, their children would call and report how they experienced the aftermath. "They talked about feeling traumatized by witnessing the symptoms of their parents. And they talked about the expectations— being traumatized by some of the expectations that the Holocaust had placed on them, such as that they are the reason their parents survived; and, therefore, there was a whole set of things that they would now have to accomplish so that all the people that died would—they could give their lives meaning," she said.

In her book *Unlike the Heart*, Nicola Redhouse searches for the locus of her postnatal dissolution and whether it was biochemical, hormonal, and genetic or whether it was emotional, built in memories and feelings. She wants to know where the sentient part of us that experiences emotion lives, where a "sorrow of fathers leaving" resides. Redhouse finds studies that conclude perinatal depression has some genetic heritability, but wonders if early infant responses to separation could influence our parental attachments. "My mother feared her mother wouldn't be there; my mother's mothering was fraught with this fear, with attempts to keep me close, perhaps made worse by my father leaving; I in turn embodied a fear of being separated from her, and when I had my own children I fell into a panic both because of the separation, bodily, from them that birth required, and the separation, emotionally, from my mother, that becoming a mother myself required." Even if Redhouse did locate in herself where the sorrow of fathers leaving slept, could she stop it from waking and disturbing her own children? I think of sorrow moving through time—traveling through molecular scars on our DNA, switching genes on and off, living in the narratives that pass from our grandmother to our granddaughter, spreading down the branches of our family trees into a complex set of actions and reactions too intricate to be observable.

Taryn knows the most dangerous thing she is likely to pass on through her genes. She found out a few weeks before we spoke. "You don't realize when you're having sex and trying to have a baby, but at some point in the process of becoming a mother you come to this crushing realization that you're not only creating a life, but you're creating a death."

Taryn and her husband both grew up in small, loving families knitted tightly together into which their baby Louis was woven in 2019. Motherhood felt at first like a psychoactive drug trip. "You're shimmering with this otherworldly energy and these hormones are just coursing through your body and you feel like you're electric," she says. "Three weeks later, exhaustion moves into your body and it just lives beside your bones for months and months and months and months." In the first year of life with Louis she was bored, exhilarated, overwhelmed, full of love, empty of sleep, heavy with responsibility and foggy-brained. "I couldn't compute basic conversations and felt like I didn't know how to function, but in the midst of that I could be having these really clear profound, almost life-changing realizations," she says. "Our relationship and our bond is constant and I feel the tug of him every time we're apart."

The demands of sleeping and feeding schedules tether new parents to the home in a way that can contract their physical world, but Taryn says motherhood expanded a space within her. "We think of an experience as going somewhere or doing something, but the experience of motherhood happens within you," she says. "Pregnancy expands you in a physical way. You fill up with this other person and then when they come out through birth they are still you, they just push out and out and you're still encompassed by this person, but they are suddenly free in the world." She begins to cry when she tries to explain what Louis has uncovered inside of her.

I feel so moved, not only by Taryn's love but by the way she has challenged a foolish misconception I started with while trying to map how we pass things on. I saw that I had believed on some level that a human came to and through parenthood as a fixed and knowable entity. Instead, she had created Louis and he had recreated her. "He has unlocked this unknown part of me that I was never able to access . . . a tenderness that I really didn't know I had in me," she says, her voice dense with emotion. "Even in the really difficult times I know these will be some of the greatest days in my whole life and it is so unusual to recognize that while you're in it."

Everyone has two copies of the breast cancer gene 1 (BRCA1) and the breast cancer gene 2 (BRCA2), often referred to as tumor suppressor genes.

When someone inherits a mutation of these genes they have increased risks of multiple types of cancer, as cells that don't contain the protein can grow out of control and become cancerous. Through genetic testing, Taryn has found out that she inherited a harmful variant of BRCA1 from her mother, who survived an aggressive breast cancer at age forty-two. Around 13 percent of the general population will develop breast cancer and 1.2 percent will develop ovarian cancer in their lifetime, while up to 69 percent of women with a BRCA1 variant will develop breast cancer and up to 44 percent of them will develop ovarian cancer. "It was a devastating couple of weeks as I had to come to grips with everything that it meant," she says. "They told me that my risk factor of developing breast cancer over the next ten years is 15 percent, but I guess for that 15 percent it is 100 percent." Taryn has been meeting with oncologists and surgeons to make plans for her eventual double mastectomy and hysterectomy. She knows she can cut out the pieces of her body most vulnerable to cancer, but she can't remove the mutation from her own genes.

Although the BRCA1 gene does slightly increase a person's risk of prostate cancer, because Louis doesn't have mammary glands or ovaries, if he does have the mutation, it won't impact his life in the way it has Taryn's. Taryn and her partner have discussed their plans to grow their family, going over the risks of passing on the variant—a one in two chance of having a kid with female sex organs, then a one in two chance of her inheriting the mutation. Now that Taryn has confirmed she doesn't already have cancer, they have decided they are going to try for another child.

"I have always known that I want two kids and that doesn't disappear just because I have this genetic flaw," she says. "If I do have a daughter and she does inherit this gene, there is a power in the knowledge. It is not something that she would grow up with thinking of a terrible, scary life-ruining thing because I'm not going to let it be that for me." Taryn and her mother did not know they had the gene until they were tested, but Taryn's embryo would be a candidate for a pre-implantation genetic diagnosis (PGD) if she chose to have her child via IVF. "They create a number of embryos and they can do a needle biopsy and test for BRCA1 and only implant the ones that don't have the mutation," she says. "We turned this option over a lot, but we have decided against it and we are going to try to conceive naturally."

When she lists her reasons for this, Taryn says she is mostly answering to the hypothetical scrutiny of others. She knows what her values are and feels this decision is in line with them. This is not a diagnosis after all; it is a risk factor. "The truth is this is a gray area, but I know PGD isn't a choice for me because I don't think this optimization process is necessary with a human being. After all, if my parents took that path I wouldn't exist," she says, adding that genes are a blueprint for your body, not for your life. "I like to think that it is not just 50 percent of my genetics that will shape and determine his whole life, but also 100 percent of my love, devotion, care, and respect." She adds, "I don't think you can decide life isn't worth coming to fruition because of potential future risk. Maybe Louis doesn't have BRCA1 and maybe he will be a rev head and die in a car accident at eighteen."

When my niece arrived, I knew what I wanted to insulate her from within our extended family and felt an immediate panic I did not feel when my nephew was born. I wanted her to be valued instantly and inherently and then praised for more than self-restraint. "I'm very resentful about it and I'm very angry," singer Mitski said of the teenage years she spent obsessed with beauty. "I had so much intelligence and energy and drive, and instead of using that to study more, or instead of pursuing something or going out and learning about or changing the world, I directed all that fire inward, and burned myself up."

My cousin and I meet up in London for coffee and find ourselves talking about the years we spent on fire. There were two ways to be the belle of our family barbecue: get a new boyfriend or lose a noticeable amount of weight. We remember a "game" in which an aunt or grandparent would ask "who is the prettiest girl?" and half a dozen hands would shoot into the air. Whoever was quickest would get to be her. It might have been a way of democratizing access to the most cherished attribute in our family, beauty, but we knew the game was redundant. It was always obvious who she was even once we grew older and the game was retired. The year I stopped eating meat and started exercising too much, I was she. My cousin and I recite like hymns the lessons we learned about which bits of our bodies were meant to be smallest (arms especially) and if you didn't have the self-discipline, at least cover them up. How did we both know the same words?

If I have a child, my body is where it will first find a home. I wondered how a habitat that spent so long trying to contract could be hospitable to new life. It took years for me to put out the flames: to stop exercising in a way that was obsessive, to strip food of morality, to see my body for what it was—a heart mercifully beating, legs generously carrying, hands helpfully typing—and not what it wasn't, to value myself the same way I had always valued others: for what was inside. Now, when I sense the burning, I imagine repeating my internal dialogue word for word to my niece and I stamp until only embers remain.

In Meg Mason's novel *Sorrow and Bliss*, a woman yells at a child who isn't hers in a changing room. Child-free Martha asks her sister, the mother of three small children, whether when you have kids you become better at tolerating cruelty in the world, especially against children. Ingrid responds no. "It makes it worse because as soon as you're a mother, you realize every child was a baby five seconds ago, and how could anyone shout at a baby? But then, you shout at your own and if you can do that, you must be a terrible person. Before you had kids, you were allowed to think you were a good person so then you secretly resent them for making you realize you're actually a monster."

In a letter to his mother, who was at times abusive, poet Ocean Vuong remembers that while preparing green beans over the sink, she suddenly said, "I'm not a monster. I'm a mother." He told her at the time that she was not a monster, but now wishes he had instead told her it wasn't the worst thing to be. "From the Latin root monstrum, a divine messenger of catastrophe, then adapted by the Old French to mean an animal of myriad origins: centaur, griffin, satyr," he writes in the letter, published in the *New Yorker*. "To be a monster is to be a hybrid signal, a lighthouse: both shelter and warning at once."

The chimera, a fire-breathing monster made up of goat, lion, and snake; forewarned rain; lightning and thunder in Greek mythology. A genetic chimera is a single organism composed of cells with more than one distinct genotype, and fetomaternal microchimerism involves cells that originate from a fetus lingering in the mother. We take our mother's cells and she takes some of ours. It happens in pregnancy whether it ends in miscarriage, abortion, or a live birth. These cells make mothers weaker and stronger—they can promote tissue repair and improve her immune system, but they can also wreak havoc, catalyzing autoimmune reactions. "It's not only us," cancer researcher Sami B Kanaan told the *Boston Globe*. "It's us, plus our mothers, plus our children if we have them, that are living with us."

Afia searches for the right word to describe herself before offering an impish smile and settling on "therapized." "I marched into motherhood armed with this real self-knowledge and awareness of how my mother's harsh parenting had scarred me," she says. "I was like 'I know what I need to do differently, and I am a confident enough person now to do it.'" Afia had thought a lot about boundaries—how she would protect her small family unit from her overbearing mother and extended family. "We moved to a different part of London before the baby arrived because I just needed to have the distance physically before I could accept I had it mentally," she says. But when her baby came, she barely slept. "Eventually I caved and I called my mother and I was so ready for a fight," she says. "I was so sleep deprived and ready to just scream the moment she was judgmental." I can sense her tensing, remembering how it felt to brace for that confirmation she had failed already at motherhood. "She came and she just silently got to work," she says. "She held the baby so I could sleep, she cooked, she cut up fruit."

Afia says she would never tell her this, but the first few months of parenthood left her in awe of her mother and how she parented three children in a new country, while learning the language and studying in a tiny flat. "We don't speak about that kind of thing culturally and I used to feel so angry about that because I wanted to be in a family where people talked about their feelings, but now I see a kind of beauty in actions over words," she says. "I just see my mother, this migrant doing the best she could with no real support or template to work off of. You know, I was so determined not to be my mother that I never really thought about how many things were outside of her control and how hard it is to tell who she really was without that level of stress." Afia's daughter has created a distance between the two women, shifting how they relate to each other. "She treats my daughter in this way she never treated us [as kids]," she says. "There's this softness in her that the child part of me almost feels jealous of, but the mother part of me can see that she's getting to do it all again more gently. Sometimes I can't tell if I'm giving her more grace because I can see her as a mother now or [if] she's giving it to me because she can see me as a mother now. I really believed people were so fixed, but I don't think I believe that anymore."

In *The Origins of You: How Childhood Shapes Later Life*, four psychologists— Jay Belsky, Avshalom Caspi, Terrie Moffitt, and Richie Poulton—explain their forty years of research involving more than 4,000 children. They map how family experience and experiences beyond the family shaped who they became later in life by picking apart how children think, feel, and behave as they move from childhood, through adolescence, and into adulthood. Research has repeatedly shown that parents who mistreated their children were disproportionately likely to have been mistreated themselves, but the authors say there are "serious problems" with the collection of this data as it relies on memory, a fallible value. They instead give more credence to evidence, tricky and time-consuming to obtain (over generations), that links actual assessments of parenting experienced in childhood with the parenting that the child, now grown up, provides for their own offspring. This research showed the way mothers parent is influenced by their experiences in their families growing up, but there was no such evidence of intergenerational transmission from fathers. In trying to describe the complexity of all that is unknown, the experts describe the science of human development as similar to meteorology. Just as studying the weather and climate must account for multiple and often competing factors and forces, human development involves many elements—emotion, cognition, behavior, neuroscience, genetics, physiology—that interact in complex ways over time and space.

The idea that success relies on securing a number of factors while failure can hinge on a single deficiency is sometimes referred to as the Anna Karenina principle, after Tolstoy's famous opening: "Happy families are all alike; each unhappy family is unhappy in its own way." Even the most rational person can't accurately appraise the positive or negative impacts their parents had on their development. I know my parents smoked through all four of their pregnancies. The advertised harms of this had changed rapidly over those decades—my mother was allowed to smoke on the maternity ward after she had her first child in 1976, but by the time she had her last child, me, in 1992, she had to go out onto the hospital balcony to light up, which she did. And yet I harbor no judgment, resentment, or concern about the documented effect this has on a fetus's brain or lung development. I feel nothing and so it means nothing to me. I never begrudge rain until I'm inconvenienced by it.

We can know ourselves, we can know our family histories, we can know that children need to be safe, loved, regarded, and respected. We can't know the unique ways in which a child of ours might suffer or inflict suffering on others, including their parents, any more than we can predict the weather. Harsh physical punishment, for example, can "and often does" foster aggression in a child, the experts write, but whether it does depends on a range of environmental factors including whether they have a sensitive nervous system or whether their other parent's love and affection can temper the impact of the abuse. Human development, like meteorology, is probabilistic, not deterministic. "Whether a storm will turn into a hurricane may depend not only on its characteristics, but also on whether air pressure in another locale will increase the time the hurricane spends out at sea, picking up moisture, before making landfall," *The Origins of You* researchers wrote.

A probability is not an outcome; history is not a forecast. In imagining what I might pass on to a child genetically or emotionally I saw how quickly I could become that person pointing at their phone screen, insisting it is currently raining because there is a cloud emoji for the day, as the sun sparkled outside my window. A realization kept recurring. It would surface late in each conversation and later still in the one I was having with myself. Beyond this fear of what we might pass on, behind the self-deprecating jokes about how dysfunctional we were, was an obscured terror about what we might not pass on. We were all uneasy and ill-prepared for how different our children might be.

Researchers found people who watched post-apocalyptic movies coped better with the pandemic as they had "mentally rehearsed" an analogous scenario. There was a sense of preparedness in the anxiety about precisely how you might mess up your kids. Adversity can cripple our capacity for trust, joy, security, stability, and hope, but it connects us to others who have suffered in similar ways. Gender is a blunt way to parse this feeling because every woman I know is so acutely aware of what they do not want the next generation of women to experience and so determined to not be complicit in repeating it. I could feel it in my self-censorship around my niece. I could feel it in Alexa's initial panic about not feeling up to raising a boy who might embody the sharpest edges of masculinity. Many women I know admit they have a preference for a girl. One recently expressed it in a way that made me instantly nauseous: "I guess maybe it seems easier to raise a victim than a perpetrator." The statement was jarring, but more uncomfortable was that I instantly knew what she meant. I worried that meant "I don't want parenthood if it is hard." I worried that meant "I don't want a child that isn't a replica of me." I worried that meant "I can only empathize with suffering that looks like mine." But when I sat with it, it just felt like ineptitude. I understood the lack of faith in your ability to best parent children who are nothing like us, who do not suffer or find joy in the ways that we do, who might live in a way that is antithetical to our values, who might cause harm to others.

My friend and I send voice memos. "I think it is wanting to know you could love a child unconditionally even if they're different from you. I don't think people are like, 'Oh no! What if my teenager has an anti-democratic opposition to equality?' I think they're more like, 'What if they're a little brat, like, worryingly so, and I couldn't connect with them or make them feel connected?'" I ramble, feeling stupid. "I just think most people's kids suck and most parents make mistakes," she says in response.

When Sarah Sentilles wrote in her book *Stranger Care* about trying to adopt a baby through foster care, she said people told her, "but you never know what you're going to get." They also said this to her friend who was considering adoption, whose two-year-old son died of a fatal genetic disease. "Belief in biology runs deep," Sentilles wrote. "Fear of the unknown, of the unrelated, runs deeper." Your children might indeed inherit something of your mental health, disposition, tendencies, or experiences, but they might not catch any of it. I have little but love in common with my parents.

"Though many of us take pride in how different we are from our parents, we are endlessly sad at how different our children are from us," writes author Andrew Solomon, who spent a decade interviewing more than 300 families with children who had what he calls "horizontal" identities like deafness, schizophrenia, or prodigal intelligence. Unlike "vertical" identities, attributes and values seamlessly passed through genetics or shared cultural norms, horizontal identities were often, at least at first, an affront, treated as flaws. In his book *Far From the Tree*, Solomon documented in detail the struggles and successes of parents trying to integrate their child's difference into their family. He began his book trying to forgive his parents, who accepted his dyslexia, but struggled at first to celebrate his sexuality, and he ended it by becoming a parent, realizing his research about parenting was also a means to subdue his own anxieties about impending fatherhood.

Solomon described a positive connection to his parents tainted with a despair at his family dynamics where he found it hard to distinguish between their emotions and his own. He wanted to understand why he had suffered so much in his childhood and to separate what was attributable to himself, what he could blame his parents for, and what he found reflected in the society around him. "I had been consumed by being a son; recently emerged from that whale's mouth, I was afraid to be swallowed by being a father. I was also afraid of becoming the oppressor of a child who was different from me, as I had at times felt oppressed."

Beyond what I fear I might replicate, beyond what I fear I might find alien, is a fear of failure. It is not only the strangeness, but the modern expectation that we should perfectly handle the strangeness that makes me feel nervous about my potential as a parent. Good parents are now more than ever defined by how accepting they are and less by historical measures of raising obedient and well-behaved children, writes philosopher Agnes Callard in her essay "Acceptance Parenting," published in *The Point*. She believes there has been a "deep tectonic shift" in parenting that leaves parents feeling like failures, despite spending more time with their children than previous generations. "Parents have always justified themselves with reference to the future—you'll thank me later!—and parents have always aimed at the happiness of their child," she writes. "[But] at no point in the past was the parental inability to accept that which strikes them as antithetical to their basic understanding of what is true and what is good perceived as a potential failure by the parents' own standards. . . . What's radically new is not, at heart, how concerned or permissive we've become, but how fully we have given over to our children the job of defining 'happiness.'"

Parents can no longer rely on values of the past to be handed on or the traditional standards on which children are to be assessed, as they are no longer trying to give their children some version of their lives, but instead this unknown life based on an unknown future. "Like all forms of freedom, acceptance parenting makes life more, and not less, stressful. If the parent is demoted from wise authority figure to tentative spokesperson for the child's future self, childhood and child-rearing become a nerve-wracking quest to find one's own footing," she writes. "The problem here is not my fear of employing discipline, or my inclination to micromanage. The problem is ignorance. Unlike my forebears, I don't know the things I need to know in order to be a good parent, and none of the people telling me to calm down know those things either. The only one who might know, my grown child, doesn't yet exist."

Writer Jacqueline Rose worries about the expectation to provide a love that can never fray or falter. "Expecting mothers to be perfect is, of course, not unrelated to the drive to perfection of the so-called whole world—a world that must be flawless—in her baby," she writes in *Mothers*. "Or to put it another way, if you're asking mothers to be perfect, why wouldn't they pass that impossible demand on to their child?"

Unlike many of the people I spoke to, Taryn is not taming ghosts hovering above her family but is facing a current and corporeal reality in which she has data to evaluate a real genetic risk. There is so much in between the medical risks and the reality of her family's future. So instead of forecasting, she is already trying to have a looser grasp on what will come, letting each projection and possibility run through her fingers while she asks herself the questions she knows she needs to answer first before having another child. "What are my values? What are my fears? What are my tendencies? What is my personality? What is my genetic predisposition? What is anxiety and what is real? What are the points in my life that I know 'this is legitimate'?" she asks. "It is when I have my son sitting on my lap. It is real, no matter how loud my anxiety is."

Years before I carried in my pocket the ability to prevent getting lost, obliterate uncertainty, or know instantly the weather forecast in real time, before spontaneity was a thing you planned to do tomorrow, it began sprinkling while my cousin and I were swimming in the ocean. We were almost at womanhood and though we had the kindling for the fire we would later subject our bodies to, we were still displaying them with pride—leaping across the netball court, practicing handstands, performing choreographed dances for our families. We looked back to the beach, now empty of men, empty of anyone, and pulled off our bikinis, laughing and cawing like seagulls as the sky cracked further open and poured down on us. A flash of lightning illuminated my cousin's bum as she mooned the clouds, diving under a wave before it crashed. Later, we carried our sopping wet towels home, shivering, yapping about how brave we were.

I thought my nostalgia for that day was a yearning for a time before my relationship with my body became complicated by rules, a time when I could just be a nude comet racing on the waves, my hips grazing the sand as I hit the shore. Now I miss something else about that moment—the ability to let go, to let life happen to me, to find joy in the unexpected, meeting it arms wide open, fully exposed. I can't remember the last time I swam in the rain. I only go to the beach between October and May, and only if I've checked that it is going to be above 75 degrees.

Conclusion

REFLECTING AND REFRACTING

I COULDN'T STOP CALLING PEOPLE. Months before I paused to consider my own perspective, I kept asking, recording, transcribing, reading, note-taking, trying to understand, reaching out toward people who allowed me to hold their stories for long enough to feel the weight of them. I would fall asleep to the sound of their voices, studying the shape of their situations as though it was a Rorschach test through which I could interpret my own. Mothers, fathers, people who knew they would never be parents willingly or unwillingly; people who wanted to tell me about their births, their miscarriages, their parental leave, the way their husbands had learned to clean. I couldn't stop having those first calls, even once I knew there were too many case studies to possibly interview, even once I realized so many of their stories were better suited to a different book, even once I knew it would be impossible to fit them all in. I sent so many emails thanking and apologizing, thanking and apologizing.

I didn't know how to explain that their stories were important and relevant and so were everybody else's. I was used to making quick summaries, neat conclusions, publishing multiple stories a day, tomorrow's fish and chip paper, a link three pages into a search result. This was not a reporting assignment and it was not research. It was not empirical. It was not impersonal.

It was a twenty-eight-year-old woman calling strangers, hoping someone would reflect back to her what she thought she wanted.

My boyfriend's genius brother sends me a philosophy paper. I can't stop laughing. Every sentence makes a mockery of the way I have gone about answering this question. The author, Laurie Ann Paul, a Yale professor of philosophy and cognitive science, argues that normal models of decision-making theory simply can't be applied to the decision of whether or not to have a child. Unlike other choices where we can assume and assign value to different outcomes based on our preferences, this question deals with what she calls a "transformative experience," one that changes the values and preferences you held before making the decision.

Paul refers to philosopher Frank Jackson's thought experiment in which a brilliant neuroscientist Mary is locked in a colorless cell from birth and while she knows all the science behind light and the human eye's response to it, she can't know the color red until she has experienced it. "She experiences redness for the first time, and from this experience, and this experience alone, she knows what it is like to see red," Paul writes. Mary does not know how it will feel to see red, but even if she could know that red might fill her heart with joy or fear, she can't know what it is to experience it. She cannot know how she will be forever changed by redness.

And so, from my "impoverished epistemic position," there is no point imagining the reds I might know—the faint line of a pregnancy test or the last unpicked bloom of period blood seizing a cotton liner as I reach menopause. Until I have experienced having children or experienced never having children, I cannot know what it is like. Asking people with or without children how their lives have changed will tell me little about my own future. You can't assign values to either choice as you don't know how it will transform what you know and how you feel and so you can't determine the relevant outcomes of each act, nor how likely they are. "The subjective unpredictability attending the act of having one's first child makes the story about family planning into little more than pleasant fiction," Paul writes.

Does it count for nothing that I have washed, changed, read to, and bargained with a child I would die for? I know the red urgent love that surfaces in specks when a child grazes his knee. Does it count for nothing that I know what it feels like to have no dependents? I know how it feels to circle my lips in rouge self-love and go out whenever and wherever I want only to come home and sleep alone diagonally for as long as I want. Throughout the paper, Paul scrunches up my chapters of dithering, my tens of thousands of words trying to prove that I am an animal of reason, my unearned fear, my unearned hope, the napkin on which I have scrawled pros and cons, and puts them all in the bin. "I suspect that the popular conception of how to decide to have a child stems from a contemporary ideal of personal psychological development through choice," she writes. "That is, a modern conception of self-realization involves the notion that one achieves a kind of maximal self-fulfillment through making reflective, rational choices about the sort of person one wants to be."

I highlight the sentence and scrawl: *Check her age!! Not a millennial.*

There is something fragile about an identity forged only through personal choices. We collapse our connections to other humans into ourselves, an isolating process of dicing ourselves into smaller pieces that the world as we know it depends on. This individualizing, this withdrawal into ourselves, is one of the reasons I first saw motherhood as unattainable for me. The fortification of the nuclear family, the formalization of so many relationships, a consolidation of the smallest community of three at the expense of participation in a larger one. I wanted to interrogate this question, I wanted to interrogate this question before I had those conversations with my partner and eventually with my friends and family. In writing, in choosing, I felt this instinct to contain my needs within my closest relationships hurdle beyond my loved ones and into my interviews as I strained to hear my own story beneath theirs.

My eyes keep getting worse. I go back to the optometrist for another test and he confirms for the third time in two years that I need stronger lenses. I have six pairs of glasses, all different prescriptions. I tell him about the increasing number of distracting gray squiggles floating across my vision. He asks me how often I look up from my medium-sized screen and not, he insists, just to look at my small-sized screen. I picture myself as I had been for months, a hunched prawn at a desk switching between screens as I transcribe

interviews and read documents, and then later relaxing in front of the very
big screen at my boyfriend's house. The optometrist tells me to look at the
horizon frequently. "You have to learn to look past the squiggles and into
the distance and you will find they don't annoy you so much. They will also
disappear when you blink." I feel unable to look far enough beyond and
unable to close my eyes and go deep enough inside myself.

A friend tells me that when she is overwhelmed, she curls up in a fetal
position under a blanket and imagines going back in time to just before she
had left the womb. "We know all babies deserve love and they haven't learned
to hate themselves yet, and I start from there," she says. "When I focus on
myself at that stage things don't seem noisy." One morning I put my quilt
over myself and close my eyes. I try to move backward to a time before I
bloomed. Before I opened myself up to the warmth and wind of other people,
before I was lavender soothing, chamomile calming, before discoloration and
asymmetry jeopardized my worth, before I knew how fragile my parts were,
before I knew they could grow back. Outside, my housemates sleep, the planes
roar above, the trains scrape past, and the lorikeets laugh. I bring my knees up
toward my chin, the ridges of my spine flaring, a seashell, listening inside of
herself for the sound of the ocean she came from. I mistake sounds for things
they're not. Bins dragged to the curb sound like the early rumblings of a
thunderstorm. I am so full. I feel swollen with other people's decisions, my
own feelings diluted. I wait until the sounds disappear, until my body is a
silent crypt but for my beating heart. Is there anything that so quickly confirms what you love and fear most about the world and yourself, like the
question of whether or not to have children? My anxieties about the world
rush forward, extroverted, bellowing about the end times. My fears about
myself are almost inaudible. I buy a tarot reading in case she can reveal my fate.

I realize no one is going to write the ending for me. I keep making calls.

The parents make me feel young and untethered. The childfree people recoiling away from parenthood make me realize I am only leaning. Their
certainty is moreish. I call Victoria, who loves being an auntie, but when she
and her husband hold babies, waiting for a sign they should procreate, they
feel nothing. Victoria says there is no bodily urge nor rational reason she

would ever want children. "So many of the things that women are expected to do are based in a tradition that no longer belongs here," she tells me. "In heterosexual relationships, you get married and you lose your last name, then you have kids and you lost your first name because you just become 'Mum' and you've lost your job in one way or another whether you go back part-time or not at all. First name, last name, job, all gone. What's left?" This is how Victoria sees motherhood—loss after loss. It would only jeopardize her personhood, distract from her wonderful relationship, and worsen the chronic migraines she lives with. Importantly, it would derail her ambitions as a writer and actor. "The only thing that I would drive myself through extraordinary pain and trauma for is career-based because that is how much I love it," she says. "My identity and what I want to do with my life is to tell stories. It is not just a thing that I do, it is who I am."

Imagine, I think later, *knowing who you are.*

There is nothing miraculous nor magical about pregnancy. "I think it is a parasite and I think it would be cumbersome," Victoria says, my eyes widening as I transcribe. "I think about how heavy you must feel and how difficult it must be. It makes me uncomfortable. It truly does."

I call Lucy, who tells me her ex-partner was planning on carrying any child they would have together. "The more I became comfortable in my butch identity, the more the idea of being pregnant and my body changing scared me," she says. "I have narrow hips and small breasts and I like that. I wonder if I had a more feminine figure if I would have taken steps to alter my body." Lucy had never felt the urge to have children. "I've still never felt those ovary pains," she says. "I've always felt a bit alien for not feeling it." But her partner wanted kids and so Lucy figured she would become a parent, not out of any compulsion of her own, but as a compromise to be with the woman she loved. "I was delaying making the decision with her and avoiding coming to terms with what the dread and overwhelm eventually meant because I was in a partnership."

It wasn't just pregnancy but motherhood itself that loomed as an unwelcome disruption to her relationship with her body and gender. "I see my relationship to womanhood as more of a collective, almost political relationship. I relate to the experiences of being oppressed in the patriarchy and of finding camaraderie with other women and within that I include trans women," she says. "But I don't have a very personal relationship to woman-hood and so being called a woman is kind of okay because it feels like I am part of a collective whereas daughter, sister, and mother feel like definitions relating to someone else . . . you're not a person anymore—you're a mother."

When she and her partner broke up, Lucy felt relief underneath the sad-ness. "Maybe I'm just a selfish prick, but I want to be who I want to be and I want to do what I want to do," she laughs. "I want to be able to dictate my own life direction and not be so worried that I'm running a small person's life and have someone else dependent on me." She wants to keep spontaneity, to spend time in her community, and have enough energy and time to offer her loved ones and their children—"and still go home to my own bed." When Lucy met her current partner she realized they weren't in a rush—to have kids, to get married, to own a home. "It gave me the space and freedom and relief to not feel like we were on a timed path and to take our time." They are happy living as they are. "There is this blankness on the horizon and this free-dom to create whatever path we want, in the past it might have terrified me, but now I get excited about the idea of it," she says. "This temporal freedom."

Timing, timing, timing. The word punctuated the transcript of my conversation with Melissa.

Seventeen years after her first abortion, she was booked in for another one a month before her thirty-eighth birthday. Melissa's first pregnancy was during university. "I knew that I wasn't supposed to be responsible for another human life and that I could not provide for it or guarantee it or myself the quality of life that we deserved." In the intervening years she had never imagined herself with or without children, but as time went on, she was content with the likelihood she would never be a mother. This time she had written a pros and cons list. Her partner did not want to keep the pregnancy, so together they decided to make an appointment. The clinic assured her she could cancel at any time. Melissa found herself sobbing in the shower. "I just broke down and I thought, 'I cannot terminate this pregnancy.'" Their baby was born a few months before we spoke. It wasn't a realization that she had wanted to be a mother all along, it was a realization that she had arrived at a position in her life where motherhood was right for her. Her partner took to fatherhood instantly and excitedly, and Melissa found herself coping with motherhood better than she had predicted. "One of the reasons why motherhood is a thing I feel confident in now is because I am in an emotional and financial position to provide for a family," she says. "Everything I had thought about timing was valid."

I go and get a facial, and by that I mean I try to purchase the confidence I need to finish writing because internal metrics of self-worth only apply to women you care about more than you do yourself. The beautician solemnly tells me I am ageing prematurely and I buy the expensive cream she recommends because her skin is gleaming like a freshly peeled lychee. On the bus home I see myself, suddenly a crone, in the reflection. I search for egg-freezing clinics near me. As I write, time hunts me like this, in bursts. Sometimes, I don't feel chased. I feel safely transported by the seasons, along tracks I cannot see. Time does not hand me my coat, press a guiding palm to the small of my back, and usher me out toward a decision like I'd hoped it might. Instead time allows me to write, and through the words I feel myself changing.

I find, as the author Deborah Levy did, not only that the idea of the mother "as imagined and politicized by the societal system, was a delusion," but that my own ideas of her did not stand up to scrutiny. A person from a family that is now only ever in the same room at a funeral did not know how to create something close, loving, and stable. A person who could not cleanly resolve her angst about the future was not fit to deliver a child into the murk of it. A person who did not inherently know she was a mother could never become one.

I began reimagining motherhood and not-motherhood. I needed time to sit with the flaws in the feminism I knew best. This feminism wanted more choice and more freedom, but it could also be fast, anti-maternal, power-hungry, self-interested, isolating, a handmaiden to capitalism. It does not value what I do—care, maintenance, community, inclusivity, forgiveness. I needed to admit that regardless of my choice, I value motherhood and do not want to participate in its degradation anymore. I do not want to buy into a binary in which mothers are not as savvy, creative, intellectual, ambitious, or interesting, just as I know they are not more selfless or caring than women without children.

I realized I want my decision to be made with the full knowledge that motherhood was not the only way to love deeply and fulfil someone else's needs and that life without children was not the only way to connect to yourself and your own potential. I want a life without my own children that is still rooted in connectivity, that is still in service of others, that still involves other people's children. I want a motherhood expansive enough to incorporate personhood, to embrace humanity. A person who makes mistakes and is not crucified for them, a person who has her own needs, a person who just wants to be a mother more days than she does not.

Every week I see updates on social media from a friend of my brother's, who he met in rehab. Her two sons were taken away from her because the family was experiencing violence and she was in addiction. The last time I saw her in person she was still trying to get full custody of her boys and needed to prove she was dry and clean. In this limbo she was recommitting to motherhood, reimagining herself as a mother again. As a good mother, she told me. She said she would spend her life making it up to them, earning their trust and keeping them safe.

They are now reunited and I see them thriving, each football game and birthday a miracle she celebrates. She reminds me that being a parent is not something you choose just once. In my efforts not to romanticize mother-hood I had spent too much time wondering how people had the strength to survive it and forgetting how it could help you to find the strength to survive.

"It's true what they say, that a baby gives you a reason to live," author Rivka Galchen wrote in *Little Labors*. "But also, a baby is a reason that it is not permissible to die. There are days when this does not feel good."

When I began writing, I saw parenthood only as permanence, an immutable relationship to another human, a shackling to the world as it is and to your-self as you are. I had decided the people around me who were choosing to have kids had reached a heroic self-possession and a peace with the future that I was incapable of. I am not sure that is right anymore. I am redefining bravery. The question of whether or not to have a child became an exercise in tracking my fear about the world and extending it beyond my own lifes-pan. Civilization is collapsing and humanity has been rendered infertile by 2027 in the film *Children of Men*. "Fugees" flee to a militarized Britain, where they are hunted down and jailed. Humans are on the brink of extinction until Kee, a fugee, falls pregnant, a miracle the world has been waiting for. The film follows her struggle to safely reach a secret scientific group so she can be studied to cure the two decades of global infertility. As Gavin Jacobson writes, the future of humanity has been placed in the body of "perhaps the most powerless, disenfranchised, stigmatized, and exploited individual in the modern Great Chain of Being"—a Black refugee woman. "Kee is the antithesis of almost everything that modern societies venerate and forgive: the rich, the male, the rooted, the documented," Jacobson writes. "She is the film's true apocalypse in the literal sense of the word—pure revelation, forcing us to confront the hollowness and turpitude of the prevailing moral order."

I thought the film would be useful to watch, to add to my growing appendix of texts in which children are synonymous with hope and so without them despair flourishes and chaos ensues. Instead, I was struck by how real this world felt. As philosopher Slavoj Žižek says, this is not an alternate reality; the directors have instead "simply [made] reality more what it already is." I do not want to be a person who, with all her privilege, with all her resources, can more easily conceptualize collapse than change. Imagining the end of procreation should not be easier than imagining a world in which we can transform the forces that make creating new life so fraught. I ask what I want from my life and how do I want to live through the horror of a virus that has only laid bare what was already there. The pandemic shattered each community differently, but we fracture along lines that were already drawn.

A pollster tweeted a graph that showed that in the four years leading to August 2021 an increasing number of Americans believed this statement was very or somewhat likely: "Given the events you have witnessed over your life-time, how likely do you think it is that we are currently living in a version of a negative afterlife (e.g., hell, purgatory, or a similar concept)?" When inter-viewed by journalist Luke O'Neil, the author Casey Taylor said the question began as a joke "at the peak of mass hysteria" when US President Donald Trump was elected, but when it became clear one in three people thought it was feasible they lived in hell he looked more closely at the data.

"When I dove into the crosstabs, it started to become clear that 'hell' acted as a proxy for cyclical, institutional problems in America," he told

O'Neil. "Women and people of color were more likely to believe it was possible. Lower classes and the unemployed. People with debt or medical problems they can't solve." I want my doom to be instructive, not conclusive.

"I think all of us Cold War children in America probably had death on our minds too young," Barbara, age seventy-one, reflects. "I remember lying next to my sister in bed when the Cuban Missile Crisis was going on and we were frozen with fear even though we couldn't have really grasped the scale of it. You know, when I hear this whole climate change discussion about having kids I really get it because we too felt like an apocalypse was around the corner. We didn't have to understand it in detail and I'm not sure kids now completely understand what global warming is, but they can feel it. They can sense what their parents feel even if they don't have that deeper knowledge of what it means. I could feel how the adults in my family were feeling and knew they were talking around it." I ask the obvious question: Is the dread now different from what came before? "I can see people are still treating hope like a jinx, some kinda hot potato they don't know how to handle," she says. "People were still having babies through a nuclear war, but I think there was that same dissociation from the future."

Inaction was the inevitable choice in the fact of existential threat—"it wasn't like I could have a say in the war"—but Barbara believes the opposite is now true.

"We were waiting for the bomb—the big bad bang that would end it all," she says. "Powerlessness can be useful in that way, you know? What else is there to do but live, to make babies, to fall in love, to build a life and get on with it? I think what's different now is we all feel part of so many problems and part of the solution. That's a little trickier."

When writer Jia Tolentino was interviewed while eight months pregnant in mid-2020, she said there isn't an "ethical justification for having kids" at a time when existing human suffering and racial and economic inequities were only escalating, especially during a pandemic. "But I am committed to the idea that the world can be better," she said. "And I have some amount of faith that being human, being able to love, is still an untouchably and unpredictably generative thing—worthwhile across unknown contexts, in and of itself." Is there a more staggering display of hope than to bring new life into a world you believe is unstable and dangerous? It looks like hope as critic Rebecca Solnit defines it is not as a "lottery ticket" that you hold feeling lucky but "an axe you break down doors with in an emergency."

Each week, I ask in different ways: Is it fair to force children to sharpen themselves in a world we have made so abrasive? Each week, I feel challenged to learn how to hope more usefully. I felt frustrated with myself that I had not already managed to do this as a person without children.

While waiting for the arrival of his son into a world he deemed mostly "bad," Tom Whyman identified three main qualities as antithetical to hope. I harbored them all. He identifies cynicism—calming our fear of our own desire for a better world by branding that desire as stupid, dangerous, and delusional; from resignation—deciding we have no power to work toward a better world; and despair—the absence of any belief in a better world. He makes a case for cultivating more hopeful virtues; charity—a "do-gooding" for others that Whyman defines as an intellectual value rather than a blanketing moral one; solidarity—acting for the collective interest; and finally modesty—a knowledge that progress isn't absolute and an awareness of what we can achieve alone and together. "To be truly hopeful, we must be able to recognize some good which transcends our own discrete self-interest—and being invested in the interests of future generations, in whatever capacity whether it be as a parent or a grandparent or a godparent or an aunt or an uncle or a teacher or a campaigner or an artist or a friend—is one (perhaps the most readily available) direct, practical way we have of realizing this transcendent good *immanently* in the world." I want to hope better. The choice to try to do so is the simplest part.

I call Whyman to find out whether his hope had changed shape since becoming a father. He tells me parenthood has confirmed for him the wisdom of two of Nietzsche's concepts. The first is that of "eternal recurrence"—the idea that everything in the world perpetually repeats itself in cycles. In Nietzsche's thought experiment—I don't possess the intellect to engage with it as an actual metaphysical theory—he tells the reader to imagine a demon who comes to them at their "loneliest loneliness" and asks them to imagine reliving their life as they have lived it with every pain and every joy.

"I used to think that was just monstrous," Whyman tells me, and I find myself agreeing. In the throes of decision-making the idea adds an unbearable, if hypothetical, weight—would I choose having kids again? Would I choose never having kids again?

"But now I realize if I'd done anything prior in my life different prior to his conception [my son] wouldn't have existed," Whyman says. "I can see why I would want everything in the universe to be the same up until now because it means he is here." This is the second idea of Nietzsche's that fatherhood has fortified for Whyman, that of amor fati or love of fate—an active embrace of all that has happened in life as necessary. I discover the philosopher Laurie Ann Paul is fifty-four. She speaks with the considered cadence of an NPR host. She paces across a stage, her hands gesticulating, adding confident exclamation marks to her words. She would never spend the time it takes to grow a baby dithering on the page about whether or not she should. She would never conceive of herself as a rational agent. Paul says she does not believe it is right or wrong to have children, nor that people shouldn't be happy with their decision. "My view is simply that you need to be honest with yourself about the basis for this choice."

Philosopher John J. Kaag believes Nietzsche was not asking people to obsess over the rightness or wrongness of their decisions, but to liberate themselves by taking responsibility for them. "Perhaps the hardest part of the eternal return is to own up to the tortures that we create for ourselves and those we create for others," Kaag writes. "Owning up: to recollect, to regret, to be responsible, ultimately to forgive and love."

I become completely invested in the health and safety of two uteruses—those of my closest friends. One is in her first trimester of pregnancy. The other is waiting to find out whether the growth pushing into her endometrium is an unusual fibroid or an aggressive cancer. A few weeks before turning thirty she is wondering whether she will need a hysterectomy. A court makes a landmark ruling in favor of climate activists and against Shell, ordering the fossil fuel giant to cut its carbon dioxide emissions and noting the company's activities constituted a threat to the "right to life." I begin spontaneously bleeding, waking in the middle of the night with cramps I haven't felt in years. I vomit from the pain. I wonder whether endometriosis is winning the war against my implant.

The elderly lady I read to dies alone. She once told me her late sister visited on her loneliest nights, lying down next to her bed to keep her company, but for two years I was her only terrestrial visitor, lockdown restrictions stopping me in the month before her death. She didn't have children because something was wrong with her ovaries, but I can't catch what, even at her most lucid when she describes her beloved cattle dogs and the never-ending blond fields she grew up on. The residents with children are rarely visited, so I will never know if motherhood would have spared her finishing her 103 years on Earth alone in a ward where pigeons roam the corridors.

I go to the pub with a former colleague, her two-year-old, and her husband, whose eyes widen excitedly as he tells us that having a child has renewed his sense of wonder in the world. Their daughter hands me pencils, listing each color. She points at the traffic excitedly. She dips her fries in ketchup as though she has never tasted it before. Her name is, of course, Hope. I know if this was a script it would be reworked to prevent scathing reviews from critics about the ham-fisted symbolism invading my life just at the denouement.

It is stories that pulled me into this question and it is stories that are helping me to answer it. Those that we tell about ourselves and about each other. The myths that live on inside us. The chronicles of everyone I called. They self-selected to be interviewed because they understood that their lives had meaning beyond themselves. They wanted to shake and calm, bruise and heal others. The tales of the end of the world. The grand theories of who owns a body. The chapter my partner wants to write next. The editing of what a mother is, who my mother is. The redrafting of what a daughter is, who I am. The story of how I would grow old without a child. The story of who I would be with a child.

The narrativizing has transformed me. It is through these stories that I feel the small heel of something true pushing outward from within me, testing the strength of the limb it is attached to.

For years I did not know how to describe a particular sensation that sometimes overcame me without someone thinking it was suicidal ideation or a fantasy of self-harm. I knew it was neither, but it looks bad on paper and so on paper was where I left it. If you were to trace a line north from your navel along your torso and pause at the last place that it is soft, just before the hard bracket of your sternum, right there, that is the spot. Every so often, I would feel a strong and sudden desire to pierce it with a knife. It happened in times of self-doubt or guilt, especially if I thought I had inconvenienced, offended, or hurt someone, but I knew it was not an urge to mutilate my body. My flesh just happened to be in the way of this rock of a feeling I wanted to shuck and drain. I could almost feel the blood rushing toward my center, looking not for violence but for deliverance—for peace.

The therapist I was seeing in my early twenties took out a piece of paper and drew a line traveling gradually up the page from the bottom left to top right corner. This was not how self-reflection and healing worked, he told me. It was not a satisfying upward linear trajectory toward enlightenment and freedom. Then he drew another line, but this time it looped around and around before reaching the top of the page. Growth was a long slow trudge in a circle on a slight incline. Again and again you would have to face your darkest parts. They might get less shadowy on approach, but they would still be there on the next lap. There was no summit. He offered me the piece of paper, blank but for the spiral and the straight line. "It's okay," I said. "I think I can remember that." I thought I knew what I would tour past. I had yet to learn that you can see and experience things that loved ones or lawmakers deem hard and still flourish. Nothing ever feels as it looks on paper. The pen circled around and around my mother. I felt a horrified guilt when I thought of the C-section scar left by my birth. I was told I was an afterthought rather than an accident, but I felt like an albatross.

I have always felt my mother's emotions as mine. We have spent more time alone together than anyone else in the family because I was born a decade after my parents' third child and my parents separated when I was still a toddler. I have always felt we are irreconcilably different yet made of the same stuff. I felt like I was the one giving her away. In my sessions I looped past her emotional needs and my incapacity to meet them or to establish boundaries so that I wouldn't feel the need to once I'd left home. I feared that I was not the daughter she wanted; a daughter with similar values who had an interest in establishing a family. It took a while to get to the truth of why I felt like this. I told the therapist in snippets of a series of memories in which, in the chaos of our family, my mother had withdrawn love, whether in stress or frustration or fear or exhaustion. They were not the nights we ended up sleeping somewhere else; they were flashes of anger and absence I knew she rarely, if ever, thought of now. She might not remember them because she had already seen too much of life and had four children. I would never forget them because I had not seen enough of life and had one mother. These moments, hard beads on a string marking the timeline of my life so far, felt unbearable to think about. I found myself unable to speak so he asked me if I could feel where in my body I was experiencing the pain of the memories. My hand moved instinctively to my chest and then down to the spot. I rested my hand there and cried silently. He told me there would be no confrontation. He said this was on-her-deathbed stuff. To make peace with it, we would revisit these moments again and again. I stopped seeing him soon after. I did not want to slowly slice myself open.

I always thought a pearl began to form when a grain of sand entered an oyster, but it is usually a tiny invading organism. "Then, something miraculous happens," the *Nat Geo* voice over tells me. The mollusk responds to the intruder by secreting a smooth crystalline substance called nacre, or mother-of-pearl. "It takes several years for thousands of layers of nacre to build up and create a smooth iridescent gem, but it's a rare event," the voice says. "A pearl of value is found in less than one in 10,000 wild pearl oysters." As author MFK Fisher wrote in *Consider the Oyster*, "the unwelcome worm is encased in its rare coffin," coated in a protective material.

Nacre is stronger and lighter than concrete. Scientists tried to work out how a random process in which different cells simultaneously secreted materials around the mollusk could result in such exemplary engineering. Faults replicated through layers "like a helix," but somehow the material ended up sturdy and uniformly structured, Dr. Igor Zlotnikov said in an interview. "How could perfection emerge from such disorder?" he marveled. The scientists discovered that defects from opposite ends of the mollusk moved toward each other until they met and synchronized. The material toughened as it was stressed.

I had long accepted that my relationship with my mother would be imperfect. I had accepted there would still be joy to be found in the future and in the past. I had accepted her not just as a mother, not just as a woman, but as a human being who, like most humans, is doing so much more than expected. I found a new gratitude for all the gifts she had given me. Her joy. The endless and infectious enthusiasm for life that turned errands into adventures. I can see her dancing down supermarket aisles, chucking discounted chocolates into the cart, testing my teenage sullenness until I joined her. Her commitment to humor. Her acute allergy to anything affected, snobbish or, in her words, "indulgent." Her unshakable loyalty. Her fearlessness in the face of other people's pain. *The turning up, turning up, turning up.* Her connection to her own pleasure and her steadfastness in pursuing it. An afternoon at the beach reading a crime novel, a bag of dresses on sale hauled home from an outlet, a freshly baked lamington bursting with cream. Her ability to multitask which I can only remember failing her once when we crashed into a driver who had swerved into our path while driving through a country town. It happened right in front of a police officer stationed with a speed camera, as if we were all trying to give him extra work. Mum had been smoking a cigarette out the window, singing along to the radio, peeling a mandarin, sipping a Diet Coke, and almost instantly answering the cryptic crossword clues I was reading out. She told the police officer it was his fault as he had distracted her, and he laughed. We bought new swimming costumes at Target and waited at a motel for the car to be repaired. Another adventure. "Thank you, thank you, thank you," I say when I feel my attention draining down my breastbone toward my belly.

Mollusks improve the quality of the water around them by removing excess nitrogen and incorporating it into their bodies as they grow. Fake pearls will stay cool and smooth, but a real pearl will warm with your skin and feel gritty if you run it along your teeth. I watch video after video of people wrenching open different oysters, mussels, and clams. They fumble around in the protective tissue, a complex filtration system that lives between the pearl and the mother of the pearl, and wrench out the gleaming gem, an unannounced visitor made precious from the organism's flesh and bone.

I will never understand why I decided to email my mother six months into this search for an answer. I have tried to retrace my steps, but it just happened. It had taken years to accept we would never have the very conversation it took me less than an hour to start. I breached the terms and conditions she had set for our relationship and then waited for my proof that maternal love was conditional. I hit send and went for a walk. I watched the sun set knowing I might have risked her withdrawing love indefinitely.

I told her how much I loved her. I acknowledged how much good and bad we had been through together. I explained how hard it was to write a book in which I was repeatedly expressing opinions she herself did not hold. I knew what she saw as political or ideological differences were not just a contest of ideas for me, but a constant reminder that I was unable to value what she did. To write this book, to write this email, was to make someone uncomfortable, to take up space, to have needs, to be visible. It was to risk love.

I did not tell her about the knife, but I tried to draw the outline of what it was trying to spear. I said that I was content to deceive my readers of my book, then half written, but I could not deceive her of a realization I'd had soon after I gave myself this deadline. Underneath the fear about the smoke in the air, the gender inequity, the precarious workforce, down past the colorless coral in the depths of myself was my relationship with her, unopened. I feared that even if I found myself wanting a child, there was a deeper and dormant not wanting that would only emerge once I had a child. In order to know I was capable of wanting, I wanted to know she had wanted me. I apologized that the years of care, love, and tenderness could not eclipse a handful of moments I felt were confirmations of my unwantedness. My mother replied at first with a text, asking for a day to respond, but assuring me that I was loved and that love was unconditional. In the email there was no defensiveness, no denial, no avoidance. It was just my mother, the clearest I have ever and will ever see her.

"I have never felt anything but love for you."

She described what motherhood feels like. I had never asked. She told me about the beauty, the terror, the singular intensity. I instantly remembered her telling me once she had slept with one hand in the crib to make sure my chest was rising and falling. I understood that parenting is mostly holding fear for someone you love. She wrote that I was the child with whom she finally had the time, space, and financial security to appreciate the wonder of me "growing, changing, and responding." We emailed back and forth, both of us crying. Salt water on my keyboard. This was what it felt like to finally believe something you wanted to be true. When I saw her in person we did not speak of it, but something had changed. We were not attacking and we were not defensive. My mother allowed herself to split open, as she had when I was cut from an incision in her abdomen, so we could see how we were together and apart from each other, our past and present illuminated. My grit within her, hers within me.

Elena Ferrante has written, in *Incidental Inventions*, that when it comes to mothers, reconciliation does not involve forgetting wrongs but seeing our mother as we did when we were children. "I was reconciled with mine when I felt those wrongs—what seemed to me wrongs—as part of myself, essential for my development. So essential that they now appear an invention of mine, a brightly colored exaggeration." Mother-of-pearl appears iridescent because its comprising platelets of aragonite are so thin they are close to the wavelength of visible light. Fake pearls will shine, but real pearls will glow, the light trapped in miniscule layers of nacre. The surface changes color because the light is not just reflecting but refracting. I felt briefly whole, nothing needing to be excised. I could feel my blood, warm and red, moving through every part of my body.

BIBLIOGRAPHY

ABC. "Australia's Shame." *Four Corners*, July 25, 2016.

Ahmed, Sara. *Living a Feminist Life.* Durham, NC: Duke University Press, 2017.

An Old Housekeeper. *The Australian Housewives' Manual: A Book for Beginners and People with Small Incomes.* Melbourne, Australia: A.H. Massina & Co., 1883.

Antigny, Lea. "Early Spring Everywhere." *The Lifted Brow*, no. 42 (June 2019): 121, 123–124.

Arbes, Vicki, Charlie Coulton, and Catherine Boekel. "Men's Social Connectedness Report." Hall & Partners, Open Mind, 2014.

Australian Bureau of Statistics. "Personal Safety, Australia." ABS Website, August 11, 2017. https://www.abs.gov.au/statistics/people/crime-and-justice/personal-safety-australia/latest-release.

Australian Human Rights Commission. "Bringing Them Home: Report of the National Inquiry into the Separation of Aboriginal and Torres Strait Islander Children from Their Families." Report. Human Rights and Equal Opportunity Commission, April 1997.

Australian Institute of Health and Welfare. "Child Protection Australia 2019–20." Report. AIHW Website, May 18, 2021. https://www.aihw.gov.au/reports/child-protection/child-protection-australia-2019-20/summary.

Australian Institute of Health and Welfare. "Pregnancy and Birth Outcomes for Aboriginal and Torres Strait Islander Women: 2016–2018." Report. AIHW Website, July 8, 2021. https://www.aihw.gov.au/reports/indigenous-australians/pregnancy-birth-outcomes-indigenous-women-2016-18/contents/summary.

Australian Institute of Health and Welfare. "Stillbirths in Australia 1991–2009." Report. AIHW Website, September 12, 2014. https://www.aihw.gov.au/reports/mothers-babies/stillbirths-australia-1991-2009/summary.

Bannah, Sylvia. *Birds, Bees and Birth Control: A History of Family Planning in Queensland 1971–2001.* PhD thesis, University of Queensland, 2010.

Beck, Koa. *White Feminism: From the Suffragettes to Influencers and Who They Leave Behind*. New York: Simon & Schuster, 2021.

Behrendt, Larissa. "Aboriginal Women and the White Lies of the Feminist Movement: Implications for Aboriginal Women in Rights Discourse." *The Australian Feminist Law Journal* 1, no. 1 (1993): 27–44, doi:10.1080/13200968.1993.11077108.

Bekkar, Bruce, Susan Pacheco, Rupa Basu, and Nathaniel DeNicola. "Association of Air Pollution and Heat Exposure with Preterm Birth, Low Birth Weight, and Stillbirth in the US: A Systematic Review." *JAMA Network Open* 3, no. 6 (June 18, 2020).

Belsky, Jay, Avshalom Caspi, Terrie E. Moffit, and Richie Poulton. *The Origins of You: How Childhood Shapes Later Life*. Cambridge, MA: Harvard University Press, 2020.

Berlatsky, Noah. "How Boys Teach Each Other to Be Boys." *The Atlantic*, June 6, 2014. https://www.theatlantic.com/health/archive/2014/06/how-boys-teach-each-other-to-be-boys/372246/.

Bezner Kerr, Rachel, Toshiro Hasegawa, Rodel Lasco, Indra Bhatt, Delphine Deryng, Aidan Farrell, Helen Gurney-Smith et al. "Food, Fibre, and Other Ecosystem Products." *Climate Change 2022: Impacts, Adaptation, and Vulnerability*. Contribution of Working Group II to the Sixth Assessment Report of the Intergovernmental Panel on Climate Change. Cambridge, UK: Cambridge University Press, 2022.

Birthrights. "Systematic Racism, Not Broken Bodies: An Inquiry Into Racial Injustice and Human Rights in UK Maternity Care." Executive Summary, May 2022. https://www.birthrights.org.uk/wp-content/uploads/2022/05/Birthrights-inquiry-systemic-racism_exec-summary_May-22-web.pdf.

Bollen, Christopher. "Ask a Sane Person: Jia Tolentino on Practicing the Discipline of Hope." *Interview*, July 8, 2020. https://www.interviewmagazine.com/culture/ask-a-sane-person-jia-tolentino-book-2020-hope.

Brannon, Robert, and Deborah David. *The Forty-Nine Percent Majority: The Male Sex Role*. Glenview, IL: Addison Wesley Publishing Company, 1976.

Brooks, Kim. "Motherhood in the Age of Fear." *The New York Times*, July 27, 2018. https://www.nytimes.com/2018/07/27/opinion/sunday/motherhood-in-the-age-of-fear.html.

Brown, Brené. *Daring Greatly: How the Courage to Be Vulnerable Transforms the Way We Live, Love, Parent, and Lead*. New York: Portfolio, 2013.

Cain Miller, Claire. "How Same-Sex Couples Divide Chores, and What It Reveals About Modern Parenting." *The New York Times*, May 16, 2018. https://www.nytimes.com/2018/05/16/upshot/same-sex-couples-divide-chores-much-more-evenly-until-they-become-parents.html.

Callard, Agnes. "Acceptance Parenting." *The Point Magazine*, October 2, 2020. https://thepointmag.com/examined-life/acceptance-parenting/.

Center for Reproductive Rights. "The World Abortion Laws Map." Center for Reproductive Rights Website. Accessed 2022. https://reproductiverights.org/maps/worlds-abortion-laws/.

Center on Poverty and Social Policy at Columbia University. "Monthly SPM Poverty for January 2022." Policy Brief. Poverty Center Website, February 17, 2022. https://www.povertycenter.columbia.edu/news-internal/monthly-poverty-january-2022#:~:text

=The%20monthly%20child%20poverty%20rate,monthly%20Child%20Tax%20Cre
dit%20payments.

Center on Poverty and Social Policy at Columbia University. "3.7 Million More Children in Poverty in Jan 2022 Without Monthly Tax Credit." Poverty Center Website, February 17, 2022.
https://www.povertycenter.columbia.edu/news-internal/monthly-poverty-january-
2022#:~:text=The%20monthly%20child%20poverty%20rate,monthly%20Child%20
Tax%20Credit%20payments.

Centers for Disease Control and Prevention. "Abortion Surveillance—United States 2019."
CDC Website, November 26, 2021. https://www.cdc.gov/mmwr/volumes/70/ss/ss7009
a1.htm.

Centers for Disease Control and Prevention. "Fatal Injury and Violence Data, 2020."
CDC Website, November 2022. https://www.cdc.gov/injury/wisqars/fatal.html.

Centers for Disease Control and Prevention. "Racial/Ethnic Disparities in Pregnancy-
Related Deaths—United States, 2007–2016." CDC Website, September 6, 2019.
https://www.cdc.gov/mmwr/volumes/68/wr/mm6835a3.htm.

Centers for Disease Control and Prevention. "Racial/Ethnic Disparities in Pregnancy-
Related Deaths—United States, 2019." CDC Website, November 2022. https://www
.cdc.gov/reproductivehealth/maternal-mortality/disparities-pregnancy-related-deaths
/infographic.html.

Chu, Judy Y. *When Boys Become Boys: Development, Relationships, and Masculinity.* New
York: NYU Press, 2014.

Cineas, Fabiola. "Reproductive Rights Have Never Been Secure. Ask Black Women." *Vox*,
July 13, 2022. https://www.vox.com/23205101/abortion-rights-reproductive-justice-black
-women.

Clarke, Edward H. *Sex in Education: Or, a Fair Chance for the Girls.* Boston: J.R. Osgood
& Co., 1873.

Clubb, Kathy. "Dear Gina, You're Helping Women Kill Their Babies." *The Freedoms
Project*, March 7, 2018. https://thefreedomsproject.com/item/184-dear-gina-youre
-helping-women-kill-their-babies.

Conrad, Marissa. "How Much Does IVF Cost?" *Forbes Health*, January 23, 2023. https://
www.forbes.com/health/family/how-much-does-ivf-cost/.

*Constitutional Amendments Relating to Abortion: Hearings on S.J. Res. 18, S.J. Res. 19, and
S.J. Res. 110 Before the Subcomm. on the Constitution of the S. Comm. on the Judiciary*,
97th Cong. 329–39 (1981) (testimony of Vincent Rue).

Coombe, J. et al. "Factors Influencing Contraceptive Use or Non-use Among Aboriginal
and Torres Strait Islander People: A Systematic Review and Narrative Synthesis."
Reproductive Health 17, no. 155 (2020). doi:10.1186/s12978-020-01004-8.

Coontz, Stephanie. "How to Make Your Marriage Gayer." *The New York Times*, February 13, 2020. https://www.nytimes.com/2020/02/13/opinion/sunday/marriage-house
work-gender-happiness.html.

Costa, Dora L., Noelle Yetter, and Heather DeSomer. "Intergenerational Transmission of
Paternal Trauma Among US Civil War ex-POWs." *Proceedings of the National Academy of Sciences USA* 115, no. 44 (2018): 11215–20, doi:10.1073/pnas.1803630115.

Crawford, Anwen. "This Isn't Working: Single Mothers and Welfare." *Meanjin Quarterly*
73, no. 3 (2014).

Davis, Angela Y. *Women, Race & Class*. New York: Knopf, 1983.

De Costa, Caroline. *The Women's Doc: True Stories from My Five Decades Delivering Babies and Making History*. Crows Nest, Australia: Allen & Unwin, 2021.

Department for Work and Pensions. "Households Below Average Income, Statistics on the number and percentage of people living in low income households for financial years 1994/95 to 2020/21." UK Government Website, last updated March 24, 2023. Table 1.4a. https://www.gov.uk/government/collections/households-below-average-income-hbai--2.

Department of Health and Social Care. "Abortion Statistics, England and Wales: 2021." UK Government Website, June 21, 2022. https://www.gov.uk/government/statistics/abortion -statistics-for-england-and-wales-2021/abortion-statistics-england-and-wales-2021.

Dombek, Kristin. *The Selfishness of Others: An Essay on the Fear of Narcissism*. New York: FSG Originals, 2016.

Dresden, TU. "Holographic X-ray Nano-Tomography Reveals How Mother-of-Pearl Self-Assembles Into a Perfect Structure." *SciTechDaily*, January 15 2021. https://scitech daily.com/holographic-x-ray-nano-tomography-reveals-how-mother-of-pearl-self -assembles-into-a-perfect-structure/.

Durairaj, Scott. "Turning the Tide: The Experiences of Black, Asian and Minority Ethnic NHS Staff Working in Maternity Services in England During and Beyond the Covid-19 Pandemic." NHS England, 2020. https://www.northeastlondonhcp.nhs.uk /downloads/ourplans/Maternity/Turning%20the%20Tide%20Maternity%20Report %20-%202020.pdf.

Erickson, Rebecca J. "Why Emotion Work Matters: Sex, Gender, and the Division of Household Labor." *Journal of Marriage and Family* 67, no. 2 (May 2005).

Federici, Silvia. *Wages Against Housework*. Bristol & London, UK: Falling Wall Press and the Power of Women Collective, 1975.

Ferrante, Elena. *Incidental Inventions*. Rome, Italy: Europa, 2019.

Fisher, MFK. *Consider the Oyster*. New York: Duell, Sloan and Pearce, 1941.

Flood, Michael. "Masculinities and Health: Attitudes Towards Men and Masculinities in Australia." Report. Victorian Health Promotion Foundation (VicHealth), 2020. https:// www.vichealth.vic.gov.au/-/media/ResearchandEvidence/Current-research/Vic Health-Attitudes-to-men-and-masculinity-report-July-2020.pdf?la=en&hash=CC6 F4938563E65E58E6D4D7C573FA8AA13286986.

Fox, Chloe K. "How Children Change Their Mothers." *The Boston Globe*, 2017. https://www .bostonglobe.com/ideas/2017/07/07/how-children-change-their-mothers-and-their -mothers-dna/N4kx56tylbhmkdMFK15LaJ/story.html.

Galchen, Rivka. *Little Labors*. New York: New Directions, 2016.

Garcia, Michael A., and Debra Umberson. "Marital Strain and Psychological Distress in Same-Sex and Different-Sex Couples." *Journal of Marriage and the Family* 81, no. 5 (June 6, 2019): 1253–1268.

Glausiusz, Josie. "Doubts Arising About Claimed Epigenetics of Holocaust Trauma." *Haaretz*, April 30, 2017. https://www.haaretz.com/science-and-health/2017-04-30 /ty-article/.premium/doubts-arising-about-claimed-epigenetics-of-holocaust -trauma/0000017f-e9b2-df2c-a1ff-fff3428d0000.

Glick, P., and S. T. Fiske. "The Ambivalent Sexism Inventory: Differentiating Hostile and Benevolent Sexism." *Journal of Personality and Social Psychology* 70, no. 3 (1996): 491–512, doi:10.1037/0022-3514.70.3.491.

Goldman, Emma. *Anarchism and Other Essays*. New York & London, UK: Mother Earth Publishing Association, 1911.

Gordon, Devin. "Why Is Joe Rogan So Popular?" *The Atlantic*, August 19, 2019. https://www.theatlantic.com/entertainment/archive/2019/08/my-joe-rogan-experience/594802/.

Gottman, John Mordechai, Robert Wayne Levenson, Catherine Swanson, Kristin Swanson, Rebecca Tyson, and Dan Yoshimoto. "Observing Gay, Lesbian and Heterosexual Couples' Relationships: Mathematical Modeling of Conflict Interaction." *Journal of Homosexuality* 45, no. 1 (2003): 65–91.

Greene Foster, Diane. *The Turnaway Study: Ten Years, a Thousand Women, and the Consequences of Having—Or Being Denied—An Abortion*. New York: Scribner, 2021.

Günaydin, Eda. "Your Life's Work." *The Lifted Brow*, February 26, 2020. https://www.theliftedbrow.com/liftedbrow/2020/2/21/your-lifes-work-by-eda-gnaydn.

Hartley, Gemma. *Fed Up: Emotional Labor, Women, and the Way Forward*. London, UK: Yellow Kite, 2018.

Heglar, Mary Annaïse. "Home Is Always Worth It." *Medium*, September 12, 2019.

Hennessy, J.R. "Who the Hell Cares What Old People Think About Climate Change?" *The Outline*, October 11, 2018. https://theoutline.com/post/6384/boomers-shut-up-climate-change.

Heti, Sheila. *Motherhood*. New York: Henry Holt & Company, 2018.

Hickman, Caroline et al. "Climate Anxiety in Children and Young People and Their Beliefs About Government Responses to Climate Change: A Global Survey." *The Lancet Planetary Health* 5, no. 12 (December 2021): 863–73. https://www.sciencedirect.com/science/article/pii/S2542519621002783.

Hicks, Neville. *This Sin and Scandal: Australia's Population Debate 1891–1911*. Canberra, Australia: Australian National University Press, 1965.

Hochschild, Arlie Russell. *The Managed Heart: Commercialization of Human Feeling*. Oakland: University of California Press, 1983.

Hoffman Kelly M., Sophie Trawalter, Jordan R. Axt, and M. Norman Oliver. "Racial Bias in Pain Assessment and Treatment Recommendations, and False Beliefs About Biological Differences Between Blacks and Whites." *Proceedings of the National Academy of Sciences* 113, no. 16 (April 4, 2016). 4296–4301. https://www.pnas.org/doi/10.1073/pnas.1516047113.

Holt, Kelsey. "Fertility Control Unjust Way to Combat Climate Change." *Los Angeles Times*, December 11, 2019.

hooks, bell. *All About Love: New Vision*. New York: William Morrow, 2015.

Human Fertilisation & Embryology Authority. *Fertility Treatment 2019: Trends and Figures*. HFEA Website, May 2021. https://www.hfea.gov.uk/about-us/publications/research-and-data/fertility-treatment-2019-trends-and-figures/.

Jacobson, Gavin. "Why Children of Men Haunts the Present Moment: How Alfonso Cuarón's 2006 Dystopian Masterpiece Became the Cultural Exemplum of Apocalypse, and a Cardinal Citation in the Time of Coronavirus." *The New Statesman*, July 22, 2020. https://www.newstatesman.com/culture/film/2020/07/children-of-men-alfonso-cuaron-2006-apocalypse-coronavirus.

Jamison, Leslie. *The Empathy Exams: Essays*. Crows Nest: Granta Paperbacks, 2015.

Jaffe, Sarah. *Work Won't Love You Back: How Devotion to Our Jobs Keeps Us Exploited, Exhausted, and Alone*. New York: Bold Type Books, 2021.

Joshi, Ketan. *Windfall: Unlocking a Fossil-Free Future.* New South Wales, Australia: NewSouth Books, 2020.

Kaag, John. *Hiking with Nietzsche.* New York: Farrar, Straus & Giroux, 2018.

Kapsalis, Terri. "Hysteria, Witches, and the Wandering Uterus: A Brief History." *LitHub*, April 5, 2017. https://lithub.com/hysteria-witches-and-the-wandering-uterus-a-brief-history/.

Keating, Shannon. "The Year in Heteropessimism," *BuzzFeed News*, December 30, 2019.

Keats, John. "Letter to George and Tom Keats in December 1817." *The Letters of John Keats*, edited by H. Buxton Forman. London, UK: Reeves and Turner, 1895.

Kilpatrick, Connor. "It's Okay to Have Children." *Jacobin*, August 22, 2018. https://jacobin.com/2018/08/its-okay-to-have-children.

Kimball, Alexandra. *The Seed: Infertility Is a Feminist Issue.* Toronto, Canada: Coach House Books, 2019.

Klinenberg, Eric. "The Seas Are Rising. Could Oysters Help?" *The New Yorker*, August 9, 2021.

Knight, M. et al., eds. on behalf of MBRRACE-UK. "Saving Lives, Improving Mothers' Care: Lessons Learned to Inform Maternity Care from the UK and Ireland Confidential Enquiries into Maternal Deaths and Morbidity 2018–20." University of Oxford, November 2022.

Lakshmin, Pooja. "Mothers Don't Have to Be Martyrs." *The New York Times*, June 11, 2021.

Leiser, Claire L., Heidi A. Hanson, Kara Sawyer, Jacob Steenblik, Ragheed Al-Dulaimi, Troy Madsen, Karen Gibbins et al. "Acute Effects of Air Pollutants on Spontaneous Pregnancy Loss: A Case-crossover Study." *Fertility and Sterility* 111, no. 2 (December 4, 2018): 341–347.

Levy, Deborah. *Things I Don't Want to Know.* London, UK: Penguin, 2018.

Lopez, Iris. *Matters of Choice: Puerto Rican Women's Struggle for Reproductive Freedom.* New Brunswick, NJ: Rutgers University Press, 2008.

Mackintosh, Sophie. *Blue Ticket.* London, UK: Penguin, 2020.

Mackintosh, Sophie. "The Desire to Have a Child Is Never Simple or Fair." *The Evening Standard*, August 27, 2020.

Mailangi, Enoch. "Family." *Queerstories*, directed by Maeve Marsden, December 9, 2020. Podcast, MP3 Audio. https://maevemarsden.com/queerstories/.

Marks, Elizabeth, Caroline Hickman, Panu Pihkala, Susan Clayton, Eric R. Lewandowski, Elouise Mayall, Britt Wray et al. "Young People's Voices on Climate Anxiety, Government Betrayal and Moral Injury: A Global Phenomenon, 2021." *SSRN Electronic Journal*, September 7, 2021. https://papers.ssrn.com/sol3/papers.cfm?abstract_id=3918955.

Mason, Meg. *Sorrow and Bliss: A Novel.* New York: Harper, 2021.

Matos, Kenneth. "Modern Families: Same- and Different-sex Couples Negotiating at Home." Report. Families and Work Institute, 2015.

McCallum, Jamie K. *Worked Over: How Round-the-Clock Work Is Killing the American Dream.* New York: Basic Books, 2020.

McGlade, Hannah. "Kaya Nidja Noongar Boodjah—Perth, Black Lives Matter Rally 2020." *NITV News*, June 7, 2020. https://www.sbs.com.au/nitv/article/kaya-nidja-noongar-boodjah-perth-black-lives-matter-rally-2020/dsxsze1m4.

McPherson, Miller, Lynn Smith-Lovin, and Matthew E. Brashears. "Social Isolation in America: Changes in Core Discussion Networks Over Two Decades." *American Sociological Review* 71, no. 3 (June 2006): 353–375.

Meaney, Michael J., and Moshe Szyf. "Environmental Programming of Stress Responses Through DNA Methylation: Life at the Interface Between a Dynamic Environment and a Fixed Genome." *Dialogues in Clinical Neuroscience* 7, no. 2 (2005): 103–23, doi:10.31887/DCNS.2005.7.2/mmeaney.

Miller, Alice. *The Drama of the Gifted Child*. New York: Basic Books, 1979.

Miller, Lisa. "The Ambition Collision." *The Cut*, September 6, 2017. https://www.thecut.com/2017/09/what-happens-to-ambition-in-your-30s.html.

Miller, Martin. *The True "Drama of the Gifted Child": The Phantom Alice Miller—The Real Person*. Martin Miller, 2018.

Milson, Veronica. "Episode Eight: Zero Future Babies." *Zero Waste Baby*, produced by Veronica Milson, September 15, 2020. Podcast, MP3 Audio. https://podcasts.apple.com/us/podcast/zero-waste-baby-with-veronica-milsom/id1531827488.

Moreton-Robinson, Aileen. *Talkin' Up to the White Woman: Indigenous Women and Feminism*. Brisbane, Australia: University of Queensland Press, 2002.

Morrison, Toni. *Beloved*. New York: Random House, 1987.

Moss, Gabrielle. "The Girlboss Era Is Over. Welcome to the Age of the Girlloser." *Medium*, June 28, 2021. https://gabriellemoss.medium.com/the-girlboss-era-is-over-welcome-to-the-age-of-the-girlloser-85a9ac0c09ee.

Murphy, Katharine. "Scott Morrison Brings Coal to Question Time: What Fresh Idiocy Is This?" *The Guardian*, February 9, 2017.

Nat Geo WILD. "Formation of a Pearl | Secret Life of Pearls." April 23, 2016. YouTube Video. https://www.youtube.com/watch?v=m07OvPEoR6g.

Nelson, Camilla, and Rachel Robertson, eds. *Dangerous Ideas About Mothers*. Perth, Australia: UWA Press, 2018.

Nelson, Jennifer. *Women of Color and the Reproductive Rights Movement*. New York: New York University Press, 2003.

New South Wales Coroners Court. "Findings in the Inquest into the Death of Naomi Williams." Last updated May 27, 2020. https://coroners.nsw.gov.au/coroners-court/download.html/documents/findings/2019/Naomi%20Williams%20findings.pdf.

Newman, Jane E., Repon C. Paul, and Georgina M. Chambers. "Assisted Reproductive Technology in Australia and New Zealand 2018." National Perinatal Epidemiology and Statistics Unit, University of New South Wales, September 2020.

Nguyen, Kevin. "RFS Firefighter Who Died When Fire Tornado Flipped Truck During Green Valley Bushfire Named as Samuel McPaul." *ABC News*, December 30, 2019.

Nietzsche, Friedrich. *The Birth of Tragedy*. New York: Oxford University Press, 1992 [1886].

NITV News. "100% of Children Detained in NT Are Aboriginal." *NITV News*, June 26, 2018. https://www.sbs.com.au/nitv/article/100-of-children-detained-in-nt-are-aboriginal/fgy1zolf3.

O'Connell, Mark. *Notes from an Apocalypse*. London, UK: Granta Publications, 2020.

Odell, Jenny. *How to Do Nothing: Resisting the Attention Economy*. Brooklyn, NY: Melville House, 2019.

Offill, Jenny. *Dept. of Speculation*. London, UK: Granta Publications, 2015.

O'Neil, Luke. "I Don't Actually Think That All of These People Believe We're in Hell." *Welcome to Hell World*. Blog, August 28, 2021. https://luke.substack.com/p/i-dont -actually-think-that-all-of.

Organisation for Economic Co-operation and Development. "Net Childcare Costs." OECD Website. Accessed 2022. https://data.oecd.org/benwage/net-childcare-costs .htm.

Paul, Laurie Ann. *Transformative Experiences*. New York: Res Philosophica, 2015.

Perel, Esther. *Mating in Captivity: Unlocking Erotic Intelligence*. New York: HarperCollins, 2017.

Petersen, Anne Helen. "How to Work Through a Coup, Culture Study." Culture Study Substack, January 7, 2021. https://annehelen.substack.com/p/how-to-work-through-a -coup.

Peyser, Alexandra, and Avner Hershlag. "Is the Increase in Egg Freezing Cycles Related to Increased Numbers of Single Women in the United States?" *Fertility and Sterility* 112, no. 13 (September 2019).

Piazza, Jo. "How I Trained My Husband to Be a Dad." *New York Times*, October 4, 2018. https://www.nytimes.com/2018/10/04/style/how-i-trained-my-husband-to-be-a-dad .html.

Plomin, Robert. "Parents Matter But They Don't Make a Difference." *Psychology Today*, September 27, 2018.

Pochin, Courtney. "When My Husband Told Me to Shush During Labour I Knew Our Marriage Was Over." *The Mirror*, October 28, 2020. https://www.mirror.co.uk/ lifestyle/sex-relationships/relationships/when-husband-told-shush-during-2291 8057.

Queensland Ombudsman. "The Indigenous Birth Registration Report." 2018. https://www .ombudsman.qld.gov.au/ArticleDocuments/514/The%20Indigenous%20birth%20 registration%20report.pdf.aspx.

Randone, Amanda. "Sexual Health Services Are Failing Black Women. It's Time to Finally Face Up to Healthcare's Colonial Roots." *Glamour Magazine*, November 17, 2021. https://www.glamourmagazine.co.uk/article/racist-sexual-reproductive-healthcare

Redhouse, Nicola. *Unlike the Heart: A Memoir of Brain and Mind*. Brisbane, Australia: University of Queensland Press, 2019.

Rees, Anne. "The Quality And Not Only The Quantity Of Australia's People." *Australian Feminist Studies*, 2012.

Rich, Adrienne. *Of Woman Born: Motherhood as Experience and Institution*. New York: W. W. Norton & Company, 1976.

Ripple, William J., Christopher Wolf, Thomas M. Newsome, Phoebe Barnard, and William R. Moomaw. "World Scientists' Warning of a Climate Emergency." *BioScience* 70, no. 1 (January 2020): 8–12.

Ritchie, Hannah. "Global Inequalities in CO_2 Emissions." Our World in Data, October 16, 2018. https://ourworldindata.org/co2-by-income-region.

Roberts, Dorothy E. *Killing the Black Body: Race, Reproduction, and the Meaning of Liberty*. New York: Random House, 1997.

Robertson, Boni, Catherine Demosthenous, and Hellene Demosthenous. "Stories From the Aboriginal Women of the Yarning Circle: When Cultures Collide." *Hecate* 31, no. 2 (2005): 34–44.

Rooney, Kristin L., and Alice D. Domar. "The Relationship Between Stress and Infertility." *Dialogues in Clinical Neuroscience* 20, no. 1 (2018): 41–7, doi:10.31887/DCNS.2018.20.1 /klrooney.

Rose, Jacqueline. *Mothers: An Essay on Love and Cruelty*. New York: Farrar, Straus and Giroux, 2019.

Ross, Loretta J., Lynn Roberts, Erika Derkas, Whitney Peoples, and Pamela D. Bridgewater, eds. *Radical Reproductive Justice: Foundations, Theory, Practice, Critique*. New York: The Feminist Press at the City University of New York, 2017.

Rottenberg, Catherine A. *The Rise of Neoliberal Feminism*. New York: Oxford University Press, 2018.

Rushton, Gina. "Australian Women Are Forgoing Groceries to Pay for Their Abortions." *BuzzFeed News*, January 23, 2017. https://www.buzzfeed.com/ginarushton/austra lian-women-are-forgoing-groceries-to-pay-for-their-abo.

——. "A Politician Has Blamed Abortions for Lost Tax Revenue." *BuzzFeed News*, May 5, 2017. https://www.buzzfeed.com/ginarushton/a-politician-has-blamed-abortions-for -lost-tax-revenue.

——. "Here's Why Mamamia Just Deleted an Article About Abortion." *BuzzFeed News*, April 23, 2018. https://www.buzzfeed.com/ginarushton/mamamia-just-deleted-this -article.

——. "We Need to Talk About the Abortion Myth Male Politicians Keep Perpetuating." *BuzzFeed News*, August 22, 2018. https://www.buzzfeed.com/ginarushton/abortion -queensland-doctors-myth-bernardi-trad.

——. "This Politician Had a Powerful Response to Other Senators Calling Women 'Murderers' For Having Late-Term Abortions." *BuzzFeed News*, September 18, 2018. https:// www.buzzfeed.com/ginarushton/late-term-abortions-senate-janet-rice.

——. "Babies Are Being Born into Smoky Delivery Rooms as Australia Burns." *BuzzFeed News*, January 2, 2019. https://www.buzzfeed.com/ginarushton/baby-delivery-canberra -bushfire-smoke.

——. "If an Aboriginal Woman Had Been from Sydney's Eastern Suburbs, She Might Have Been Treated Better, Coroner Says." *BuzzFeed News*, March 14, 2019. https://www .buzzfeed.com/ginarushton/naomi-williams-inquest-coroner-hospital.

——. "An Anti-Abortion Group Told Its Members the Bushfires Should Continue Until We Reject 'Moral Degeneracy.'" *BuzzFeed News*, December 20, 2019. https://www .buzzfeed.com/ginarushton/anti-abortion-group-bushfires-australia-ordained-by -god.

Saad, Layla F. *Me and White Supremacy: Combat Racism, Change the World, and Become a Good Ancestor*. New York: Sourcebooks, 2020.

Sacks, Alexandra. "The Birth of a Mother." *The New York Times*, May 8, 2017.

SAFIRE: Black Women for Wages for Housework. Pamphlet. Fall 1977. https://collect ions.barnard.edu/public/repositories/2/archival_objects/6296.

Salsberg, Edward, Chelsea Richwine, Sara Westergaard, Maria Portela Martinez, Toyese Oyeyemi, Anushree Vichare, and Candice P. Chen. "Estimation and Comparison of Current and Future Racial/Ethnic Representation in the US Health Care Workforce." *JAMA Network Open* 4, no. 3 (March 31, 2021).

Sandberg, Sheryl. *Lean In: Women, Work, and the Will to Lead*. New York: Alfred A. Knopf, 2013.

Seals Allers, Kimberly. "Rethinking Work-Life Balance for Women of Color." *Slate*, March 5, 2018.

Sentilles, Sarah. *Stranger Care: A Memoir of Loving What Isn't Ours*. New York: Random House, 2021.

Seresin, Asa. "On Heteropessimism," *The New Inquiry*, October 9, 2019. https://thenew inquiry.com/on-heteropessimism/.

Servigne, Pablo, and Raphaël Stevens. *How Everything Can Collapse: A Manual for Our Times*, translated by Andrew Brown. Cambridge, UK: Polity, 2020.

Smiler, Andrew. *Is Masculinity Toxic? A Primer for the 21st Century*. London, UK: Thames & Hudson, 2019.

Solnit, Rebecca. *Hope in the Dark: Untold Histories, Wild Possibilities*. New York: Nation Books, 2004.

Solomon, Andrew. *Far From the Tree: Parents, Children, and the Search for Identity*. New York: Simon & Schuster, 2012.

Stewart, Kitty, Ruth Patrick, Aaron Reeves, Mary Reader, Kate Andersen. "Needs and Entitlements: How UK Welfare Reform Affects Larger Families." The London School of Economics and Political Science, University of York, July 2022.

Stopes, Marie Carmichael. *Radiant Motherhood: A Book for Those Who Are Creating the Future*. New York: G. P. Putnam's Sons, 1920.

Strand, Ginger. "The Crying Indian." *Orion Magazine*, November 2008. https://orionm agazine.org/article/the-crying-indian/.

Sweetman, Rosita. *Feminism Backwards*. Cork, Ireland: Mercier Press, 2020.

Talaga, Tanya. *All Our Relations: Indigenous Trauma in the Shadow of Colonialism*. Melbourne, Australia: Scribe Publication, 2020.

Talbot, Margaret. "On the Road with Mitski." *The New Yorker*, July 8, 2019.

Taylor, Matthew, and Jonathan Watts. "Revealed: The 20 Firms Behind a Third of All Carbon Emissions." *The Guardian*, October 9, 2019. https://www.theguardian.com/env ironment/2019/oct/09/revealed-20-firms-third-carbon-emissions.

"The Royal Commission on the Birth-Rate." *The Sydney Morning Herald*, 1904.

"The Slave Tragedy in Cincinatti." *The New York Times*, 1856. https://timesmachine .nytimes.com/timesmachine/1856/02/02/76452571.pdf.

Tokumitsu, Miya. *Do What You Love: And Other Lies About Success and Happiness*. New York: Regan Arts, 2015.

Tolentino, Jia. "We're Not Going Back to the Time Before Roe. We're Going Somewhere Worse." *The New Yorker*, June 24, 2022.

"Toni Morrison, in Her Novel, Defends Women." *The New York Times*, August 26, 1987. https://www.nytimes.com/1987/08/26/books/toni-morrison-in-her-novel-defends -women-from-morrison-s-beloved.html.

Tyson, Alec, Brian Kennedy, and Cary Funk. "Gen Z, Millennials Stand Out for Climate Change Activism, Social Media Engagement with Issue." Pew Research Center, May 26, 2021.

Umberson, Debra, Mieke Beth Thomeer, Amanda Pollitt, and Sara E. Mernitz. "The Psychological Toll of Emotion Work in Same-Sex and Different-Sex Marital Dyads." *Journal of Marriage and the Family* 82, no. 4 (May 11, 2020): 1141–1158.

Unamuno, Miguel. *Tragic Sense of Life*, translated by J. E. Crawford Flitch. New York: Dover Publications, 1954.

United Nations. "IPCC Report: 'Code Red' for Human Driven Global Heating, Warns UN Chief." *UN News*, August 9, 2021. https://news.un.org/en/story/2021/08/1097362.

Vuong, Ocean. "A Letter to My Mother That She Will Never Read." *The New Yorker*, May 13, 2017.

Wade, T. J., and Justin Mogilski. "Emotional Accessibility Is More Important Than Sexual Accessibility in Evaluating Romantic Relationships—Especially for Women: A Conjoint Analysis." *Frontiers in Psychology* 9, (May 14, 2018).

Wallace, Maeve et al. "Homicide During Pregnancy and the Postpartum Period in the United States, 2018–2019." *Obstetrics & Gynecology* 138, no. 5 (2021): 762–769, doi:10.1097/AOG.0000000000004567.

Wang, Yuhe Faye. "Heterosexuality and Its Discontents." *The Outline*, January 28, 2020.

Ward, Jane. *The Tragedy of Heterosexuality*. New York: NYU Press, 2020.

Ward, Mary. "*You're* Asking One Person to Give You What an Entire Village Used to Provide." *The Sydney Morning Herald*, June 5, 2019. https://www.smh.com.au/lifestyle/life-and-relationships/youre-asking-one-person-to-give-you-what-an-entire-village-used-to-provide-20190603-h1f0qx.html.

Whyman, Tom. *Infinitely Full of Hope*. London, UK: Repeater Books, 2021.

Williams, Zoe. "Marie Stopes: A Turbo-Darwinist Ranter, But Right About Birth Control." *The Guardian*, September 2, 2011.

Wolynn, Mark. *It Didn't Start with You: How Inherited Family Trauma Shapes Who We Are and How to End the Cycle*. New York: Viking, 2016.

Wright, Alexis. "The Inward Migration in Apocalyptic Times." *Emergence Magazine*, October 26, 2022.

Wyndham, Diana H. "Striving for National Fitness: Eugenics in Australia 1910s to 1930s." PhD thesis, University of Sydney, 1996.

Yehuda, Rachel, Nikolaos P. Daskalakis, Linda M. Bierer, Heather N. Bader, Torsten Klengel, Florian Holsboer, and Elisabeth B. Binder. "Holocaust Exposure Induced Intergenerational Effects on FKBP5 Methylation." *Biological Psychiatry* 80, no. 5 (September 1, 2016): 372–380.

Yehuda, Rachel. "How Trauma and Resilience Cross Generations." *On Being with Krista Tippett*, July 15, 2014. Podcast. https://onbeing.org/programs/rachel-yehuda-how-trauma-and-resilience-cross-generations-nov2017/.

Žižek, Slavoj. *Children of Men*. DVD commentary. Universal Studios Home Entertainment, 2007.

ACKNOWLEDGMENTS

Thank you so much to my agent, Rach Crawford, without whom this book would not exist, and Kate Johnson, without whom it wouldn't have traveled across oceans and into the hands of new readers.

Thank you to Alessandra Bastagli for your brilliant edits and insights and to everyone else at Astra. I will be forever grateful to you all for granting me the thrill of seeing this book in a New York bookshop. Thank you to Rodrigo Corral for the incredible cover design. Thank you to every friend who gave hearts, brains, eyes, and ears to the first edition of this book, either directly or indirectly: Casey Willoughby, Gyan Yankovich, Rebecca Slater, Léa Antigny, Hannah Ryan, Sarah Krasnostein, Aden Knaap, Ruby Munsie, Alex McClintock, Freya Newman, Tahlia Pritchard, Alex Christie, Humyara Mahbub, and Laura Southern. Thank you to the team at Pan Macmillan Australia for supporting me to write the first edition of this book, and the team at Indigo Press, particularly my wonderful UK editor, Susie Nicklin, for your thoughtful and thorough edits. Thank you to every person who shared their stories of ambivalence, miscarriage, abortion, trauma, joy, hope, despair, care, solitude, community, anger, and labor. Thank you to everyone in the reproductive healthcare and rights space who has supported my journalism vocally and protectively from the very beginning. Thank you to my family. Finally, thank you to Tim for every moment of support while pitching, writing, publishing, and promoting this book. In these pages I've tried to get better at asking and answering hard questions, something I want to keep doing off the page with you. I love you!

PHOTO BY SLY MORIKAWA

ABOUT THE AUTHOR

Gina Rushton is the editor of the Australian news and politics website *Crikey*. Her work has been published in *BuzzFeed News*, the *Guardian*, *Vogue*, *Australian Associated Press*, the *Sydney Morning Herald*, and the *Monthly*. This is her first book. Follow Gina on Instagram at @ginarushton-author and Twitter at @ginarush.